Moderate Learning Difficulties and the Future of Inclusion

Brahm Norwich and Narcie Kelly

RoutledgeFalmer
Taylor & Francis Group

LONDON AND NEW YORK

First published 2005 by RoutledgeFalmer
2 Park Square, Milton Park, Abingdon, Oxon OX14 4RN

Simultaneously published in the USA and Canada
by RoutledgeFalmer
270 Madison Avenue, New York, NY 10016

RoutledgeFalmer is an imprint of the Taylor & Francis Group

© 2005 Brahm Norwich and Narcie Kelly

Typeset in Baskerville and Gill by BC Typesetting Ltd, Bristol
Printed and bound in Great Britain by
TJ International Ltd, Padstow, Cornwall

British Library Cataloguing in Publication Data
A catalogue record for this book is available from the British Library

Library of Congress Cataloging in Publication Data
A catalog record for this book has been requested

ISBN 0–415–31974–9 (hbk)
ISBN 0–415–31975–7 (pbk)

Moderate Learning Difficulties and the Future of Inclusion

Children with mild to moderate learning difficulties (MLD) make up the largest sub-group requiring special educational needs, and yet they are often neglected in terms of research and their influence on future government policies. This book, based on a Nuffield Foundation research project, considers the perspectives of children with moderate learning difficulties, reviewing relevant issues such as:

- identification of children with MLD;
- appropriate curriculum and pedagogy;
- inclusion in mainstream schools;
- their identity and self-perception.

The authors weave their findings into a wider review of current research in the MLD field and use a range of perspectives, from professional, to psychological and sociological.

This is a contemporary look at MLD that discusses the historical and policy context by discussing the origins and justification for having a category for MLD and including this group in the area of special educational needs. It challenges the reader to examine carefully the options for future policy and practice.

Students, researchers, and academics that are active in the field of inclusive education will find this an insightful and comprehensive text.

Brahm Norwich is Professor of Educational Psychology and Special Educational Needs at the School of Education and Lifelong Learning, University of Exeter. **Narcie Kelly** is Research Fellow at the School of Education and Lifelong Learning, University of Exeter.

Contents

Figures

Tables

Acknowledgements

We would like to thank the children who participated in our perspectives study, the local education authority (LEA) and schools who hosted and supported the study, the LEA officers who participated in the policy survey, Margie Tonbridge for reading a draft and the Nuffield Foundation for funding the perspectives study.

Abbreviations

AAMR	American Association of Mental Retardation
AD/HD	Attention deficit hyperactivity disorder
AEN	additional educational need
CMO	Chief Medical Officer
DfES	Department for Education and Skills
DS	Down Syndrome
DSMIV	*Diagnostic and Statistical Manual* (4th edition)
EAL	English as an additional language
EBD	emotional and behavioural difficulties
ESN	educationally sub-normal
ESN(M)	educationally sub-normal to a moderate degree
HMI	Her Majesty's Inspectorate
IEP	individual educational plan
ILEA	Inner London Education Authority
IQ	intelligence quotient
KS	Key Stage
LCD	language and communication difficulties
LD	learning disability
LEA	local education authority
MLD	moderate learning difficulties
MMR	mild mental retardation
MT	mental retardation
NC	National Curriculum
OECD	Organization for Economic Cooperation and Development
SATs	standard attainment tests
SEN	special educational needs
SENCo	SEN coordinator
SLD	severe learning difficulties
SN	special needs
SpLD	specific learning difficulties
UNESCO	United Nations Educational, Scientific, and Cultural Organization

Chapter 1

Introduction

Rationale for the book

The term 'moderate learning difficulties' (MLD) was introduced formally in the Warnock Report (DES, 1978), to replace what was then the formal term for a group identified as being 'educationally sub-normal to a moderate degree', or ESN(M). The ESN(M) term was introduced in 1945 as one of eleven categories of educational handicap. Prior to this other terms were used to refer to a group of children who have been widely seen as constituting the largest group of children designated as having special educational needs. These have included mental deficiency, mentally defective, feeble-minded, mentally retarded, the backward child and the slow-learning child.

The introduction of the term MLD following the Warnock Report sat uneasily alongside the new framework for identifying children's individual need for additional or different provision based on their learning difficulties. One of the main reasons for the Warnock recommendation to abandon categories like ESN(M) was that categories like this did not indicate specifically what provision was required for the individual child. Nor did they take account of a child's other characteristics, perhaps significant assets, nor of the child's context, which might be supportive or inhibiting of their learning. Another reason was that categories like this became negative labels that were associated with stigma and personal devaluation. So, the concept of special educational needs was built on the assumption that special provision would be based on an individual needs assessment and that decisions about provision would not be in terms of general categories of difficulty or disability. The key concept introduced by the Warnock Report was that of a continuum of needs, such that those with special educational needs (SEN) could not be distinguished clearly from those without SEN. There was no definitive basis for a general qualitative difference. This thinking still underpins the current system of identifying children with SEN and decision-making about suitable educational provision.

Despite this, the Warnock Report and subsequent Government guidance still made use of general concepts, but replaced terms like educationally sub-normal (ESN) with softer, less negative-sounding terms, such as moderate and severe learning difficulties. The term MLD, which is a derivative of the term learning difficulty, and is built into the current legislative framework, shares some of the benefits of this latter term. Learning difficulties does not mark out a group as different with as much negative connotation as does a term like educationally sub-normal. Learning difficulties can be seen as an inclusive term in that we all share difficulties in learning to some degree at some times; it is a term well suited to the continuum concept. However, since the Education Act 1981, which set up the current legislative framework for special educational needs, the term MLD has come to be used as a general category that referred to a kind of special school and as a general label to identify a child's kind of difficulty. In this sense, the term MLD has perpetuated some of the uses of the previous term ESN(M) in its use to distinguish one group of children from others with SEN, for example severe learning difficulties or specific learning difficulties, as well as distinguishing the MLD group from those without SEN.

About twenty years ago Sally Tomlinson completed a study on the decision-making about children identified as ESN(M). In this she questioned the status of the concept 'educational sub-normality' on the basis that it was socially constructed by the judgements and decisions made by professionals about children, rather than 'being an innate quality within the child' (Tomlinson, 1982, page 2). From a sociological perspective she aimed to question the status of this category and asked how some children came to be 'excluded from important institutions of "normal education", and included instead in a category which for historical reasons carries a stigma of inferiority and difference' (page 3).

Tomlinson rejected the view that this group of children presented educational characteristics that could be identified and assessed objectively with tools of diagnosis, like the IQ (intelligence quotient) test. This was partly on the grounds that the ESN category had a disproportionate number of children from manual working class backgrounds and that in the 1960s there had been a disproportionate number of children from an Afro-Caribbean background being sent to ESN(M) special schools. Her case was based partly on an analysis of the various and sometimes contrary definitions used by different professional groups involved with children identified as in the ESN(M) category. Though much of her case was based on contemporary issues and the framework of two decades ago, the underlying themes that she was dealing with continue to present challenges for education and social policy and practice more generally.

The reason for focusing this book on inclusive education provision for the group identified as having MLD is similar to those that moved Tomlinson to examine the ESN category twenty years ago, though the style and orientation of this book may be different and the context has changed considerably over this period. The MLD group is widely recognised to be the largest within the larger group of those with special educational needs (Fletcher-Campbell, 2004). Despite this it is an area which attracts less interest by educational researchers and social scientists than others, such as specific learning difficulties (dyslexia), emotional and behaviour difficulties and autism, for example. It is a poorly defined area of special educational needs and, as we will explore in this book, it is contentious whether it is rightly considered to be a special educational need in many respects. Tomlinson based her critique of ESN on the differences between professionals in how they defined that term. The problems of defining MLD nowadays reflect many of the issues that she confronted then. It is relevant that the Department for Education and Skills, in issuing the new classification of types of special educational needs in 2003, noted that they had difficulties in defining the term MLD.

At the root of these issues are questions about whether these children are more like those with sensory impairments, where there are identifiable organic impairments, or more like those children whose school attainments are below and well below average. As often remarked, these children come to be identified only once they have started their formal schooling, unlike those with sensory, motor and more severe intellectual difficulties. This might indicate that there is something about their difficulties in learning which is specific to the demands made by mainstream school curriculum and teaching. It has been noted over many decades that there has been confusion about what used to be called 'high-grade defectives'. The great majority of those who came under this administrative term did not come to official notice, except in schools, where they were considered 'educationally sub-normal'. It was held by some that there was no reason why those identified as 'high-grade defectives' should not be regarded as anything other than ordinary, if somewhat limited, citizens (Clarke and Clarke, 1974). As educationalists and special educationalists have noted for well over a century, the predominant feature of this group is that they come from lower socio-economic class families. This was the basis for Tomlinson's critique of the ESN category which argued that the so-called 'dullness' was being attributed to children from manual working class backgrounds. She argued that this implicated the wider social functions of schools and the role of schools in industrial society. Special schools for the ESN were seen from this sociological perspective to have various functions. One was to assist the smooth functioning of mainstream schools by acting as settings to receive those who were troublesome and difficult to teach. The second function was to legitimise the segregation and labelling of those who did not fit the mainstream and prepare them for low socio-economic positions in society, which has been called the 'transmission of ignorance'.

However, over the last two decades there has been a social movement to retain and provide support for children who are struggling in mainstream schools, and to transfer children from special schools into the mainstream. Though it is difficult to quantify, it is likely that many children who in the past would have been identified as being ESN(M), or more recently MLD, and transferred to MLD special schools, have been retained in mainstream schools with support for their learning difficulties. This process would have contributed to the reducing proportions of MLD pupils in special schools. It is also likely that some children in special schools for MLD would have come to have been included back into mainstream schools with various support arrangements. This phenomenon of school inclusion provides the other reason for examining in this book what the move towards greater inclusion means for MLD. This is the group that many might consider to be the easiest to include in mainstream schools that are adapted for a greater diversity of children.

In a recent study of the views of professionals in relation to inclusion, Evans and Lunt (2002) concluded that many of these professionals, including educational psychologists, teachers, social workers and health service professionals, saw obstacles to 'full inclusion' and considered that schools as currently organised frequently find it difficult to meet the wide range of needs. Though these authors discuss their findings in relation to conflicts between different Government educational policies, their study did indicate that these professionals had views about which areas of SEN were more or less difficult to include. Those with MLD were widely recognised as being 'easy to include' along with those with sensory and physical difficulties, speech and language difficulties and specific learning difficulties. This contrasted with those who were 'difficult to include', such as those with severe and profound learning difficulties and those with emotional and behaviour difficulties. These conclusions are clearly over-generalised given the wide variety of difficulties within these different categories. However, it is clear that the MLD group is seen here to be one which can be accommodated within the mainstream, yet there are many children identified as having MLD who are still not in mainstream schools. This raises the question of why this is still so. Relevant to this, it is interesting that some ten years ago Phillip Williams, in a review about the integration of students with MLD, claimed that:

> The integration of children with MLD is the acid test of integration policies: they constitute the largest group in the special school population, their parents are not as strong a lobby as parents of other children with special needs, and they do not command the same degree of sympathy as do children with obvious sensory and physical handicaps.
>
> (Williams, 1993, page 314)

If inclusion is to proceed as it has over the last two decades, then clearly the future of inclusion for this group is the 'acid test' for inclusion. Also, as Williams notes, this group does not have the same voice in lobbying Government as other areas of special needs. This means that there has also been less advocacy on behalf of this group, less policy and practice focus on the group and, as discussed above, less research interest and less written about it. Despite the relative size of the MLD group, children in this area of SEN do not have a clear identity, unlike those with severe learning difficulties. Nor are they like those described as low attainers, who are not identified as having SEN. One of the questions to be considered in this book is whether this situation will persist or can be resolved.

One interesting development has been recent work undertaken under the title of 'special needs education' in which the Organizatioon for Economic Cooperation and Development (OECD) undertook an international survey of the incidence and indicators used by different countries with respect to students with disabilities, difficulties and disadvantages (OECD, 2000). They adopted a system similar to the one introduced by the Warnock Report in the United Kingdom and built into aspects of the legislative system established by the Education Act 1981. Rather than focus on the nature of the child's disabilities, they adopt the term 'special educational needs' to refer to those who require additional support. But in doing so they see the SEN concept as extending 'beyond those who may be included in handicapped categories to cover those who are failing in school for a wide variety of reasons that are known to impede the child's optimal progress' (OECD, 2000, page 8).

This is an interesting concept of SEN in that it goes beyond the one that has come into use in this country. Though the SEN concept established in UK legislation is also defined in terms of additional provision, it does not explicitly include those who require additional provision for non-disability or impairment reasons, such as social disadvantage. In fact the current English legislation defines special educational needs in terms of learning difficulties, and defines these in terms that are confined to areas of disabilities and difficulties with connotations of impairment. The legislation also explicitly excludes English as a second language as a causal factor for learning difficulties. By contrast, the OECD recognises such linguistic factors in its category C. They are:

1   Category A: educational needs where there is substantial normative agreement, such as blind or deaf, severe and profound mental handicap and multiple handicap. These conditions affect students from all social classes and occupations . . . In medical terms they are considered as being organic disorders attributable to organic pathologies.
2   Category B refers to educational needs of students who have difficulties in learning which do not appear to be directly or primarily attributable to factors which would lead to categorisation A or C.
3   Category C refers to educational needs of students which are considered to arise primarily from socio-economic, cultural and/or linguistic factors.

There is some form of disadvantaged or atypical background for which education seeks to compensate.

(OECD, 2000, page 9)

The OECD survey shows that there is consistency with students across countries in allocations to categories A (impairments) and C (disadvantage). However, in some countries children similar to those identified as MLD in this country might be in the impairment category A, or category B (neither disadvantage nor clear impairment). In some countries children with learning difficulties associated with social disadvantage might be in category C. It is interesting that the OECD report fails to classify the UK system in its three-way classification on the grounds that the UK uses a non-categoric system. Perhaps this arises because those involved in this country in the project took the UK framework as having literally abandoned categories. In practice categories have been used, as we will discuss in later chapters. Where the MLD group would fall under this OECD system is open to contention, as we will set out in the following chapters.

This three-way classification of SEN can be linked to the difference between what have been called the social and medical models of special educational needs. Category A connects with the medical model, while category C reflects aspects of the social model. However, category B, which is defined as neither based on impairment nor social disadvantage, appears to leave open whether special educational needs, and MLD in particular, can be simply attributed to external or internal causal factors. This would not suit those who advocate the social model as one to replace the medical model. The so-called medical model has been criticised as inadequate because it medicalises or pathologises difficulties in education in terms of within-child conditions and disorders, and in so doing ignores social factors. In the social model, difficulties in learning, such as with children described as having MLD, are seen to reflect schools which have not accommodated the learning needs of these children. They are interpreted as calling for organisation change, not for labels which implicate the child's deficiency in a way that comes to justify separate provision outside the mainstream education system.

This opposition of social and medical model is unfortunate for various reasons. It confuses the role of the medical profession with assumptions often held in medical, but also other, circles. The medical profession has traditionally had power and influence in special education, but less so recently, with the growth of the influence of other groups, such as psychologists. One version of the medical model criticises excessive professional power relative to the influence and voice of the parents and the children said to have special needs. The other interpretation of the medical model is the focus on individual within-child causal factors. In this interpretation the model is better represented as an individual model where the analysis is in terms of causal factors impacting on individuals experiencing difficulties in learning. It is quite rare to find professional and medical practitioners who would deny the significance of environmental and social factors in the development of difficulties such as MLD. In this book we assume that there is a false opposition between social and individual models. There is a place for individual and social perspectives, the preference for one or the other depending on whether the focus is on individuals or social organisations, what is called the level of analysis. If the focus is on identifying additional provision required for an individual child, then some analysis of the interaction of within-child and environmental factors is relevant. If the focus is on planning curriculum and teaching programmes for groups and classes of children at the level of the school, then how they accommodate and include the diversity of children is relevant.

Inclusive planning at a school or class level requires taking account of individual children's additional educational needs. This implies that an individual model cannot exist outside the context of the social, as a social model cannot exist without reference to individuals. It is difficult to make sense of an individual's additional or special educational needs without considering how institutions and society accommodate and respond to diversity. Similarly, when education institutions accommodate diversity it is necessary to consider what that diversity is in individual terms.

The kind of conceptual model or framework that we need for the education of children and others with learning difficulties and disabilities is what has been called a bio-psycho-social model (Engel, 1977; Norwich, 1990; Cooper, 1996; Kiesler, 2000). This is an inter-disciplinary, multi-level and interactive framework. It is one where factors and processes within and between these three broad levels of analyses would be considered. When processes within a particular level might be seen as dominant, other levels might still be seen to have some contributory interactive impact. It is a framework which enables us to avoid *over-individualising* problems in education, a tendency criticised by proponents of social models, while still recognising individual factors, if they can be shown to be relevant. Also, it is a framework which enables us to avoid *over-socialising* problems, as those who assert the reality of individual difficulties and disabilities would contend. The social model has become the more dominant and popular model and this can be understood as a necessary development and corrective to over-simplistic and over-individualised models (Lindsay, 2003). However, the way that the social model has been presented and advocated has been exaggerated and over-simplified. Much of the persuasive force of the social model has come from the commitment to the value of the social and academic participation of all children and young people in mainstream schools. The social model has provided the basis for an agenda to remove barriers in society and schools to the greater participation of all in mainstream schools. How the model has come to be represented and used owes much to its role in justifying the push towards greater inclusion and less to the complexities about the origins and causes of learning difficulties and disabilities.

Another reason for this book on MLD and inclusion is to consider inclusion from the child's perspective. Much of the debate around inclusion in general has been in terms of the academic and social outcomes for children educated in different settings (separate versus mainstream). There has been a tendency to neglect the experiences and perspectives of children themselves about how and where they have their schooling. The original SEN Code of Practice (DfE, 1994), which set out the procedures for identifying, assessing and providing for pupils with SEN in 1994, promoted practices which took account of children's views and feelings about their special provision. In the revised SEN Code (DfES, 2001), these principles have been further emphasised. Recognising the child's voice in education is part of a wider movement across various areas of social provision. The Children Act 1989, the current cornerstone of care and welfare legislation, for instance, recognises that children's and young people's perspectives should be included in decisions about care. In this book we therefore report and discuss the findings from a recent research study which examined the perspectives of children and young people who received special education provision for their moderate learning difficulties in mainstream and special schools.

Organisation and contents of chapters

This book is organised into eight chapters. The next two chapters introduce the area in terms of historical and current issues. Chapter 2 addresses the question of whether there are children with MLD as a distinct group who can be clearly distinguished from other children who have not been seen to be in need of special education. It deals with historical issues that relate to relevant education policy and practice over the last 100 years in this country. It deals with questions about the nature of the category, its definition, the terms or labels used and the causal assumptions. Recent and current policy relevant to SEN generally and MLD in particular are discussed. This chapter also introduces the framework of dilemmas as a way of making sense of some of the tensions that arise in this field. This is the perspective which recognises hard choices in policy and practice about how to respond to differences between children – dilemmas of difference. This leads into Chapter 3 which addresses issues and questions about the curriculum and teaching for this group. To what extent is the common curriculum entitlement as set out in the National Curriculum appropriate for this group, and is teaching children with MLD different from teaching children without MLD? This chapter further examines who goes to special schools for MLD, the diverse nature of the MLD group, whether research about social and academic outcomes is relevant to the question about inclusion and what recent studies have found with respect to the MLD group. There is also a brief discussion of what happens to pupils with MLD when they leave school. The dilemmatic theme also runs through this chapter as a way of illuminating policy and practice issues that arise.

Two separate studies are reported and discussed in this book. The next three chapters set out the findings from the first study, which looks at the perspectives of children with MLD on their special educational provision and themselves. In each chapter the findings from the study are set within a discussion of similar and relevant research studies. The findings of the study in each of the three chapters are reported in quantitative and qualitative terms to give an overall analysis of these perspectives, on one hand, and to give an in-depth account of these perspectives, on the other. Chapter 4 is about these children's perspectives on their educational provision in special and mainstream schools. One of the main findings from the study about pupils' experiences of bullying and teasing did not arise from the starting aims of the study. This is the focus of Chapter 5, which also reviews other studies about the nature and quality of social relationships between children with and without learning difficulties in this and other countries. One of the aims of the study was to examine how children with MLD perceive them-selves. This is the focus of Chapter 6. Chapter 7 examines the findings of a survey of English and Welsh local education authorities (LEAs) about their policies and practices with respect to the MLD group, the second study reported in this book.

The final chapter pulls together the main themes, points and conclusions from the preceding chapters. It sets out explicitly to address the question set in the title of book – whether inclusion means the end of MLD as a category of special education. The question is set in its historical context as well as within the context of current deliberations at local and central Govern-ment level. The question is addressed by posing several options which are examined and evaluated. This is where the dilemmatic perspective is again used to explain that whichever option is chosen there are risks and potential drawbacks. The argument in this book is presented as an example of how theoretical and research matters bear directly on policy and practice issues in a neglected area of special education that has wider significance and impli-cations for education and social policy.

Chapter 2

Are there children with MLD?

Categories, history and current issues

MLD as a category

The use of the term moderate learning difficulties in the UK reflects much of what is loosely defined and lacking in clarity in the system of additional and different provision for children with difficulties and disabilities. The term was recommended in the Warnock Report (DES, 1978) to replace the term educationally sub-normal with the more positive sounding term *learning difficulties,* and then to qualify this phrase by moderate and severe to correspond to the terms moderate and severe ESN. However, the Warnock Committee also recommended the term mild to correspond to slow learning as part of its adoption of the continuum notion, so connecting severe ESN with slow learning. However, the term mild learning difficulty has never come into common usage. It could be that the term MLD has come to be used beyond the range of what was the coverage of the ESN(M) term, to include those who were slow learners, or who more recently have been called low attainers.

One of the confusing aspects of the term learning difficulties, whether with the qualifier severe or moderate, is that in the current UK legislation, first set out in the Education Act 1981, all children with special educational needs are defined as having learning difficulties. This meant that whether a child had a sensory, motor or intellectual difficulty, she or he would be defined as having a learning difficulty. In one sense this was an understandable turn in the 1981 Act, which was re-focusing special education as being about difficulties in learning and not as about medical categories. But, to avoid confusion between these two meanings of learning difficulties – as the replacement for the term ESN and the historic focus on children assumed to have limited intellectual abilities, and as the term to cover all kinds of special educational needs – it would have been wise to abandon the Warnock terminology and adopt some other term for children with moderate to more significant degrees of low intellectual functioning. It is also interesting that, a quarter of a century after the Warnock Report, there is still little comment about this matter. One possibility might be that to clarify the distinction between learning difficulties as the generic term for special educational needs, and as the more specific term for intellectual difficulties, a system for classifying degrees of intellectual difficulties would need to be endorsed. This might have raised the prospect of building the new system of special education on the contentious system of IQ testing and classification. Using the term learning difficulties in this loose sense might have been a way of avoiding this option.

The Warnock Committee philosophy was one of abandoning categories of child handicap or disability and of focusing educational interest on childrens' individual educational needs. There were two key aspects to this – first, the focus on needed education provision and second, the focus on individual needs, not on general categories of needs. This came to be expressed in the system of producing Statements, as formal individual records of appropriate needs and provision, and as legally binding contracts between LEAs and parents. It has been continued in the SEN Code of Practice expectation for individual educational plans (IEPs) for those with lesser degrees of special educational needs under the SEN Code of Practice (DfE, 1994). Yet, alongside this individualising approach was the inconsistent one of using general categories, but ones with more positive connotations such as MLD, to refer to kinds of provision and to children, such as MLD special schools and the MLD child or the child with MLD. In 1994 with the first SEN Code this came to be formulated in the following definition of 'learning difficulties':

> Their general level of academic attainment will be significantly below that of their peers. In most cases, they will have difficulty in acquiring basic literacy and numeracy skills and many will have significant speech and language difficulties. Some may also have poor social skills and may show signs of emotional and behaviour difficulties.
>
> (DfE, 1994, paragraph 3:55)

It is notable that the first Code did not actually use the term 'moderate' in front of 'learning difficulties'. But this implied MLD as can be seen by the way 'learning difficulties' is contrasted with 'severe or profound and multiple learning difficulties' (paragraph 3:56), on one hand, and specific learning difficulties (example dyslexia) (paragraph 3:60), on the other hand. This is clearly a continuation of the historic line of terms – mentally defective, mental deficiency, moderate ESN leading to MLD. However, there is very little in the first Code which helps to define the Moderate LD–Severe LD distinction, nor the boundaries between general 'learning difficulties' and 'specific learning difficulties'. Specific learning difficulties is defined in terms of an uneven level of performance – where performance in literacy or numeracy is not typical of 'general performance'. But, whether 'general' is a reference to attainments in other areas of the curriculum, or whether it is a coded reference to intellectual abilities involved in various kinds of reasoning, is not clarified.

This move away from aspects of the Warnock philosophy was halted to some extent in the 2001 version of the SEN Code (DfES, 2001), reflecting the continuing ambivalence about the use of categories. In the revision, the case against 'hard and fast categories' is stated in terms of the child's unique circumstances. However, the term 'impairment' was introduced alongside the position that there were areas of needs that were interrelated, so that individuals may have needs which spanned two or more areas. This move dealt with the continuing problem that many children have more than one kind of difficulty that can impact on their learning. The second SEN Code identified four areas or dimensions of need related to:

1   communication and interaction;
2   cognition and learning;
3   behaviour, emotional and social development;
4   sensory and/or physical.

Within the dimension of cognition and learning, the 2001 Code refers to 'children who demonstrate features of moderate, severe or profound learning difficulties or specific learning disabilities' (DfES, 2001, paragraph 7:58). This shows that the four overlapping areas of need were still not used to replace the term MLD.

That the Department for Education and Skills has found the term indispensable is also shown by its research into the costs and outcomes for pupils with moderate learning difficulties. As soon as some research is required that asks general questions about children with learning difficulties, some general categories are necessary. Otherwise, generalisations about learning outcomes and economic costs cannot be addressed. Crowther *et al.* (1998) had to grapple in this research with the complexity of the MLD reference. This it did in a novel and interesting way by proposing a three-dimensional approach which has some similarities to the areas of need approach used in the second SEN Code. MLD's determining characteristic was defined in terms of *milder or more severe difficulties*, i.e learning progress in relation to the National Curriculum. Milder was 'making slow but discernible progress'; while more severe was 'making only limited progress'. These terms were then defined in relation to National Curriculum test levels for each Key Stage (KS) of the assessment process. For example, 'milder' in Key Stage 3 (KS3) would be attaining at Levels 2/3 in KS3 Standard Attainment Tests (SATs); while 'more severe' would be attaining at Level 2 and below in KS3 SATs. The other two dimensions were about the presence or absence of significant emotional/behavioural difficulties and the presence or absence of significant sensory/medical difficulties. This resulted in a complex classification system with six different combinations relevant to MLD (see Table 2.1).

Though this three by two breakdown of the broad area of MLD goes further than previous attempts to outline a definition system, there are still

Table 2.1 System for defining MLD by Crowther *et al.*, 2001

Associated with	Milder learning difficulties	More severe learning difficulties
No other significant difficulties		
Significant emotional and behavioural difficulties		
Significant sensory/medical difficulties		

two areas where the scheme does not go far enough. There is a gap between the notion of 'progress within the National Curriculum' which implies breadth, and the narrow use of indicators concerned with literacy and numeracy in the system. Nor does the reference to Key Stage SATs levels deal with the evenness/unevenness of attainments across subjects areas. Is science as a core subject included, or only literacy and numeracy, and what about unevenness within subject areas? Some unevenness of attainments across subjects is to be generally expected. So the degree of unevenness that is compatible with generally low attainments needs specifying, as high degrees of unevenness mark the boundary between MLD and specific learning difficulties (SpLD). The main positive aspect of this three by two scheme is that it recognises the association between levels of MLD and other kinds of difficulties. But there are two points about this. First, there is no recognition of combining a level of MLD with both areas of significant difficulties, only with one or the other. Second, it does so only to the extent that the other difficulties are judged to 'create significant additional needs'. It is not clear exactly what is meant by this in terms of provision, nor why this condition is applied only to the associated difficulties, but not to the primary one of MLD.

Complexity of MLD group

The sample used in one of the studies which forms part of this book illustrates well the degree of association between MLD and other areas of difficulties. All pupils in one LEA in the south-west of England with Statements of SEN, in which mild to moderate general learning difficulties was a main feature, were identified from their database of Statements. The LEA used the broad definition of learning difficulties based on the SEN Code of Practice (see above page 00 and DfE, 1994). The final sample was selected randomly to have 50 children in mainstream schools and 50 in special schools, so that half within each setting was aged 10 to 11 years and half 13 to 14 years, each balanced for the numbers of boys and girls. Mainstream children with MLD were found to be in 29 different primary and secondary schools, while the special school children with MLD were in four different special schools.

Details of difficulties were recorded from each pupil's latest Statement, and the most recent National Curriculum attainment levels in mathematics and English were also collected. This enabled a comparison between the nature and severity of difficulties of the participants in the different school settings. Table 2.2 shows the differences between the mainstream and special schools in terms of the combination of other recorded areas of difficulties in addition to recorded moderate learning difficulties.

More pupils were recorded as having a language and communication difficulty (LCD) with MLD than MLD alone. In all, 61 per cent of the sample had some form of LCD with MLD and 16 per cent had emotional and behavioural difficulties with MLD. It is clear that pupils in special schools were recorded as having more additional areas of difficulties: for example, 75 per cent of pupils with MLD only were in mainstream schools, while 25 per cent were in special schools. For pupils with MLD plus two other areas of difficulties, only 29 per cent were in mainstream schools, while 71 per cent were in special schools. These data, although based on one LEA's identification of pupils with MLD, also show that more than a third of the sample had more than two associated areas of difficulties, on one hand, and only 16 per cent of the sample had no associated difficulties. It calls for a definition scheme which accommodates additional areas, one that is even more sophisticated than the one devised by Crowther *et al.* (1998).

Table 2.2 Range of difficulties in learning in special and mainstream schools

	Mainstream	Special	Total
MLD only	12	4	16
MLD + LCD	19	13	32
MLD + Motor	4	5	9
MLD + EBD	5	2	7
MLD + Sensory	1	0	1
MLD + LCD + Motor	6	9	15
MLD + LCD + Sensory	2	4	6
MLD + LCD + EBD	1	2	3
MLD + LCD + Epilepsy	0	2	2
MLD + LCD + Autism	0	1	1
MLD + Motor + EBD	1	3	4
MLD + Motor + Epilepsy	0	1	1
MLD + Motor + Sensory	0	1	1
MLD + Sensory + EBD	0	1	1
MLD + Motor + Sensory + LCD	0	1	1
MLD + Motor + LCD + EBD	0	1	1

Key: MLD: difficulty in acquiring basic educational skills
LCD: language and communication difficulty
EBD: emotional and behavioural difficulty
Motor: motor impairment
Sensory: visual or hearing impairment

This contemporary picture can be compared with the historic findings from the National Child Development Study, which followed up 16,000 children born in one week in 1958. At age 7, there were 74 children identified as ESN(M), 0.53 per cent of the cohort, while at age 11 this rose to 1.71 per cent or 266 children (Fogelman, 1983). When identifying the ESN(M) group in terms of the IQ range 55–70, it was found that 28 per cent had associated sensory or motor impairments and 28 per cent other impairments and conditions. This ESN group was likely to have been identified by tighter criteria than the recent MLD sample because it was based on a research sample using consistent IQ scores, which could not be assumed with the MLD group. Despite this, at least 58 per cent had some associated difficulties. The classic Isle of Wight study in the mid 1960s also showed a similar picture (Rutter et al., 1970). It is notable that these authors distinguished between intellectual retardation, defined in terms of intellectual functioning (IQs below 70) and the contemporary term of mental sub-normality. The latter was seen as an administrative term which related to those who needed 'care and control' in an institution. The authors referred to previous studies which showed that there were people in such institutions with intellectual functioning within the normal ranges (i.e. IQ above 70). In the epidemiological study of all children on the Isle aged 9, 10 and 11 (2,334 children), they found 2.53 per cent with intellectual retardation, defined as below two standard deviations below the mean of the Isle of Wight control group. This group was also found to have an increased rate of neurological difficulties, in all aspects of speech and language, and clumsiness as well as emotional and behavioural difficulties. It is worth noting that among this group identified as having 'intellectual retardation' were some children with IQs below 50, which has traditionally been the threshold between moderate and severe intellectual difficulties. The social class difference between those with and without neurological difficulties was also explored in this study: 1 of 11 (9 per cent) from a non-manual family had no neurological difficulties compared to 13 of 48 (27 per cent) from manual backgrounds.

More recent research by Male (1996) also shows the extent to which pupils at special schools for MLD have associated difficulties. From a sample of 54 MLD special schools (about 14 per cent of all such special schools in England in 1993), it was found that head teachers reported a wide range of associated difficulties, from sensory, to physical and medical to emotional and behavioural difficulties and autism. The two most frequently associated difficulties were language and communication difficulties, and emotional and behavioural difficulties (EBD); 87 per cent of heads reported that up to a half of their pupils had associated LCDs, and 80 per cent reported that up to half had associated EBDs. High percentages also reported associated sensory impairments (visual and hearing impairments) and physical disabilities, but at a lower level, from 67 to 70 per cent of heads.

Current SEN classification scheme

Most recently, the Government has opted to collect data about individual pupils across the country which includes details of any kind of special educational needs (DfES, 2003a). In deciding to do this it has finally re-introduced formal definitions of 11 areas of SEN, similar in principle to the 11 categories of education handicap defined in 1945, which formed the basis for the pre-Warnock system of special education. It is interesting that these definitions have been re-introduced as part of the Government's push to monitor special educational provision with more precision; they were not introduced as part of the SEN Code nor as part of a curriculum development. MLD is defined in the following terms:

> Pupils with moderate learning difficulties will have attainments significantly below expected levels in most areas of the curriculum, despite appropriate interventions. Their needs will not be able to be met by normal differentiation and the flexibilities of the National Curriculum.
> **They should only be recorded as MLD if additional educational provision is being made to help them to access the curriculum.**
> Pupils with moderate learning difficulties have much greater difficulty than their peers in acquiring basic literacy and numeracy skills and in understanding concepts. They may also have associated speech and language delay, low self-esteem, low levels of concentration and under-developed social skills.
>
> (DfES, 2003a, emphasis in original)

The consultation over the new classification system resulted in the MLD definition being subjected to the most critical comment. About a third of these responding expressed the view that the initial definition was either unclear or inaccurate. The Government summary of these responses noted that respondents considered the initial definition to be too broad, admitting it was one the hardest areas of SEN to define.

This new classification system applies to children with Statements and those at School Action Plus, not to the larger groups of children with SEN at School Action. It picks up elements of definitions from the initial and second SEN Code. From the first Code it refers to attainments significantly below peers/expectation, to difficulties in acquiring basic and literacy skills and to difficulties in speech, language and social skills. From the second SEN Code it places MLD within the cognition and learning area of SEN, one of four broad SEN areas. And it recognises the need to have a classification that allows for individual children to have more than one area of SEN and, where appropriate, a secondary area, as in the Crowther *et al.* (1998) scheme.

The latest definition reflects attempts to deal with respondents' criticisms that previous versions were too broad. To do this, the definition now includes further limiting criteria. One is that 'needs will not be able to be met by normal differentiation and the flexibilities of the National Curriculum', another is reference to 'much greater difficulty than their peers in . . . understanding concepts'. By referencing MLD to needs not met by 'normal differentiation and flexibilities' of the National Curriculum, a determining distinction is drawn between normal and non-normal, or typical and atypical curriculum differentiation and flexibilities. The problem with this lack of specificity is that it perpetuates the definitional issue by introducing yet another unspecified dimension. This recent definition also needs to be reconciled with requirements placed on schools to provide a differentiated curriculum for all (see SEN Code, DfES, 2001) and for an inclusive curriculum as part of the National Curriculum 2000. The second limiting criterion about difficulties in understanding concepts is a revealing reference to limited conceptual skills and abilities, which perpetuates the historical definitions of the precursors of MLD (mental deficiency, ESN(M)) in terms of limited intellectual abilities. Reintroducing the historical assumption of low intellectual abilities raises the persistent questions about its assessment, the role of IQ and other methods and measures. Whether this was introduced to reduce the breadth of the previous attempt to define MLD is questionable, as there is a general reminder in the introduction to the new classification that a 'lack of competence in the English language is not a SEN' and that 'underattainment may be an indicator of SEN but poor performance may be due to other factors such as problems in the child's home or family circumstances or poor school attendance (see SEN Code of Practice 7.38–7.45)' (DfES, 2003a).

International perspectives

Despite the fact that broad categories of special educational needs have been used in official documents since the first SEN Code in England, the UK system is represented in international terms as having a non-categorical system (OECD, 2000). It was thought that the UK does not use a range of categories within the broad special educational needs group for statistics-collecting purposes, although informal categories of SEN are still used. The UK is similar to Denmark, which also distinguishes between significant SEN and less significant SEN – in UK terms SEN with and without Statements – within a philosophy which responds to exceptionalities rather than defining student categories. The OECD has analysed the definitions used in 23 countries to collect data and identified four basic patterns:

1 use of disability categories only (e.g. France, Germany);
2 use of disability categories *and* disadvantaged students (e.g. Greece, New Zealand);
3 use of disability categories *and* disadvantaged students *and* gifted students (e.g. Spain, Turkey);

4   base provision on the need to respond to exceptionalities rather than defining students (e.g. New Brunswick, Canada, UK, Denmark).

It is not clear whether with the new English SEN classification, the OECD classification of the UK system would change from pattern 4 to pattern 1. The reason for doubting this is because there is a distinction between the use of categories for general national and local provision planning, on one hand, and for the identification of individual educational needs decisions, on the other. In the UK, identification and provision planning are made in terms of individual, non-categoric terms; IEPs and Statements are planned in terms of the child's individual strengths and difficulties. The individualised plan may then be categorised as being of a certain broad kind, but this would come at the end of the identification and assessment process. For individual assessment and provision planning, it may be possible to work in a non-categoric way, while specific categories are used for general monitoring and planning of provision. The OECD four patterns, set out above, do not make this key distinction, even though it states, 'those with special educational needs are defined by the additional public and/or private resources provided to support their education' (OECD, 2000, page 8).

The focus on 'additional resources' shifts the focus away from child charac-teristics to the available educational provision and its flexibility and appro-priateness – it is about the 'normality' of provision, what is called 'generally available provision' (to use the UK legislative term).

The OECD study also designed a system of cross-country categories for the 18 countries in the OECD study which used some form of categoric system (patterns 1, 2 and 3 above). These were represented as:

1   Category A – where there is substantial normative agreement about the categories, e.g. sensory, motor, severe, profound intellectual disabilities;
2   Category B – difficulties which do not appear to be attributable to factors which lead to categories A and C; what could be called contended dis-abilities;
3   Category C – difficulties that arise from socio-economic, cultural, and/or linguistic factors; some disadvantaged or atypical background which education seeks to compensate for.

What is so interesting about the use of these broad categories is the wide variations between countries. For example, the USA is reported to have 5.6 per cent of all primary and lower secondary aged children in category A (normative agreement about disabilities) and almost 70 per cent of these children are in regular classrooms; whereas Holland, which only has 1.8 per cent in this category, has 87 per cent of them in special schools. There is some agreement between countries about which SEN areas are under category B – the contended disabilities (neither category A – normative disabilities – nor category C – socio-economic/linguistic based difficulties). Both Dutch and US panels judged that specific learning disabilities (corresponding to specific learning difficulties in the UK) fell within category B; but only in the US was emotional disturbance in category B.

This study also illustrates the variations between countries in the reported percentage of students with what was called 'moderate learning difficulties'. In New Zealand, where the term referred to students with IQs between 35–50, only 0.03 per cent of primary and lower secondary students were deemed to have 'moderate learning difficulties'; all were in special schools. In Hungary, by contrast, educable mental retardation was defined as IQs between 51–70; some 3.56 per cent were deemed to have 'moderate learning difficulties', with 70 per cent in special schools, 30 per cent in special class, and none in regular classes. In Italy, where they use the term 'moderate mental handicap', in which the IQ range is 35/40–70, some 0.9 per cent were identified, with most in regular classes and only 0.9 per cent in special schools (see Table 2.3).

The degree of international variation is also evident in two other features of the use of terminology. First, the use of the term 'mental' to refer to some form of intellectual disability or difficulty is widespread; for example, 'mental handicap' in Germany and 'mental disability' in Portugal. In several countries the term 'mental' is reserved for the more severe degree of disability and 'learning' for a lesser degree or specific kind of disability; for example, in Korea 'mental retardation' is used to refer to those with IQs less than 70, and 'learning disabilities' is the term used for specific learning difficulties. Second, in some countries, lesser degrees of intellectual disabilities were judged to be in the contentious category B (neither normative agreement nor difficulty based on socio-economic disadvantage); for example in Finland 'mild mental impairment' was judged to be in category B while 'moderate mental handicap' was judged to be in category A.

Table 2.3 Examples of international variations in 'moderate learning difficulties'

	IQ range	% with MLD	% in different placement	National term
New Zealand	35–50	0.03	All special school	Intellectual disabilities
Hungary	51–70	3.56	70% special school; 30% special class, none regular class	Educable mental retardation
Italy	35/40–70	0.9	Most regular class; 0.9% special schools	Moderate mental handicap

Historical context

The other context in which to consider the category of MLD is the historical one, which has already been touched on in the above sections. The above analysis of the contemporary MLD category in the wider context of the international OECD (2000) study shows two key features of this area:

1   the contentious nature of the category – uncertainty and disagreement over whether this is a clear-cut disability and to what extent it is attributable to socio-economic factors;
2   whether to define it in terms of difficulties in learning (school curriculum terms) or in terms of intellectual ability (usually in IQ terms).

This section sets these two key issues in context and shows the continuity in the UK over at least 100 years of these persistent questions.

In a recent history of this field, Copeland (2002) identifies the interaction between two Royal Commissions in the 1880s as critical to establishing the framework that divided 'exceptional' children from 'ordinary children' and subsequent policy and practice in this country. The Royal Commission on the Elementary Education Acts (Cross Commission) handed over the issue of the 'feeble-minded' to the Egerton Commission, which was initially set up in 1886 to examine provision for 'the Blind, Deaf and Dumb', but came to widen its terms of reference to include 'other cases as from special circumstances would seem to require exceptional methods of education'. Copeland's point is that this sowed the seeds of segregated provision, the basis for the continuing divisions between the exceptional and the ordinary, or what is nowadays called the special and the mainstream. This move shifted the focus away from mainstream school practices to a focus on exceptional cases and their distinctive needs.

The Egerton Commission was much influenced by a Dr Shuttleworth, who was the medical superintendent of an asylum for 'idiots and imbeciles' in Lancaster. His classification included the terms 'idiot' and 'imbecile', and he constructed a hierarchy in which 'idiocy is a deeper defect than imbecility', and in which there are three levels:

1   those capable of learning to read and write (about 40 per cent) – 'educational imbeciles', which the Egerton Commission came to refer to as being 'feeble-minded';
2   those capable of benefiting to some extent from school instruction and discipline (about 40 per cent), also referred to as 'imbeciles';
3   the 'ineducable' group (about 15 per cent) – referred to as 'idiots'.

This could be seen as a positive position about the potential impact of education, but the Commission also accepted Shuttleworth's case for separate residential institutions for the education of 'imbeciles'. His separatist approach contrasted with the more inclusive approach practised even then in Norway and was based on four arguments which are still voiced down the decades to this day. The first was in terms of economies of scale – numbers being too small to make special classes in mainstream elementary schools viable. The second, linked, argument was that there was a need for specially trained and experienced teachers. The third argument was that residential schooling was needed because progress also depended on care outside the classroom, and the fourth was that the specialised nature of the curriculum might be inappropriate for mainstream schools. However, as Copeland notes, there were already separate schools for those who were blind and deaf, and the Commission was only extending this approach to those who were 'feeble-minded'. Unlike Shuttleworth, whose professional base was in residential institutions, another leading doctor in the field at that time was a paediatrician, a Dr Warner, who identified about 5 per cent of school children as not coping in elementary schools of the day. Warner's approach concentrated on family circumstances, physical symptoms and treatment within the school system, clearly a less separatist one. He proposed the establishment of special classes in mainstream schools and ways of identifying children in need of these classes by more objective methods.

The Egerton Commission recommendations in 1889 were for a distinction between 'feeble-minded children' and the 'educable imbeciles', the former to be in special classes in mainstream elementary schools, the latter in separate institutions. Copeland interpreted this division as one where the feeble-minded were regarded as children like other children, while the 'educable imbeciles' were a category based on the then-current medical terminology of the day. It can also be noted that the boundary between the mainstream schools of the day and the separate institutions was marked by a separation of professional territory between the doctor, who certified 'educability' in the separate institution and the teacher in elementary schools with special classes. So, two models of provision were established in the early 1890s, for example the special classes in elementary schools in Leicester, and the special centres in London.

Another feature of Government commissions of that period was the tentativeness of recommendations in the field of 'mentally defective' children (Sutherland, 1984). The persistence of terms which were not clearly and specifically defined is noted by Copeland, who illustrates how a term like 'feeble-minded' was defined as different from some other terms which were also not clearly defined, for example the feeble-minded were not 'idiots' or 'imbeciles'. Official Government positions also recognised that there were no clear separating criteria and that differences were a matter of degree (Copeland, 2002, page 97). Despite this recognition there was a need in practice for a dividing line and this was found by reference to 'the ability to earn a living' (Departmental Committee on Defective and Epileptic Children,

1898, quoted by Copeland, 2002, page 98). The assumption was that the 'dull' or 'weak minded' can 'earn a living', whereas the 'imbecile' was unable to do this.

There was continuity of these hierarchical views, but with further distinctions and ordering being made. In 1913 the Chief Medical Officer of the Board of Education, for example, identified five groups of children (from a quote in Copeland, 2002, pages 109–110):

1   the mentally normal child;
2   the dull or backward child;
3   the feeble minded child;
4   the imbecile child;
5   the idiot.

By contrast to the other groups, the 'idiot' is not described as a child, and the 'imbecile child' and the 'idiot' are seen as 'ineducable'. But this classification distinguishes between the 'feeble-minded' and the 'dull or backward child', a distinction not made by the Egerton Commission, some 24 years before. The Board of Education also recognised in 1913 that there was considerable variations across the country in the identification of children as 'backward' and that this showed that there was no recognised standard for this category.

Despite the introduction of statistical techniques through the development of psychometric tests of mental abilities (or what are called cognitive abilities tests or IQ test more recently) and their international use, the persistence of the problem of the boundary between the 'normal' and 'sub-normal' continued into the 1920s. Burt, the British psychologist who is best known within education for promoting and developing mental testing, was clear that there were no sharp demarcation lines. Burt accepted that what he called 'mental deficiency' was an administrative category rather than a psychological one, because the cut-off 'corresponded with the general practice of the more experienced teachers and school medical officers when nominating or certifying cases in need of education at special school' (Burt, 1921, page 81). He also accepted that the boundaries were 'somewhat arbitrary' but, as they had to be fixed somewhere for practical reasons, these boundaries had to take account of schools themselves and the actual number of available places. There have been several contemporary critics of Burt's approach to this, as part of his wider legacy. Copeland (2002) bases his criticism on a Foucauldian analysis of the operation of the power–knowledge nexus at work. In other words, those in positions of power, like Burt, could use their position to define what counted as knowledge – the boundary for scholastic 'normality' – even when there was uncertainty. Corbett (1996) has been more critical of Burt's reference to the question of fixing the time for the daily lighting up to consider the boundary issue, as this was neither objective nor scientific. Gipps *et al.* (1985) have criticised the reliance on available places in special settings as this was not an objectively justifiable boundary and was therefore problematic. However, Norwich (1990) made the distinction between basing a boundary on the actual numbers of places in special settings compared to the number judged to be in need of such placement. The latter might be preferable, but this depends on the justification for the judgement about education needs. This also raises the questions of expectations and responsibilities; what range of children should teachers in ordinary schools teach, and when is it legitimate for ordinary schools to withdraw responsibility for teaching children who have difficulties in learning? It is interesting that these wider questions arose in relation to boundary questions many decades ago. They are questions that are still central to current debates, though they probably have added significance more recently, with emphasis on inclusion and questions about the responsibilities of mainstream schools.

The Wood Committee, which included Burt amongst others, was established in 1924 to examine questions relating to 'mental deficiency among children of school age', though it only reported in 1929. Copeland (2002) explains the establishment of the committee as being prompted by a further desire to surveil and control the system given the persistent difficulties (definitional, wide variation in identification, placement uncertainties, rural provision). By contrast Pritchard (1963) saw setting up a committee as a defensive move to provide a breathing space for the Board of Education. The Wood Committee approved the then-current system that LEAs were required to make provision for all children who were 'capable of deriving benefit from education in the ordinary acceptation of the term'. By this it was meant that children who were not able to attend a day school or could not 'make substantial progress in scholastic and manual work' should be transferred out of the school system to be the responsibility of the local Mental Deficiency Authorities; and be considered 'ineducable' (quote from Copeland, 2002, page 153). This set the lower limit for what was considered to be 'mental deficiency' within the education system – this was judged to be an IQ of 50 and below. This distinction between the 'educable defectives' and 'ineducable defectives' was one of the Committee's main recommendations; the 'educable defectives', covering the feeble-minded, the dull and backward, were all to be regarded under the single category of 'retarded'. It has been commented by Copeland (2002) that the category of retarded broadened the range of children judged to be 'educable defective' by including those who were 'dull' or 'backward'. This is a similar point to the one that was made about the Warnock Committee's more recent move to bring together those who were regarded as 'slower learners' into the broadened concept of SEN – widening it from 2 per cent to 20 per cent of school-age children (Tomlinson, 1985). Another interesting recommendation by the Wood Committee was that ascertainment prior to entering special schools should be dropped, and only retained for notifying the Mental Deficiency Authority in cases of children who were 'ineducable'. This proposal was never realised.

During the 1920s the school leaving age was increased, requiring the re-organisation of post-primary schooling with implications for 'retarded' pupils. For example, Her Majesty's Inspectorate (HMI) produced a pamphlet on these implications in 1937, while the Chief Medical Officer (CMO) referred in his annual report in the previous year to the increasing number of LEAs taking the 'retarded' into account in their re-organisation plans. From this period there was a move to tighten the use of the definition of 'educable defective' by specifying its practical operation through the use of IQ tests and the following of detailed procedures by school medical officers. This strategy of responding to uncertainties in defining what counted as a 'defective' pupil by specifying procedures rather than criteria was not new in the 1930s. Newman, who was CMO in the 1920s also recognised the definitional problem in the Education Act 1921, which described children who were 'incapable of receiving proper benefit from instruction in ordinary public elementary schools but . . . not incapable of receiving benefit from instruction in . . . special classes or schools' (Education Act, 1921). Newman's response had also been to provide for a more detailed schedule of assessment or 'ascertainment'. This traditional strategy has persisted to the present day with the problems in the definition of special educational needs (Audit Commission/ HMI, 1992), and the use of the SEN Code of Practice as a way of responding to uncertainty of definition by specifying identification and assessment procedures.

In the historic 1944 Education Act, terminology changed; 'defect' was replaced by 'handicapped' and the form of legislation became more inclusive in bringing the provisions for the 'handicapped' into the formulations of the provisions for primary and secondary schools. The associated regulations in 1945 introduced 11 categories of educational handicap. Those who were identified as 'mentally defective' came to be referred to as 'educationally sub-normal', 'pupils, who by reason of limited ability or other conditions resulting in educational retardation, require some specialised form of education, wholly or partly in substitution for educational normally given in ordinary schools' (Ministry of Education, 1945). The position here was that the 'educationally sub-normal' were not just those with limited ability but were also ESN(M) from other causes. These other causes were adverse family and domestic circumstances. Limited ability referred to low intelligence, which was assumed to have an innate basis and by 'general agreement . . . cannot be substantially improved by any methods known . . . at present' (quoted in Copeland, 2002, page 198). Despite this, the Government position still managed to make reference to the school system as a cause of retardation, such as large classes, and poor buildings.

The Government position was that the ESN category consisted of those who were retarded by more than 20 per cent of their age, but not so low as to be 'ineducable'. Some 10 per cent were estimated to fall into this category, though the basis and justification for this figure was not specified. Of these, a small minority (0.2 per cent) would be in residential special schools with about 1 per cent in day special schools (those with IQs between 55–70/75), this figure being determined, as it had been historically, in terms of available special school provision. The assumption was that even some with IQs of less than 70, if they were stable and received support from parents and others, could remain in ordinary schools. This implied that special schools would receive those presenting behavioural difficulties and/or where parent and other support was not forthcoming. It also meant that pupils with IQs above 70, with behavioural difficulties and/or where parent and other support was not forthcoming, would find their way into special schools for the ESN(M). This would explain to some extent the significant growth in the numbers of children with ESN between 1950 and 1970 – from 9,205 to 31,338, a rise from 0.27 per cent to 0.64 per cent of the school population (DES statistics quoted in Copeland, 2002).

There was and continues to be confusion about the connection between ESN(M) and limited ability as indicated by IQs in the 55–70 range. It is clear from the 1945 regulations (quoted above) that it was meant to be about low educational attainment. Jones-Davies (1975), writing in the period before the introduction of the SEN framework, believed that this was the correct understanding of the ESN(M) term, but that its more limited meaning in terms of intellectual abilities was its practical interpretation. Perhaps this interpretation came to be reinforced by the LEAs taking responsibility for children with IQs below 50 in 1971. This group came to form the category of children with severe ESN. It may be that the extension of the ESN category to those with more severe intellectual disabilities came to influence the association of ESN(M) with low intellectual ability. It is also interesting that between the 1950s and early to mid 1970s the term 'slow learning' came to have wide currency (Cleugh, 1957; Tansley and Gulliford, 1960). This term might have been popular because it may have been less offensive to parents than ESN. However, its use was also inconsistent; it was used for children failing in school (e.g. Education Pamphlet, 1964) as well as those with limited intelligence (e.g. Williams, 1970). Jones-Davies argued that the wider usage, for up to 15 per cent of pupils with lowest attainments, was more justified as it included those called 'backward' and 'remedial' and did not suggest an intellectual ability limitation. 'Slow learning' came to be used for a wider group including those experiencing adverse socio-economic conditions, those with emotional and behavioural difficulties, those with specific impairments and those with low intellectual abilities. However, as Jones-Davies also argued, it was not a very useful term for identifying different educational needs and planning provision, except as a blanket one to orient or alert to a broad area of educational concern.

To conclude this historic section, more needs to be said about the assumptions about intelligence as an largely innate, general and testable characteristic and the role of intelligence testing in identifying children as mentally defective. There have been many serious criticisms over the years which have constituted a serious challenge to their design, purpose, use and abuse. These have included the following:

1   IQ tests have been a limited measure of the functioning of people with intellectual disabilities (Ryan, 1972), leading to the development of measures of social competence – a version of the wider criticism about abilities that IQ tests do not measure.
2   IQ tests assume innate fixed intellectual abilities that ignore the develop-ment of acquired abilities from genetic–environmental interactions.
3   IQ tests are not measures of abstracted cognitive abilities; they measure performance, which is determined by the interaction of contextual and personal factors, with cognitive as one of several factors – leading to the development of dynamic or assisted forms of assessing intellectual abilities (Feuerstein, 1979; Haynes, 1971). This is a version of the wider criticism that IQ tests have been misrepresented as measuring innate intellectual abilities.
4   IQ tests assume general intellectual abilities and ignore distinct areas and kinds of intelligence – leading to multi-dimensional models of abilities (Guildford, 1967; Gardner, 1993).
5   The historic standardisations of IQ tests did not include children from less advantaged and ethnic backgrounds, so identifying disproportional numbers from these groups as below thresholds.
6   IQ test reliability (the margin of error in IQ score and the consistency of scores over time) and validity in predicting future learning outcomes have been exaggerated.
7   IQ tests depend on quantification that requires the use of standard pro-cedures outside 'real' contexts – leading to contextual and teaching assess-ment methods based on qualitative descriptions of abilities (Vygotsky, 1978; Feuerstein, 1979; Gardner, 1993).
8   IQ tests have been used for high-stakes decisions about placements in stig-matised special schooling based on biased and erroneous assessment of potential for future attainments.
9   IQ tests provide limited useful and practical evidence about how to teach children with learning difficulties – leading to the development of curri-culum based assessment methods (Ainscow and Tweddle, 1978; Solity and Bull, 1987).

These nine broad areas of criticism, some of which are interconnected, pro-vide the historic context for the above analysis of the definitional problems surrounding the identification and assessment of children with moderate learning difficulties. The social need for a theory of intelligence and a prac-tical means of assessment for use in mass schools systems is evident from the above history. Psychologists played a major part in this history in particular in relation to the ESN/MLD group discussed here (cf. Binet in France and Burt in the UK) and their work came to define one of the most influential, albeit contentious, areas of psychology in the twentieth century (Wooldridge, 1994). The current UK situation is that cognitive ability measures have ceased to have any official use in regulations and guidance about general special education policy and practice (such as assessing whether children have 'difficulties in understanding concepts': part of the definition of MLD in the new SEN classification, DfES, 2003a). Nor are they recommended in the identification and assessment procedures for individual children set out in the SEN Code. Despite these criticisms they have continued to be used by educational psychologists who play a key role in the statutory assessment procedure which provides the advice to LEAs about whether to issue a Statement or not (see Chapter 7 for examples of LEA practices).

The problems underlying categories of special educational need

Over the last two decades there has been persistent criticism of the concept of special educational needs from a critical sociological perspective, as part of a wider critique of the special education system (Tomlinson, 1982; Barton and Tomlinson, 1984; Tomlinson, 1985). Tomlinson (1985) argued that 'the whole concept of special needs is ambiguous and tautological. It has become part of the rhetoric that serves little educational purpose'. That is, needs are defined in terms of additional provision without specifying who is to have this additional provision, other than that it is for those with special needs. Tomlinson's point is that while the identification problem had not been resolved, the SEN concept was expanded by the 1981 educational legislation. Barton and Tomlinson (1984) recognised that there was normative agreement about certain categories of special needs, such as blind, deaf, severe intellectual disabilities, but others, 'maladjusted', 'disruptive' and 'ESN', were described as 'not normative' (page 7). This led to the assertion that there were normative and non-normative SENs; the latter including the then-ESN and now the MLD category. It has not been clear whether this distinction was one of causation or of severity of disability or both. If it were one of causation, then it parallels one made traditionally in medicine between organically and functionally or psycho-socially caused conditions. However, this is currently not a clear-cut medical distinction as even organically based conditions might also be associated with psycho-social causal conditions. Also, all medical disorders, whatever their causation, are initially identified in terms of social norms and values (Kennedy, 1980). To use a current example, whether over-activity and attentional difficulties are interpreted as an attention deficit hyperactivity disorder (AD/HD) or as an emotional deprivation and behavioural difficulty, either way it implies some 'problem' in terms of behavioural norms. The issue is not that some difficulties and impairments are normative and others not so, as all are normative in the above sense, but that for some there is agreement over the norms and for others less agreement over norms. More disagreement is found with difficulties in learning which are not so different from the average. Less disagreements are found over what are called severe and profound difficulties, which are less frequent in number and further from the average than moderate and mild difficulties.

Tomlinson's initial study of decision-making about ESN (Tomlinson, 1982) aimed to show that this category was socially constructed by the judgements and decisions of professionals rather than being 'an innate quality within children' (page 2). The study rejected the assumption that these children had educational characteristics that could be identified and assessed by objective tools. The focus was switched onto professionals and the system within which they operated. Tomlinson aimed to show in this study that:

> there is no normative consensus amongst professionals about what constituted the ESN(M) child and that beliefs about qualities other than 'educational' are used to account for the categorisation . . . by 'informal procedures' during which professionals can reinforce their characterisations of the child and parents – the parents being involved in the process as 'cultural inferiors'.
>
> (Tomlinson, 1982, page 28)

Tomlinson assumed that the ESN(M) categorisation process served the social order in two key ways, first, within the school system to remove troublesome children, and second, in the wider society by legitimising the 'reproduction of a troublesome section of the population as an inferior stigmatised group' (page 29). Part of her argument was based on the disproportionate over-placement of children of West Indian origin in ESN special schools (Coard, 1971), in itself a criticism of the British school system in making these children ESN. However, this was as much a question of the use of behavioural criteria for placing children in special schools, as the extent to which appropriate forms of assessing intellectual functioning were used by psychologists. Nevertheless, the study did focus attention on important questions about ethnic tolerance and discrimination in schools and the extent to which referrals for ESN special schools reflected inflexible and unresponsive schooling.

Tomlinson concluded in her influential study that professionals did differ in their beliefs about what was an ESN(M) child, though a closer reading of the findings does raise the questions of the extent to which they supported this general conclusion. She used nine types of accounts to analyse the range of perspectives she identified from head teachers, psychologists, doctors and parents: functional, statistical, behavioural, organic, psychological, social, school, tautological and intuitive. A close analysis of the data and graphs in her book was undertaken to show that despite some differences between these professionals, there were still agreements about the types of accounts used. Mainstream school referring heads, receiving special school heads, educational psychologists and parents mostly used functional types of accounts – in terms of what the child could/could not do, usually in learning and intellectual functional terms. Doctors differed from other groups in mostly referring to family, cultural and socialisation factors; this was called a social account. This difference of accounts may be interpreted as showing an implicit functional account, as a social one implies a causally based one. Causal accounts might be expected from doctors, who aim to identify medical conditions in terms of their aetiology (causation) rather than in simple descriptive terms. Statistical accounts (which refer to ability and attainment tests) were used only by psychologists and doctors. However, they are refinements of functional ones and the kind of definitions to be expected from professionals who specialise in quantitative assessment methods. Behavioural accounts (inappropriate behaviour, uncontrolled, etc.) were also widely used; they were second most frequently used by referring and receiving head teachers and third most frequently used by parents. Social accounts were also widely used; most frequently by doctors, second most frequently by psychologists and special school head teachers and third most frequently by referring heads. Organic and psychological accounts were less frequently used overall. Organic definitions (genetic, disorder, damage, condition) were used by all groups, but to varying degrees; by doctors and parents most frequently, by special school heads less frequently and least frequently by psychologists and referring heads. Psychological accounts (emotional disturbance) were only used by referring heads and psychologists, and less frequently so. All groups used school accounts, except referring heads, but these were used more frequently by psychologists and receiving special school heads.

This summary of the Tomlinson findings, taken from her concluding chapter, indicates that although there were clear differences in professional accounts, there were still important similarities. The differences can be attributed to the expected specialist roles of the different professionals. The similarities were about functional learning and ability difficulties which, as we have discussed, have been recognised since the late nineteenth century. Tomlinson's professional perspectives analysis does not relate directly to her more significant sociological explanations of the existence of special schools as a 'safety valve allowing the smoother running of the normal education system' (1982, page 49) and the product of power struggles and vested professional interests. As Copeland (1993) has pointed out, there are problems with both kinds of explanations. From a historian's perspective, Cole (1990) has questioned whether there is historical evidence for Tomlinson's vested interest and 'separating out the defectives' claims.

Have the categories SEN and MLD outlived their usefulness?

The argument over categories has to be set within the persistent contradiction in the Warnock Committee Report (DES, 1978). The Committee rejected the current special education categories (by denying a clear dividing line between disability and no disability) but recommended more positive categories, like moderate learning difficulties. At the time, their proposals distracted attention from this contradiction, by distancing medical categories from their educational and schooling implications, by focusing attention on educational needs and provision, and by highlighting the individuality of needs that could not be captured by crude general categories. That its recommendations were still based on traditional categories is clear from its use of well-known epidemiological studies, like the Isle of Wight study (Rutter *et al.*, 1970), which was based on evidence from psychometric tests, such as IQ cut-offs of below 70, for identifying children with 'intellectual retardation'.

A key element of the Warnock philosophy which was embedded in the Education Act 1981 was the relativity of needs, by which was meant that SEN were seen as the product of an interaction between a child's particular impairment/s and the social and learning environment. This interactive model has been interpreted as implying that educational needs can be changed according to the quality of the environment (Gray, 2003) and as implying that 'the system fails to adapt to the characteristics of the child' (Dyson, 1990, page 59). However, it can be argued that an interaction model implies that changes in either child or environmental factors or both would affect the interactive outcome. To focus, as these and other commentators do, on the impact of environmental or systems change makes sense, as the environmental factors are more easily changed for intervention purposes. However, the interactive outcome can be affected by changes in child factors themselves too. This argument against an overly environmental interpretation of the interactionist model can be seen as a challenge to the Warnock orthodoxy about SEN (Gray, 2003). Challenge has also come from other quarters by members of the disability movement, who consider that 'needs' imply a paternalistic and professionally controlled system, rather than one based on the rights of those with disability as equal citizens. A third challenge to the Warnock orthodoxy has come, as discussed above, from a management perspective, best exemplified in the recent case for common national definitions of need (Audit Commission, 2002a).

The contemporary case for defining national common categories of SEN is based on the need for planning, monitoring and ensuring equal opportunities. Gray (2003) summarises these as follows:

1 Strategic planning of the education services is possible only if there are clear and consistent definitions of need; the comparison with health planning is made here.
2 Government is asked for statistics about different areas of need.
3 Consistency of service requires common definitions across schools and LEAs, cast as an equal opportunities issue.
4 Categories will provide the basis for monitoring the progress of different groups, what is called 'value added' as well as judgements of 'value for money'.

These points are reinforced, according to Gray, by other background factors:

1 the increasing recognition of the value of disability labels; for example, the growth of disability voluntary organisations, benefits conferred by labels;
2 the move towards within-child models of SEN; the growth of parent interest groups and teacher interest in specific disabilities;
3 new specialisms; for example, specialist support teams.

Gray's criticism of the new Government SEN classification is based on questioning its validity, desirability and necessity. The validity issues also include the consistency of category use. However, it is important to distinguish between the validity of the principle of categorisation and the actual practice of it. There may be difficulties in practice that call for more specific, sophisticated category systems, better training and moderation. This does not affect the principle of categorisation. The validity of educational categories is about whether categories, such as MLD, have implications for additional or different educational provision or interventions for those with MLD compared to those without MLD. However, a test of validity in this sense is full of difficulties and uncertainties to which we will return later in this chapter.

The issue of the desirability of categories is connected with the validity issue, as categories give access to additional resources and have been shown to create pressure to increase identification of children with SEN, what are called 'perverse incentives'. This depends on the practical system for applying categories, which is why outside professionals, first doctors and then psychologists, were employed to provide an identification system that was less influenced by parent and school interests. The large scale and complexity of the identification of children with SEN in the SEN Code system, which goes well beyond those in special schools, has involved the use of pupil audits. These audits vary in the areas and levels of SEN identified across LEAs, but they are all completed by teachers, subject to some moderation across schools. The role of the external professional advising on identification has been retained only for the 3 per cent of children undergoing statutory assessment when a Statement is being considered. This process has been

increasingly criticised for being expensive, alienating to parents, bureau-
cratic and unnecessary in many cases, as expressed in another Audit Commission report (Audit Commission, 2002a). As we pointed out before in this
chapter, despite the non-categoric assumptions in the current system, even
the pupil audits have used general categories, such as 'general learning
difficulties'.

The issue of 'perverse incentives' can be dealt with in two broad ways.
One way is to counter the pressures to over-identify or under-identify (for
example, to boost value added measures) – by using less alterable (but for
some still questionable) indicators, such as standardised group test scores
and by better systems of moderating pupil audits. The other is not to use
categories at all, but this potentially undermines the basis of a system of additional educational resourcing for children with SEN and disabilities. There
are clearly some hard decisions here to which we will return.

Gray's position over the question of the necessity of categories is that there
are alternatives to them. He favours a strategy of developing services that
are flexible in response to individual variations, and based on clarity of
principles and desired outcomes in contrast to an approach which specifies
processes and procedures. This strategy is backed by reference to research on
more inclusive LEAs, which showed that they were characterised by an
ethos of determination and a clear focus on what was to be achieved (Croll
and Moses, 2000). However, what is missing from this alternative is not the
focus on outcomes, but criteria for deciding when additional resources are to
be allocated and additional provision planned under the heading of SEN
and disabilities. This point relates to Gray's response to the rationale for categories that claims that they would ensure consistent allocations to children
with similar needs. Here he draws on what he calls the 'emerging wisdom' of
moving the funding of additional needs to a school level, based on baseline
pupil performance or social disadvantage data. However, like others advocating this alternative (Dyson, 2002), he is not advocating the replacement
of pupil level resourcing and planning. In so doing, some decision is needed
about which children to cover by the SEN category and individual identification and planning SEN framework; the category question does not go away,
just the number of children covered by it is reduced.

As a response to the rationale that categories enable the comparison of the
attainments of children within categories across schools for benchmarking
purposes, Gray argues that it would be better to use progress data and link
these with demographic and expenditure factors rather than pupil categories.
However, if the argument is that categories such as MLD are of dubious
validity and if used, done so with serious validity cautions, then would this
not also apply to categories such as 'low attainers'? There are similar issues
about defining the generality of low attainment and the threshold for identifying it. In fact as the discussion in this chapter, and the findings from a

national survey in Chapter 7 (page 143) show, this is exactly one of the issues with the current MLD category.

Issues underlying defining SEN and MLD

Any discussion of the MLD category and its use has to address the basic critique of categories – that they are mere social constructions, fabricated by social institutions and professionals to serve particular purposes and interests. As discussed above, Tomlinson (1982) identified these with the smooth running of ordinary schools by removing 'troublesome children' and by legitimising the reproduction of a 'troublesome section of the population as an inferior stigmatised group' (1982, page 29). This sociological perspective has been very influential, especially in encouraging the idea that a non-labelling approach is possible. Socially and philosophically, this perspective assumes that social realities become meaningful only through socially constructed and shared symbols. This implies that difficulties and disabilities are defined by the meanings attached to certain deviations of functioning, by the labels and the labelling process used. It is clear that some form of social constructionism captures some aspects of the history of how institutions and professionals within them have come to construct categories of people for certain purposes. But the problems arise when it is presented as denying the prospect of objectivity (that MLD is a mere fabrication expressing subjective perspectives) and that there is no external reality at the base of a social or human construction of it (that neural, cognitive, behavioural nor environmental characteristics could in principle be identified as associated with low intellectual functioning).

Searle (1995), in trying to make sense of social constructionism, has argued that it is possible to recognise the importance of the social construction of reality without denying that there is some external reality. To do so, he distinguishes between the nature of judgements or statements in the domain of language and knowledge and the domain of what exists; the distinction between epistemology and ontology. Figure 2.1 illustrates the relationship between these epistemological and ontological dimensions.

Some statements can be considered to be objectively true in so far as they are consistent with the facts, while other statements might be subjective as they express personal perspectives (horizontal epistemology dimension). Independently of this distinction, some things can be considered to exist objectively, in the sense that they exist independently of any human attitude or knowledge of them, while other things are subjective or related to some human use (vertical ontology dimension). Some features of the world, such as the existence of a mountain, can be regarded therefore as intrinsic and are quite independent of any human construction for their real existence. Other features of the world, by contrast, may depend on human construction or

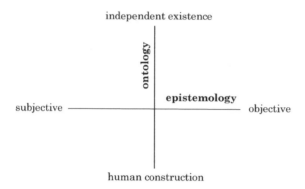

Figure 2.1 Relationship between epistemology and ontology, based on Searle, 1995

use, being ontologically subjective, but can be described in epistemologically objective terms (the bottom right area in Figure 2.1).

For example, that a child is identified as having moderate learning difficulties is a social construction in the sense that this attribution derives from social aims and institutions, but this constructed ontological feature does not prevent it from being represented by objective statements. Also, as Searle points out, for there to be a social construction of reality implies that there is something there in external reality to construct. Whether we construct low intellectual functioning and slow progress in overall school learning as 'MLD', as 'low attaining' or in some other way is a question of which is a more valid way of categorising the phenomena; it does not justify denying such phenomena. We do not, therefore, have to choose between recognising the human or social dependence of certain features of the world and objective statements about these features.

Soder (1989), a Norwegian educationalist, has criticised social constructionist perspectives, which assume that difficulties and disabilities come into existence through a process of labelling. He has also criticised the influence of social constructionist perspective on the development of non-labelling approaches to services, not unlike that recommended by the Warnock Committee. It leads, as Soder argued, to the false belief that if something is undesirable, the way to change it is by changing the meaning ascribed to it. Soder contends that this belief is superficial as social meanings cannot readily be changed as they are anchored in systems of meaning that stand as an external reality in themselves. A non-labelling approach is not an option, as shown by historic and recent attempts to avoid negative labelling (for example, ESN); these have involved replacing them with more positive ones (for example, MLD). But over time, what were acceptable as more positive labels come to have more negative connotations. In the twenty years since the proposal to introduce labels like SEN and MLD, some commentators now recognise them as negative labels (Solity, 1991; Corbett, 1996). However, a study of English trainee and experienced teachers' evaluations of different labels showed that learning difficulties and SEN were still more positively evaluated than medical or traditional ones, such as ESN (Norwich, 1999). It has also been suggested that there is a labelling cycle over a period of about twenty years in which what start out as positive terms come to develop negative connotations (Hastings and Remington, 1993). That terms go through this social process indicates that it is not the terms themselves, as much as the attitudes and treatment meted out to those referred to by them, the intolerance, discrimination and contempt for those showing some degree of incapacity, that are significant. It is relevant to this point that while many of the pupils in the first of the two studies (see Chapter 4), were aware that they went to devalued, stigmatised schools, the majority were unaware of the term SEN, and therefore did not have negative evaluations of it. However, they had experience of being called 'stupid' and 'thick', and held very negative evaluations of these terms.

Concluding points

In concluding this chapter, it is important to draw out some of the features of an educational classification of special educational needs. As the legislative definition of SEN is in terms of learning difficulties which call for special educational provision, so sub-areas of SEN need to be defined in terms of the dimensions of educational functioning and the factors that impact on them. For functioning to be educational, it needs to be defined in curriculum terms; broad and balanced educational goals that go beyond basic skills and academic learning to include personal and social development. This is to be contrasted with other types of definitions, such as medical ones, which are based on health and wider social goals. This is not to deny the clear relevance of medical conditions to decisions about educational needs, but to recognise that educational provision or interventions are judged in different terms. They are concerned with the goals, objectives, methods for access and teaching and its context. These are about curriculum, teaching and learning contexts and their adaptations that are appropriate to learner variations.

In addressing the educational functioning aspect, there is a need for a sophisticated system of categories that takes account of the multiplicity of difficulties. This has come to be recognised in relation to MLD in the new Government classification (DfES, 2003a) and more elaborate systems like that suggested by Crowther et al. (1998), discussed above. This requires a multi-dimensional system of classification, similar in principle, if not in practice, to the four-dimensional model set out in the revised SEN Code (DfES, 2001). However, this is only one side of the issue, the other side is about the validity of a category in terms of the impact of additional or different provision. This is where a category, such as MLD, is relative to what is provided for those without MLD. To justify a category it is necessary to show that those categorised benefit more educationally from this additional or different provision than they would from what is generally provided to those not so categorised. The additional or different provision has to be specifiable in curriculum, teaching and learning context terms. It is not enough just to show that those categorised are different in educational terms, for example, functioning at a lower level intellectually. There is a need to break out of the circularity of the historical definitions, which have defined those who have been 'slower in learning' as not benefiting from teaching in ordinary schools and therefore benefiting from teaching in special schools. These definitions did not explain why the difficulties were with the children and not with the inflexibilities of the ordinary school, its differentiation of curricula and teaching approaches. These definitions did not identify specific aspects of provision which were distinctive or specialised. The distinctiveness criterion is key to the justification of the MLD category, in particular the distinctiveness from these traditional groups:

- those with severe learning difficulties;
- those with specific learning difficulties;
- those with cross-curricula low attainments (slow learners).

The broad and diverse MLD group has occupied a place along the continua of intellectual and social functioning and curriculum attainments between the severe learning difficulties (SLD) and low attainers groups. From one perspective, the identity of the MLD category and group derives from being in neither the SLD nor low attainer groups. For parents, having a MLD identity is to distinguish their child from children with even lower attainments, and cognitive abilities with more organically based impairments. For teachers in mainstream schools, pupils who come to be identified as MLD are those who attain at even a lower level than those with low attainments in the broad spectrum of above and below average attainments. If social identity has played a key role in the historical construction of the MLD category, it has not been underpinned by clear-cut and distinctive curricula and teaching adaptations which do not also apply to some degree to these other allied groups. For example, if it were proposed that distinctive provision for MLD pupils was in terms of cognitive enrichment programmes (Feuerstein, 1979), then this would have to address the question of why these programmes were not also relevant to low attainers and SLD groups. It might be argued that there may be different ways in which enrichment programmes could be applied to those with MLD, but if this were so, it is likely that the teaching strategies would not be qualitatively distinctive, only differ by degree. Similarly, if it were proposed that there was a distinctive programme focusing on underlying social and family conditions, then this too would have to address whether these programmes were not also relevant to those in the low attainers group.

The point of these examples is to show that any additional programmes and teaching approaches cannot be confined to the MLD group, and this raises serious doubts about validity of the general category. The issue of the differentiation between moderate general learning difficulties (MLD) and specific learning difficulties (SpLD) is more complex partly because of the varying conceptions of these categories. As MLD can be defined in terms of low cognitive abilities and low overall curriculum attainments, or just low overall curriculum attainments, so SpLD can be defined using cognitive abilities or not. There are two versions of the discrepancy model; in one, literacy attainment levels are referenced against expected literacy attainments based on the child's cognitive ability levels. When the discrepancy is greater than a pre-defined cut-off then the child is identified as having a SpLD. In the other, literacy attainments are referenced against attainments in other curriculum areas (as in the DfES's latest classification of SEN). More recently, the definition of dyslexia has be re-focused on severe and persistent difficulties in word reading and spelling despite appropriate learning opportunities (BPS, 1999). This departs from the previous discrepancy model, in both versions, in not referencing it against attainments in other areas, whether in curriculum subject or cognitive ability terms. The effect is to broaden the group of those identified as having dyslexia/SpLD to include those with more general and severe learning difficulties (Reid, 2004). In this broader definition of dyslexia/SpLD, it becomes difficult to distinguish between SpLD and MLD. However, with the discrepancy definition (in either version), it might be argued that the SpLD group might be distinguished from the MLD group in terms of teaching provision which focused on phonological awareness and skills (BPS, 1999). However, as reviews of research on teaching children with SpLD/dyslexia have concluded, there is no distinctive dyslexia specific approach (Lewis and Norwich, 2004; Reid, 2004). A systematic and intensive phonological approach might be more relevant to those with SpLD/dyslexia, but also to others; it is a matter of difference by degree not kind.

In concluding that the MLD category cannot be justified in terms of distinctive additional or different educational provision (curriculum and teaching strategy) from these other three allied groups, it is still possible that its continued use can be justified in terms of compensatory additional resource allocation. The differentiation marks the threshold at which some children would get more educational resources than others. Though this does not justify the specific category of MLD, it might support the general principle of differentiating between more and less resource-worthy groups. Perhaps the current groups referred to as low attainers, MLD, SLD and SpLD may be re-grouped in terms of a more appropriate system of differentiation for resource allocation purposes. However, this leads to hard decisions or dilemmas about difference and differentiation – whether or not to identify differences such as difficulties in learning (Norwich, 1993, 1996). There are positive and negative conceptions in our society about human differences and what we call differentiation in education. The negative perspective is that 'difference' reflects lower status, less value and perpetuating inequalities and unfair treatment. The positive perspective is that 'difference' reflects the recognition of individuality, individual needs and interests. It is this tension between these conceptions of difference which leads us to confront dilemmas of difference. The dilemma is that both options, to recognise or not to recognise difference, have negative risks. Recognising difference can lead to different provision which might be stigmatised and devalued; but not recognising difference can lead to overlooking and ignoring individuality. The tension is between the values of inclusion and individuality.

Of course, differences are addressed throughout education, not just in the field of disability and difficulties. So, we would expect to find some expressions of the difference dilemma in other areas and aspects of education. But the argument is that as we deal in special education with exceptional or significant differences, we would expect to confront the general dilemmas in a more accentuated form here. Specifically, these difference dilemmas are evident in these three areas:

1   the identification of individual children as having SEN or a disability in the first place;
2   what children should learn – the curriculum;
3   where children should learn and with whom

In a study several years ago (Norwich, 1993), it was shown that there was a widespread recognition of dilemmas in these three areas amongst professionals at all levels of two large education systems in England and the USA. The tensions which they talked about were those to do with stigma versus access to needed provision; participating in a common curriculum and learning settings versus learning programmes relevant to their individual needs. Many of these professionals also suggested ways of resolving these dilemmas. These resolutions corresponded to a range of ways of combining the values of meeting individual needs in inclusive ways, while trying to minimise the negative implications. The point of referring to dilemmas is that resolutions have some negative aspects, not meeting all individual needs and/or not being quite as inclusive as hoped for. The dilemmatic perspective means that balancing and trade-offs are required. One of the themes of this book is to show how this perspective can illuminate the issues confronted in educating children referred to as having MLD, as it can other children identified as having special educational needs. This theme will pursued in the following chapters.

Chapter 3

MLD and inclusion

Curriculum, teaching and inclusion issues

Introduction

This chapter will focus on a range of issues relevant to the education of pupils identified as having MLD. It will consider who goes to special schools designated for MLD, whether there is a distinctive curriculum and teaching approach for MLD and what the principles are of inclusion that are relevant to this diverse group of pupils. It will also focus on policy issues and practices in LEAs in the context of the Government's commitment to inclusion, as well as what happens to pupils with MLD when they leave school. The chapter is based on recent research that is relevant to these questions and also picks up the theme at the end of the last chapter of how a dilemmatic perspective can illuminate the policy and practice issues that arise.

Who goes to MLD special schools?

There is a scarcity of evidence that is relevant to considering questions like who goes to special schools and have there been changes in the number of children identified as having MLD. This arises, as discussed in the previous chapter, from problems of definitions, but also a weak tradition of research in the field. Government statistics since the Education Act 1981 have not included any breakdown of areas of special educational needs. This can be attributed to the Government's interpretation of the Warnock Committee philosophy that general categories be abandoned, and are not relevant to specifying needed provision for individuals. However, as discussed in the last chapter, with the recent classification of SEN for all pupils in the country who have Statements of SEN, more data about specific areas like MLD will now become available. But, this raises questions about the specific interpretation of the category, the evidence used in decisions and the reliability of the use of the category by teachers in schools. In Chapter 7 the results of a survey of LEA policies and practices with respect to MLD will be presented and discussed. In this chapter the findings of a survey of MLD special schools will be discussed (Male, 1996).

From a sample of 54 MLD special schools, about 14 per cent of all such special schools in England, Male provided some very useful data about the characteristics of pupils and their implications for school provision. One in four schools had been re-organised in recent years from all-age to single phase schools. Of the 54 schools in the survey, the most frequent size was between 101–150 pupils, though there was one school with less than 50 and another with more than 200 pupils. Though the data relates to a period in the 1990s, there was no trend towards a reduction in the number of pupils, with most schools reporting an increasing number of pupils, and only 10 per cent reporting a decrease. The predominance of boys to girls was clear from the finding that 85 per cent of the schools reported that between half to three-quarters of the pupils were boys. Male notes that this ratio is consistent with earlier ratios from Williams (1966) and even earlier studies by Burt and Schonell, quoted by Williams. I have summarised Male's data on the proportions of pupils with associated difficulties in the previous chapter. But, this study also showed that two-thirds of the head teachers considered that up to 10 per cent of their pupils had severe learning difficulties, not MLD. The reasons given by head teachers are relevant to questions about the future of MLD special schools. One head reported that the school was chosen by parents of children with SLD because they were looking for a more 'normal' kind of school. As Male explains, 'in the case of SLD pupils in the sample, there seemed to be something of an "upward percolation" in terms of placement, in some cases influenced by parental choice' (Male, 1996, page 37). As regards changes in the special educational needs catered for, by far the greatest reference was to an increase in children with associated emotional and behavioural difficulties; this was reported by 73 per cent of head teachers. This compared with 38 per cent mentioning severe or complex needs. The survey also showed that most pupils came from mainstream schools regardless of the phase of the special school. For secondary and all-age schools, the second most frequent previous placement was another MLD special school.

Heads reported that about 1 in 12 pupils in their schools overall would have their needs better met somewhere else. These were children whose learning difficulties were too severe or complex or who required provision specialising in emotional and behavioural difficulties. Half the head teachers reported that at least some of their pupils would be better in mainstream provision. The significance of these judgements is reinforced by the incidence of temporary or permanent exclusions from these schools – almost three in four schools reported some exclusions in the last year.

This survey also confirmed the historical and recent picture of MLD special schools as having an over-representation of children from a 'working class' background (as discussed in the previous chapter). Heads reported an over-representation of pupils from 'unskilled' and 'unwaged' families compared to other schools in the area; and an under-representation of skilled, managerial and professional families. However, the concern in the 1970s about over-representation of children from Afro-Caribbean backgrounds in MLD special schools was not found in this mid 1990s study. Male's conclusion is pertinent to the themes of this book, that if there is a continuing role for special schools that cater for children identified as having MLD, then 'it is likely that they will be required to become even more generic in the future in terms of pupil in-take' (Male, 1996, page 41). The findings from this mid 1990s study will be compared to aspects of the national survey of LEA policies and practices with respect to MLD, to be presented and discussed in Chapter 7. What this study shows is the diversity of intake, which raises the question of whether these schools have become in practice for mild to moderate mixed or varied difficulties, despite official designations. Surveys like the Male one indicate that a basic national review of the future of special schools with this designation is needed.

Curriculum and teaching

Given the relatively high proportion of MLD special schools of the total number of special schools, there has been little research into curriculum and teaching questions for this broad and diverse group. There has been some literature bearing on curriculum design questions, but not with a strong research base (Brennan, 1979, 1985). Towards the end of the 1980s a Government-funded project focused on curriculum development in MLD special schools (Evans et al., 1987; Redmond et al., 1992). This illustrated the different styles of planning and delivering the curriculum related to different curriculum models, process- versus objectives-oriented, and the influence of underlying ideological factors. This research was based on the principle that there was a common curriculum that needed to be adapted or modified in its implementation for the needs of this group. It related to the period immediately before the introduction of the National Curriculum in 1988. Therefore, it did not address the initial design and specificity of the common curriculum in terms of subjects and fairly tight age-related content requirements. However, there was some research after the introduction of the National Curriculum which did call into question the relevance of the subject-based requirements for MLD special schools (Costley, 1996). This was a study of 251 MLD special schools using questionnaires to senior teachers about the extent to which the then-National Curriculum met the needs of their MLD special schools.

Costley concluded that there was considerable confusion across the country about the education of those with MLD. She argued on the basis of this survey that the National Curriculum established the principle of a common or inclusive curriculum, but left open the question of the extent to which all should have the same schooling and same opportunities. She suggests that this is a question of how to have a common curriculum, while adapting it to meet diverse needs. In doing so, she made reference to the common curriculum dilemma, discussed previously in relation to dilemmas of difference. It is interesting that her survey was done at the time that the Dearing Committee was about to recommend changes to the National Curriculum to occupy less time in the school curriculum and to make it more flexible. Her respondents were all in favour of this more flexible process and this was interpreted in terms of the national changes enabling teachers in special school to create a better balance between the common entitlement and adaptations for individual needs. Halpin and Lewis (1996) addressed similar themes in another study using in-depth interviews with 12 head teachers of a range of special schools (MLD, SLD and emotional and behavioural difficulties [EBD] designations). Halpin and Lewis showed that head teachers experienced a tension about the balance between the commonality of their work with that in mainstream schools and the uniqueness of the work they do in their special schools. These authors refer to the tension between equality and individuality in terms of the dilemma about the common curriculum. They found this tension to be expressed in schools in several ways: differing curriculum priorities between these head teachers; how the head teachers related to the wider educational world; the head teachers' interpretations of the significance of cross-curricular strategies; and how the head teachers put curriculum balance into practice. These two studies illustrate how the dilemmatic perspective helps in understanding the tensions in planning school curricula for pupils with MLD (and others), and the way in which the national changes since its introduction, after 1988, have moved away from tight common curriculum programmes towards greater flexibility about content and the timing of specific programmes with ages.

More recently this process has gone even further, with the introduction of national guidelines for planning, teaching and assessing the curriculum for pupils with learning difficulties (QCA, 2001). This has been a significant development in the national curriculum framework, as it confirmed the national entitlement to learning for all pupils, building on inclusion principles, while endorsing greater flexibility in planning a curriculum suited to the needs of those with learning difficulties. It also provides frameworks and materials to support schools in curriculum development, but it is aimed at a very diverse group of children and young people ranging from profound and multiple learning difficulties, through severe to moderate learning difficulties. What the guidelines provide (QCA, 2001, page 7) is a scheme which tries to integrate aspects of:

1   the full range of National Curriculum subjects, including citizenship and religious education;
2   the foundation stage for the early years of education;

3   the statement of inclusion (three broad statements);
4   a preparation for adult life;
5   the key skills framework;
6   thinking skills;
7   personal priority needs in terms of therapies.

This development marks a move to considerably more flexibility at school level in determining the balance and mix of elements that make up the particular curriculum offered by a school. However, the suitability of the guidelines are much clearer for those with more severe and profound learning difficulties, and less clear for those with moderate learning difficulties. In fact, reference to MLD is confined only to general statements which state its applicability to MLD, such as in the introduction (page 4).

Despite these learning difficulty curriculum guidelines, it can be concluded that there has been no serious attempt to develop a curriculum or pedagogy for the MLD group. This was the conclusion in a review by Lewis and Norwich (2000) of pedagogic approaches to teaching different kinds of learning difficulties, including MLD. Pedagogy was defined in this review as 'the cluster of decisions and actions that aim to promote school learning' (page 7). The review aimed to identify whether there were specific or distinct kinds of pedagogy for the different areas of learning difficulties. It was based on the assumption that we can identify three broad kinds of pedagogic needs: needs common to all, needs specific to a defined group and needs unique to individuals. Two broad positions were proposed that adopted different combinations of these three kinds of needs: the general differences position and the unique differences position. In the general differences position, pedagogic needs are informed by common needs and group-specific needs, in this case it would be the MLD group, and then adapted to unique individual needs. By contrast, in the unique differences position, pedagogic needs are informed by common needs that are adapted to unique individual needs (see Figure 3.1). Differences are recognised in both positions, but in the former these differences are identified in terms of some general category, such as MLD, while in the latter position, they are identified at the particular level of the individual pupil.

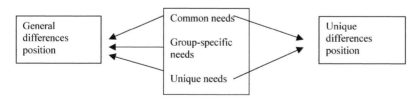

Figure 3.1 General differences and unique differences positions

No evidence was found for a distinct MLD pedagogy in this review, even though some studies were identified which examined the learning characteristics of children with MLD. However, these did not relate specifically to the teaching implications of these characteristics. There was evidence, for example, from a single study of children with MLD difficulties that they responded less well to science teaching based on inductive reasoning (Mastopieri et al., 1997). But this showed up a particular kind of difficulty in learning, not a distinct kind of pedagogy which only related to the MLD compared to other groups, such as low attainers or those with severe learning difficulties. Another area where there has been research relevant to the MLD group is that of children with Down Syndrome, whose learning difficulties fall into the MLD/SLD range. There have been a range of studies of the learning characteristics of children with Down Syndrome which have shown systematic differences from other children (Wishart, 1990, 1993). However, these studies do not test explicitly the need for differential teaching strategies, even though they are seen as indicative of the need for different strategies such as:

- error-free versus trial-and-error learning;
- the use of novelty to counter the tendency to perseverate;
- using visual rather than auditory presentations;
- explicit consolidation of learning;
- monitoring of off-task behaviours.

However, as Lewis and Norwich (2000) concluded, such work does not examine the validity of group-specific pedagogy for children with Down Syndrome, with its relevance to the MLD groups. In this respect, it is interesting that where the case is made for a specific pedagogy, it does not relate to specific groups, like those with MLD, but to the very general group of those with learning difficulties or disabilities. In the USA, Fuchs and Fuchs (1995), for example, pursue this line in their proposal that there are two distinctive aspects of a SEN specific pedagogy: (1) the use of empirically validated procedures, and (2) the intensive databased focus on individual pupils. This is similar to the main conclusion of the Lewis and Norwich (2000) review that, although there is not a MLD specific pedagogy, common pedagogic principles apply, but with greater density or intensity depending on the individual needs, in keeping with the unique difference position, explained above. The concept of continua of pedagogic strategies is proposed as a useful way to distinguish between more commonly found adaptations for most pupils, and less frequent and more specialised adaptations or high-density teaching, for those with SEN. These broad conclusions have not been revised with further work which has examined the question of whether there are group-specific distinctive educational needs in terms of pedagogy, curriculum and teachers' knowledge, in a recent book by Lewis and Norwich (2004).

Fletcher-Campbell (2004), in her chapter on children with MLD in that book, presented the lack of a MLD specific pedagogy as a challenge to the future of the MLD category.

Inclusion: the term and its links with integration

Much has been said and written about inclusion, even though the term is fairly new in policy and practice discourse. When the Education Act 1981, the foundation of the current system, was introduced in the UK, 'integration' was the current term. The Warnock Report (DES, 1978) referred to three forms of integration: locational, social and functional. Functional integration was about including children with SEN in the mainstream class in teaching and curriculum terms. If it meant anything it required the adaptation of teaching programmes in class and wider school developments to make available the content and objectives of the class teaching and learning programmes to these children. But integration came to be associated with locational placement in mainstream schools and perhaps some extra-curricula social mixing, and as such came to be seen as a process of assimilation in which children with SEN adapt to fit in with the culture and practices of mainstream schools (Ainscow, 1997). Integration was taken to mean that mainstream schools did not make changes to accommodate a more diverse group of learners. This growing critique of integration in its limited locational and social sense was in terms of the social processes of assimilation and accommodation, which had been transferred from social critiques of the issues arising from race and ethnic relations between the dominant white culture and those from ethnic minorities. In the same way that assimilating ethnic minorities in the dominant white culture was seen as signalling a non-acceptance of the 'difference' and a reluctance of the dominant culture to change, so the integration of children with SEN and disabilities came to be seen negatively.

Another term with different connotations was needed, and so inclusion came to be used, as it also linked into a wider discourse in progressive political circles about social inclusion (Thomas, 1997; Dyson, 2002). Social inclusion has come to be a key value which underpins the current Labour Government's social and economic policies. It stands for belonging and participation in society, having the means, in terms of skills and knowledge, to be economically independent and contribute to society. It has re-focused progressive policies on the values of solidarity and equal opportunities, while moving away from the more left wing commitments to equality, in order to avoid interpretations of equality in terms of equal outcomes. Social inclusion can be seen to be a 'third way' alternative to a more critical and traditional politically progressive commitment to equality, and as such is not a radical political value. It is therefore interesting that those looking for a more radical educational term than integration would look to social inclusion for it. That integration as understood in the 1980s and early 1990s was associated with organisational accommodation is clear from the focus on developing whole school policies and practices for mainstream schools. Those who currently propose inclusive schools were then proponents of SEN whole school policies and practices (for example Thomas and Feiler, 1988). It is notable that Booth, who has been associated with the recent Inclusion Index (Booth *et al.*, 2000), has noted that proponents of integration saw it in terms of changing the nature of ordinary schools, seeing integration as part of the tradition of developing comprehensive community education (Booth, 1996a).

It is clear that there is at least some continuity between previous ideas of integration and current conceptions of inclusion, and that forcing the concepts into a dichotomy of integration versus inclusion cannot be justified. There are two other aspects where inclusion goes beyond integration. One is that inclusion is not only about those with special educational needs, it is about all aspects of diversity, in particular those who are considered to be vulnerable and at risk of exclusion from schools and other social activities. The other is that it puts considerable emphasis on schools having to change to accommodate this diversity. However, in going beyond integration in these ways, the term comes to be used in more abstract and rhetorical ways. It is difficult enough to specify the range of children who are to be identified as having special educational needs; the wider group of those who are vulnerable and at risk of exclusion is even more ambiguous. It ultimately requires that we talk about all children, and so come to imply that inclusion means nothing if it does not refer to a full inclusion of all children in a population. In focusing on school change for this diversity it becomes more difficult to specify what makes a school inclusive. We will discuss a recent research review on this topic below, but for the present it is worth considering how far the current discourse of transforming schools helps to clarify the meaning of inclusion. However, what these two additional aspects of inclusion do is to move discourse to a level of generality which loses contact with operational reality.

One working definition of educational inclusion is that it is about the presence, participation and achievement of all students in local mainstream schools (Ainscow *et al.*, 2003). What this definition shows is the link between previous concepts of the forms of integration and current notions of inclusion. The term 'presence' connects with what was called locational integration, and participation relates to social integration, though participation also relates to contexts of learning. A working definition like this one functions to broaden the scope beyond those with SEN/disabilities, but it does not address the question, raised above, about defining this wider group, other than to refer to 'all students'. This kind of definition also does not specify what is meant by participation in local schools. Does it mean participation in the same classes, as indicated in the following definition – 'inclusion refers to being in an ordinary school with other students, following the same curriculum at the same time, in the same classrooms with the full acceptance of all' (Bailey, 1998, page 173)?

In many schools which are called inclusive there may not be fully inclusive classrooms as some children may be attached to resource units and spend only part of their time in mainstream class settings. In such schools ability grouping may be practised. This may be judged to be necessary if some children are going to have provision that takes account of their individual educational needs. It is clear that a more adequate definition of inclusion will address this question of the degree of participation in mainstream classes. These are some of the issues and problems that we encounter in considering inclusion. These points show that invoking terms like inclusion and inclusive practices cannot tell us much about what we are referring to, other than orient us to a general field and a set of value commitments. This orienting function is important, but it is a serious mistake to believe that these terms can be used to conceptualise and justify specific decisions in this field.

Inclusive schools

Including children with special educational needs into mainstream schools is one of the most challenging developments in educational policy and practice in this country and internationally. It is one of the central policy commitments of the Labour Government with its 'inclusive vision' of 'excellence for all'. In the 1997 Green Paper (DfEE, 1997), the Government committed itself to several areas of development:

1 A growing number of mainstream schools will be willing and able to accept children with a range of special educational needs. This means that an increasing proportion of those children with Statements of SEN currently placed in special schools will be educated in mainstream schools.
2 National and local programmes will be in place to support increased inclusion.
3 Special and mainstream schools will be working together alongside and in support of one another.

There has been a trend over the last decade towards greater inclusion of pupils with significant SEN, who would have been in special schools in the past. Figure 3.2 shows that there has been a continuing downward trend in the percentage of pupils in special schools in England since the introduction of the Education Act 1981, from 1.72 per cent in 1982 to 1.32 per cent in 2001. However, this indicator does not include those children who are excluded from schools. Data on the rate of permanent exclusions shows that

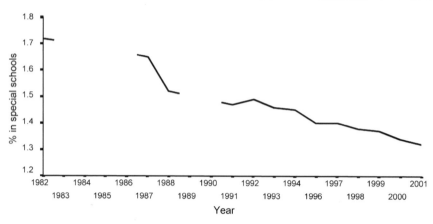

Figure 3.2 Percentage of pupils in English special schools between 1992 and 2001

Source: Norwich (2002a)

this went up until the mid 1990s and then fell a little; there has been no decrease in exclusions corresponding to special school decreases. This is of particular relevance to the question of the inclusion of those with SEN, as other research shows that high proportions of those excluded have SEN with or without a Statement. The Audit Commission (2002b) showed in a study of 22 LEAs that 87 per cent of those excluded from primary school had SEN, as did 60 per cent of those excluded from secondary school. Hayden (2000) showed a similar set of findings: 79 per cent of permanent exclusions had been identified as having SEN and 67 per cent of all exclusions (fixed term and permanent exclusions).

There are no data for the percentage of pupils identified as having MLD in special schools over these two decades. With the introduction of a SEN classification into the national collection of pupil-level data, it will now be possible to monitor trends at the level of the SEN categories. However, some data were collected about MLD trends in a survey which will be discussed fully in Chapter 7. This showed that in just over half of the sample of LEAs (n = 29) there was judged to be a decrease in the number of pupils with MLD in special schools. This corresponded with reported data over the last three years. Between 2000 and 2002 the reported percentage of pupils with Statements for MLD in special schools fell from 54 per cent to 43 per cent. These data also indicate that a significant proportion of children with Statements for MLD difficulties have been in mainstream schools for some time.

It is clear that SEN is a general and loose concept that covers a diversity of kinds and severity of difficulties. When we talk about pupils with special educational needs, we are referring not only to those with mild or specific learning difficulties and sensory and motor difficulties. Also included are those with severe and profound learning difficulties and those with severe emotional and behaviour difficulties. Much international research indicates that it is these latter groups which many teachers believe that they cannot accommodate in mainstream classes (Avramidis and Norwich, 2002). These points begin to explain what is meant by complexity when we talk about inclusion, inclusive schools and inclusive practice. The breakdown in the areas of difficulties in the sample of children with MLD from our study in one LEA, described in the previous chapter, illustrates the diversity, within just the MLD category.

As Croll and Moses (1998) have argued when examining changes in schools towards becoming more inclusive, 'such aspirations for school reform are, at least at present, of such a general nature that it is hard to specify what makes a school inclusive' (page 14). Attempts to identify factors and processes involved in schools being inclusive in the broad sense tend to be in general terms. For example, in the USA, Lipsky and Gardner (1998) have identified seven factors based on a national study in 1,000 school districts. These were judged to be consistent with factors identified in a smaller study of 12 schools, as follows:

1   visionary leadership;
2   collaboration;
3   refocused use of assessment;
4   support for staff and students;
5   funding;
6   effective parental involvement;
7   use of effective programme models and classroom practices.

Such factors require further detailed explanation, as Lindsay (2003) argues. Dyson and Millward (2000) make a similar point about another such list of generalised factors from these US authors. Their criticism goes further, that such lists seem to contradict research and professional experience which indicates the complexity, ambiguity and tensions in school life. For example, reference to teacher collaboration ignores some of the documented issues in such working practices. Such lists can also be criticised because they are descriptions of inclusive schools and this raises questions about the status of these factors. Are the factors causal or enabling of schools to become inclusive or are they defining characteristics of inclusive schools? Unless there are some outcome studies, as in the tradition of school effectiveness research (Rutter et al., 1979; Mortimore et al., 1988), this type of list reduces to a circularity and cannot provide a sound basis for informing professional practice and school developments.

In a recent review of international research on effective school-level actions to promote participation of all students, Dyson et al. (2002) found that there is a limited number of good-quality research studies. They reported that many studies were 'small scale, non-cumulative, poorly designed or

poorly reported'. This can be seen in the gap between the number of potentially relevant literature citations they started with (14,692), the number
meeting the inclusion criteria (325), the number they identified for data
extraction (49) and the number identified as key studies of 'high quality' (6).
Inclusive schools were defined in terms of 'maximising the participation of
all students in their cultures, curricula and communities', and were not confined to one group, such as those with SEN. The review was based on studies
from the USA, UK, Spain, New Zealand, Canada and Australia. Most of
the studies were descriptive, focusing on school developments. There were
fewer evaluations of either the process of developing inclusive schools, or process and outcome studies. The summary of the evidence from this review does
not seem to go beyond the kind of summary identified and criticised (Dyson
and Millward, 2000) in the previous paragraph. The evidence is summarised
in terms of schools having an 'inclusive culture' where there is 'some degree of
consensus amongst adults around values of respect for difference and a commitment to offering all students access to learning opportunities' (page vii).
This conclusion is countered by asserting that there may not be a full consensus nor the removal of tensions and contradictions. It is also not explained
what the evidence has to say about how far-reaching and on what aspects
there needs to be such a consensus. Staff collaboration and joint problem
solving are also identified as important factors, though as general factors they
are also found to be relevant to effective schools; defined in terms of optimis-
ing attainments for most pupils (Stoll and Mortimore, 1995). This indicates
that general factors, like those about consensus and collaboration, might be
relevant to school-level actions that aim to promote differing ends (effectiveness and inclusion).

The review also concedes that it was unclear to what extent 'inclusive
cultures' lead directly to enhanced student participation. Some aspects of the
culture are inherently participatory, which raises the problem identified
above, of whether these factors are causal of inclusive schools or defining of
them. The other factor identified in the review was the presence of leaders
and leadership styles committed to inclusive values. As with staff collaboration and problem solving, leadership factors are identified as relevant to
other kinds of school developments, leaving the review's conclusions as not
going much beyond the definition of an inclusive school, in its search for
effective school-level actions and organisational development strategies
relevant to any development. Though there are recommendations coming
out of the review, there is no comment about the style and orientation of
research implicit in the search for effective school-level actions. What is
required is research informed by aspects of the tradition of the school effectiveness model, in which the school-level processes associated with schools
that have enhanced student outcomes are identified. Perhaps the field is not
developed enough to justify such a large-scale review. There can also be

doubts about whether some researchers of inclusion have a commitment to this kind of scientific style of research.

Inclusion: a matter of evidence about what works or about values and rights?

One of the basic questions to be addressed is the relative contribution of value and evidence based considerations in the inclusion debate and in formulating policy and instigating practice. This question focuses on decision making rather than the detail of the arguments for and against inclusion. It is about the kinds of considerations that we take into account in making decisions. These include:

1 policy positions at national, local and school levels: the plans, their implementation and the relationship between different policy initiatives;
2 empirical matters including the efficacy of inclusive practices: such as, trends in the incidence of inclusive practices, statements about the current receptivity of mainstream schools and teachers and the consequences of inclusive educational practices;
3 conceptual points and value judgements: about the meaning and definition of inclusion and the nature of the principles and values underlying education.

The case will be made for the position that we cannot avoid dealing with all of these considerations when we address questions about inclusion. There is a need to find a constructive synthesis of value, conceptual and empirical matters in considering the future of educating all children and young people, including those with difficulties in learning and disabilities. Put like this, it may appear to be a fairly uncontroversial position and one around which there is or could be much consensus. However, this position may sound acceptable, but may be harder to accept in practice in particular situations. The reason for this is that it involves hard decisions and some sacrifice of cherished values.

The case will be made by starting with a consideration of some issues about the concept of inclusion and the values underpinning it. It is rare to read or hear about inclusion nowadays without someone commenting that we are unclear about what it means. It has been argued that those who talk about 'inclusive education' or 'inclusive schools' do not define clearly what they mean by these terms. Given these diverse assumptions and definitions, it is best to consider inclusion to be an 'orienting' term, a term which draws our attention to a set of issues and commitments to belonging and participation. Beyond that it ceases to be much help as other considerations come into play. One major difference in use is whether inclusion and its derivative terms are about belonging and participation in an educational context, where they are often used to describe the participation of children with SEN into main- stream schools. Or, is it about inclusion in society, a broader concept of social inclusion, which is about home, family, community and occupational settings?

This difference is sometimes marked by reference to inclusive education versus social inclusion. However, this is not a clear-cut distinction, as social inclusion is used in the school system to refer to issues about attendance and exclusions as opposed to provision for those with SEN and disabilities. The social inclusion agenda has also sometimes been used to find a legitimate place for education in separate settings, such as special schools. For example, based on fairly recent research in Scotland, it has been argued that reformed special schools can be part of an inclusive policy and system (Allan, 1999). The recent Government working party on special schools also seemed to be taking this line, when it concluded that special schools are part of a spectrum of provision for children with SEN (DfES, 2003b). This contrasts with a pre- dominantly school-focused conception, as in the quote above by Bailey (1998).

Inclusion is also commonly seen as referring to all forms of diversity, not just disability, as discussed above. From this perspective, those with special educational needs will be seen as one of several groups coming under this general umbrella of inclusion. There are clearly common interests between different groups and individuals at risk of exclusion, that can give some force to the case for a broad inclusivity in education. But, like all social values, inclusion is a general, abstract principle which can ignore important differ- ences in peoples' experience of exclusion. A commitment to a broad inclusion is important, but can also risk ignoring the interests of those with disabilities in education, especially those with severe and profound disabilities and those with very challenging emotional and behaviour difficulties. There is some choice about how the term 'inclusion' is used, but if it is used in the broad sense then the specific conditions and experiences of those with disabilities, which are themselves very diverse, need to remain in focus, whatever terms of reference are used.

Regarding the values and rights issues underpinning inclusive education, there has been much reference to fundamental rights, such as those asserted in the United Nations Educational, Scientific and Cultural Organization (UNESCO) Salamanca declaration (UNESCO, 1994). It is rarely noted that the statement refers to a fundamental right to education, but not to an inclusive education (Lindsay, 2003), which calls into question the idea that basic human rights can underpin an inclusive education commitment. Assertions of basic rights also introduce complexity and uncertainty. For example, if inclusion means that students have several rights, what might they be? Based on various definitions of inclusion (Lunt and Norwich, 2000), it may be argued that there is:

1   a right to participate in the mainstream;
2   a right to acceptance and respect;
3   a right to individually relevant learning;
4   a right to active involvement and choice in the matter.

If this is the kind of case for a rights approach, then it is clear that there is plenty of scope for confusion and tensions between these rights with the four elements in this formulation. It can also lead, if coupled with a commitment to inclusive purity, to confusion about whether a practice is inclusive or not. For example, if inclusion means participating in the same learning programmes in the same location and being accepted and respected there, then any separate provision, say in a withdrawal setting, could come to be considered as exclusionary, whether it provided relevant learning for individual pupils or not.

The problem that arises from asserting multiple rights is that rights are not always compatible in principle; the rights of the minorities may undermine the rights of the majorities, or the right to individual preference for educational provision in a separate setting may conflict with participation in mainstream settings. These tensions are only too evident in the current debates and uncertainties around inclusion. They arise from the fact that as a society we hold multiple values about education which leads to policy and practice dilemmas, especially around the question of difference, what was introduced in the previous chapter as dilemmas of difference. The basic dilemma, as explained before, is whether or not to recognise difference, as both options have negative risks. Recognising difference can lead to different provision that might be stigmatised and devalued; but not recognising difference can lead to not providing adequately for individual needs. Here is a tension between what we call the values of inclusion and individuality.

As explained above, these dilemmas of difference centre around three key aspects of education:

1   identification: whether to attribute SEN/disability or not;
2   curricula: how specialised can common curriculum programmes be?
3   location: whether to place in mainstream or separate settings, have ability or mixed ability classes and groupings within classes.

The research of Dyson and Millward (2000) into the changes and functioning of four secondary schools through case studies illustrates how this perspective about dilemmas can help us to understand the nature of inclusion and inclusive education practices. Despite many surface differences between these schools, Dyson and Millward claim to have detected a common model of what an inclusive school might look like and how it can come into operation. In each of their case study schools there was leadership which was committed to inclusive principles and which promoted developments according to these principles. This meant that there were attempts in these schools to abandon the structures and practices applied traditionally in special needs. For example in one school the role of the SEN co-ordinator was distributed amongst a range of senior and middle managers. In these schools there was also a reliance on in-class support as a means of supporting these students in ordinary classes. This strategy was linked to the one where professional development was emphasised as a way of facilitating responses to diversity. In three of the four schools there was also an attempt to extend the range of their intake. As these authors comment, these characteristics resemble other accounts of 'inclusive schools' (Clarke *et al.*,1995; Ainscow, 1999).

It is interesting that Dyson and Millward also note that the commitment to inclusion for the four head teachers in their case studies was more part of a personal agenda than an external requirement. This was associated with some difficulties in establishing a whole school view about inclusion. These difficulties were interpreted as partly due to resistance within these schools, but also where there was apparent consensus, idealistic visions came to be translated into something different in the classrooms. The softening and deflecting of the inclusive vision in the process of translation was associated with what these authors call the 'technologies of inclusion' which were 'all seriously problematic' (page 139). In particular, the system of in-class support provided by a range of specialist teachers and teaching assistants was observed to be variable in quality. There was also a gap between demand for support and its availability. The expectation that support teaching would produce significant changes in ordinary classrooms and the practices of teachers was also not realistic:

> it was never entirely clear that the effect of support was to transform teaching, or even simply to help class teachers – or whether it was simply to maintain the status quo by offering teachers a trouble-shooter whenever things 'went wrong'
>
> (Dyson and Millward, 2000, page 140)

In addition, differentiation practices were traditional: widespread use of setting by attainment, small groups of students with low attainments, withdrawal for individual and small-group teaching – these were all standard practices in these 'inclusive schools'. These tensions were also evident in how these four schools handled behaviour problems. These included diverting support teachers and teaching assistants to trouble spots, excluding troublesome students from classes and the school and adopting punitive class management approaches.

Dyson and Millward present their case analyses as evidence that the recent theorising about inclusion in terms of 'moving schools' (developing schools) (Ainscow, 1999) or 'adhocratic schools' (schools that make flexible ad hoc developments) (Skrtic, 1995) is of limited value, as these authors do not take account of the interaction of power within schools, interest groups or the wider policy context. These concepts are also criticised because of the circular definition of these school characteristics and inclusiveness. Being a moving school and being inclusive are defined in terms of each other. These authors argue, therefore, that their case study schools can be better understood in terms of theoretical perspectives which focus on power, interest and tensions. This is where they invoke the dilemmatic perspective and refer to dilemmas of difference. However, it is interesting that they interpret the dilemmas of difference as more basic than the commitment to inclusion:

> Inclusion does not offer an escape from the contradiction but rather arises out of it. In particular, inclusion is one attempted resolution of the dilemmas of difference amongst many, and like all such resolutions, has emerged at a particular point in time and will, our theoretical framework suggests, disappear at some future point of time.
>
> (Dyson and Millward, 2000, page 169)

Their interpretation of the dilemmatic perspective makes sense when they use it to reject the idea that inclusion is a final solution to problems in the education system. But in accepting that there is a basic tension in seeking to educate a diverse population within a common framework, they fail to recognise that the dilemma arises from a commitment to a common or inclusive system. Inclusion represents the value which sets up the dilemma in the first place. It is not an attempted resolution of the dilemma of difference. Inclusion is too vague and abstract a concept to act as a resolution. As argued above, underpinning the dilemma and the tensions are the dual commitments to inclusion and different needs. This version of the dilemmas of difference is illustrated in research conducted ten years ago in a study of professionals at all levels of two large education systems in this country and in the USA. A widespread recognition of dilemmas was found in these three areas (identification of pupils as having SEN, curriculum and location of provision) (Norwich, 1993). The tensions which these professionals talked about were those to do with stigma versus access to needed provision, on one hand, and participating in a common curriculum and learning settings versus learning programmes relevant to their individual needs, on the other. Many of these professionals also suggested ways of resolving these dilemmas which covered a range of ways of combining the values of meeting individual needs in inclusive ways, while trying to minimise the negative implications and consequences.

This professional recognition that values were being balanced can be taken to be an expression of a dilemmatic position. A more recent study of high-attaining inclusive secondary schools also illustrates this balancing. High-attaining inclusive secondary schools were identified using Government performance data in 1998–99. Out of 3,151 secondary schools in England (excluding independent and special schools), 94 schools were in the top 30 per cent of school GCSE point scorers and the top 30 per cent of schools with most pupils with Statements (Lunt and Norwich, 2000). When the exercise was repeated in 1999, only 43 of the 94 were still in this group (top 30 per cent GCSE points and top 30 per cent with Statements). What was most notable about this group of high-attaining inclusive schools was that they were in mostly county rather than metropolitan LEAs (80 per cent). A sample of these schools was then surveyed with questionnaires and some with case study interviews of staff and pupils, between 2001 and 2003. Interviews with senior and classroom staff showed the commitment to the twin priorities of raising standards and inclusion with some clear expressions of contradictory views about compatibility. For example, in one school, a recent Ofsted inspection report described the schools as inclusive, but the head, when probed in interview, held some contradictory views about compatibility, while some staff saw clear incompatibility. For example, the head teacher said:

> Opportunities for all pushes up standards for all, there is no incompatibility of raising standards and inclusion.

Then went on to say that inclusion was:

> the heart of everything we do, an overt policy that we will promote inclusion. That's what we are here for, pastoral system, learning support base, SENCO are all involved

But:

> inclusion has a cost to all staff and politics/LEA are remote from the classroom

While one class teacher said:

> if you put emphasis on high quality teaching and learning for all pupils, then the ideals of raising standards and inclusion are incompatible . . . there are tensions, particularly with pupils with severe emotional and behaviour difficulties. We try to tackle such tensions in this school by offering a high level of support to all pupils and staff in all aspects of school life.

Another class teacher said:

EBD is extremely difficult . . . it affects the learning of others, ideologically yes, but practically no. Other children suffer, who is most
important, thirty or one?

This dilemmatic framework has its origins in political ideas deriving from
philosophers and political theorists like Isaiah Berlin (Berlin, 1990), David
Marquand (1992) and the social psychologist Michael Billig (Billig *et al.*,
1988). However, it is a model which applies not only at a macro-social level
of analysis but also at micro social and individual levels too. The first key
step in dealing with these tensions is to accept that there are such dilemmas.
The second is that, in seeking a resolution, potentially contrary rights and
values need to be balanced. This means that some values and rights may not
be met or met fully. This implies that there is some loss; something has to be
given up. Another way of putting this is that there is no purity in education,
no pure version of inclusion. For all those making decisions in the education
system, including class teachers, policy and practice becomes a matter of
finding the best ways of having it both ways while minimising the loss – the
traditional case of how do you have your cake and eat it? It is a question of
resolving how do you do this, without it undermining that – where both this
and that are valued? It is a model which draws our attention to the value
bases of dilemmas and calls for a positive acknowledgement of multiple
values, the balancing of values and thus the acknowledgement of ideological
impurity (Norwich, 1996).

The efficacy and outcomes of inclusion

Valuing the presence and participation of children with significant difficulties in learning in mainstream schools and classes entails the position that
these conditions have positive benefits for them. Whether the comparison is
with the outcomes for them in separate provision settings or with outcomes
for other children without such difficulties is an issue. The point is that the
benefits can in principle be tested empirically. This does not mean that negative outcomes undermine critically the value commitment to inclusion, but
they do have a bearing on how the various values (inclusion, meeting individual needs, for example) are balanced with each other in making decisions.

Most reviews of the research evidence about inclusion indicate that there
can be no firm general conclusions from the studies which have been conducted (Lunt and Norwich, 2000). These reviews go back over two decades
and relate to studies in various countries, though the large-scale and most
systematic ones have been in the US. Some have noted that inclusion is
advocated without firm empirical evidence; others note how few studies there
have been of children with more severe kinds of difficulties in learning.
Systematic large-scale longitudinal studies which focus on broad multiple

outcomes are also very rare in this country. Some leading researchers (for instance, Hegarty, 1993; Lindsay, 2003) have argued that a global view is not the way to approach the contribution of empirical considerations. This is because inclusion is a multi-faceted and multi-levelled process and phenomenon. It operates across different levels in the education system; what applies to children whose main area of difficulty is a specific learning difficulty, may not apply to those with severe conduct difficulties. What applies in one setting or country might not apply in others, and so on.

But, even if empirical generalisations about the outcomes of inclusion are multi-faceted, there are different perspectives about the value of research. One position, argued by Lindsay (2003), supports a positive stance that good quality research using case studies and effectiveness studies can contribute useful knowledge about what supports children in mainstream settings, and what outcomes can be expected. Another position, one argued by Booth (1996b), is more critical of research. The contention is that inclusion represents a value commitment which is not subject to empirical evidence or validation. From this perspective, it can be argued that, if children who are included into mainstream classes are found to perform less well academically and socially, than, say, similar children based mainly in resourced units, then this reflects the need to examine how the mainstream classes can be adapted to remove this difference. It does not constitute evidence against inclusion. This is the position which rejects the idea that empirical evidence about efficacy impinges on provision decisions. To give another example, if children were making fewer academic and social gains in a mainstream class, despite the use of optimal teaching and management approaches, this would not impinge on the inclusion commitment. In one sense this line of argument is correct in maintaining the distinction between values and facts and guarding values against empirical facts which are sometimes alterable. However, its weakness is that it focuses on a single value, like inclusion, over other relevant values (for example, meeting individual needs, being realistic about current techniques and resource availability) that may also bear on practical decision making. How these different values are prioritised is critical for practical decision making. These other values and empirical considerations about outcomes all affect how and to what extent the inclusion value commitment is put into practice. They do not, however, undermine the value itself. The difference is between what can be called an ideologically purist position (Norwich, 1996), which holds inclusion as the overriding value, and an ideological pluralist position which considers inclusion to be a key, but not the only value relevant, to social and educational decisions (Low, 1996).

The evidence relating to different placements for pupils with MLD, the specific focus relevant to this book, has been reviewed at different times in various countries. Carlberg and Kavale (1980) in the USA undertook a meta-analysis comparing integrated and segregated provision. This synthesised statistical information across a range of 50 systematic empirical studies for academic and social/personal outcome measures. Their key conclusion was that there were different outcomes for different areas of disabilities. The advantage towards inclusive placements was for those described as 'slow learners' (IQ 75–90), who may not be considered for separate provision in the UK. There was a smaller but still positive outcome for children identified as 'educable mentally retarded' (IQ 50–75), corresponding more closely to what has traditionally been identified as ESN(M) and then MLD in the UK. This contrasted with the more positive outcomes in special settings for those identified as having 'emotional disturbance' or 'behaviour difficulties'. In a later review by Epps and Tindal (1987) there was also no clear evidence favouring separate settings for those with 'mild disabilities', which would include what is called MLD in the UK. This review also showed that placement is not the same as provision; outcomes may differ within mainstream settings depending on the particular kind of programme or provision available.

In the UK review, Crowther *et al.* (1998) suggest that the findings across different studies (mainly from the USA, for example Madden and Slavin, 1983) and reviews of these studies (some from the UK: Galloway, 1985; Williams, 1993) are ambiguous, with different studies showing different outcomes. However, they conclude, based on reviews like the ones discussed above, that there is no evidence that pupils in full-time segregated placements for MLD do better in terms of academic outcomes than those in mainstream settings. Where there are differences, these favour those in the mainstream. There was also evidence in line with the US review of Epps and Tindal (1987) that positive academic outcomes were associated with mainstream placements where pupils received appropriate levels of support in that setting. As regards personal and social outcomes, Crowther *et al.* (1998) also reviewed studies of pupil self-perceptions of children with MLD type difficulties in different settings. They conclude that where differences in academic self-concept are found, it tends to be lower in mainstream than in separate settings (link to page 105 for relevant findings from our research study). They explain this difference in terms of social comparison or reference theory – small fish: big pond effect. However, these authors also highlight some of the key weaknesses of research in this field. Assessing outcomes for the MLD group involves technical difficulties, as few of the measures have been designed for this group and there may be reliability and validity issues with them. Sample sizes may be small, intervention and controls groups not randomly allocated, limited follow-up of intervention impacts and inadequate accounts of the kind of interventions or the control groups.

Despite these weaknesses, including the question of relevance of US studies to the UK, some of the US studies illustrate interesting nuances in the findings as well as the degree of sophistication needed in studies of inclusive practices. For example, Manset and Semmel (1997) reviewed eight US inclusive models for primary-age students with mild disabilities. Though these

Table 3.1 Details of some model inclusion programmes: reviewed by Manset and Semmel (1997)

Authors/model	Goals	Students	Curriculum changes	School/class changes
Jenkins et al. (1994)	Accommodate individual differences in mainstream classes without ability grouping	Remedial, mild disabilities	Collaborative integrated reading and composition (CIRC); cross-age and peer tutoring, targeting basic reading skills 15 minutes daily instruction for selected students	Two-weekly planning meetings: teachers, special needs teachers and assistants; in-class teaching by specialist and assistants; withdrawal for some students
Schulte et al. (1990)	Trial consultation meetings between specialist teachers and mainstream teachers; with and without direct services by SEN teachers	Learning disability	Lesson plans modified during weekly consultation meetings; in-class modification by consultants, including identifying objectives, task analysis, performance monitoring, re-teaching, self-monitoring	Consultation with and without direct SEN (in-class/individual teaching/tutoring)
Wang and Birch (1984) Adaptive Learning Environment Model (ALEM)	Accommodate special needs of individuals in mainstream class	Mild disabilities	Individualised, hierarchically organised basic skills programme; diagnostic–prescriptive monitoring system; self management system	Family involvement; special teachers consult with mainstream teachers and provide support in classes; flexible, multi-age grouping; evidence based staff development

programmes involved mainly children with 'learning disability', corresponding to specific learning difficulties in the UK, there were also students with general low attainments. It is useful to summarise the key aspects of some of these reviewed models to show what kinds of adaptations were being made to mainstream settings. These are shown in Table 3.1. As Manset and Semmel conclude, these model programmes incorporate highly structured teaching practices that include individual teaching of basic educational skills and frequent monitoring and assessment of learning and performance. Opportunities for intensifying and individualising teaching are supported by additional resources or redeploying existing resources – such as reducing class size, increasing staff or using peer tutoring. Curriculum changes were required rather than just suggested, with these adaptations being 'hosts as opposed to guests in the mainstream classroom' (Manset and Semmel, 1997, page 175). One of their conclusions was that just providing mainstream teachers with additional training, or special needs teachers consulting with them, may not be enough. More positive outcomes were associated with models which adapted the mainstream curriculum. This review indicates that special education services were not eliminated in these models, but reconceptualised and redistributed. In some cases they were renamed; for example, special needs teachers did provide direct services and sometimes taught in mainstream classrooms. They also conclude that in some cases these models resembled the special education programmes they were designed to replace. For example, in the Jenkins *et al.* (1994) model (see details in Table 3.1), there was an element of intensive one-to-one teaching by specialist teachers who were previously special needs teachers in withdrawal settings.

On the question of whether these kinds of inclusive programmes are effective for students with mild disabilities, Manset and Semmel concluded that only two of the eight models had statistically significant positive findings in terms of reading and only two of the five models for maths. They summarise, 'inclusive programming effects are relatively unimpressive for most students with mild disabilities, especially in view of the extra-ordinary resources available to many of these model programs' (page 177). However, a relatively greater improvement of average students involved in the programmes was found, compared to the control group average students. This indicates that adapting the mainstream classes into appropriate learning environments for those with these kinds of SEN (mild/moderate) can have broader positive impacts. Their final conclusion is that:

> The evidence presented does suggest that inclusive programming for some students with mild disabilities can be an effective means of providing services, but evidence clearly indicates that a model of wholesale inclusive programming that is superior to more traditional special education services does not exist at present. In addition, the data from

these studies does not constitute support for the dismantling of special education.

(page 178)

The US Manset and Semmel (1997) review is referenced in the UK review by Crowther *et al.* (1998) in their conclusion that structured interventions and support in mainstream classes have more positive outcomes than programmes outside the mainstream classroom. Though there may be evidence for this tentative conclusion from one of the eight reviewed models, this was not one of Manset and Semmel's general conclusions. Nor is it the conclusion of the US study by Marston (1996), comparing in-class only, withdrawal only and combined withdrawal and in-class support models. Though this study was also about students with learning disabilities, its findings are relevant to the focus on MLD. The study showed that most of the special education teachers in the survey had experience of withdrawal and in-class models and that most (71 per cent) favoured a combination of withdrawal and in-class models, not either as the sole model. Reading gains of the students involved in these different models also showed that the gains were highest in the combined model. What is interesting is that though the special education resource teachers were required to deliver their services in 'integrated settings', they continued to provide withdrawal services for up to about 59 per cent of their cases. Also, most of the time that they allocated to direct teaching of these children with LD was in withdrawal settings. These teachers certainly did not pursue fully inclusive models, when they had the option to make their own decisions.

The most comprehensive research in the UK, which bears on the question of comparative outcomes, has been conducted with children identified as having Down Syndrome (DS) (Buckley, 2000). Many of those with Down Syndrome would be in provision designated for moderate learning difficulties. Research over a 15-year period has been summarised as indicating that there were no distinct educational benefits of special school education. For teenagers with Down Syndrome, those in mainstream settings had the same levels of functioning, or higher levels on all measures, compared to those in special schools. Teenagers in mainstream schools were more than two years ahead on spoken language measures and more than three years ahead on literacy measures. The one difference in favour of special school pupils with DS was in the area of interpersonal friendship skills. The methodological weakness with this kind of comparative study is that the special and mainstream groups would not have been allocated randomly to provision in the two placements and therefore those in the special school may have more severe and more additional difficulties in learning. This was one of the main features in the comparative samples used in the study reported in the next three chapters.

Post-school outcomes for pupils with MLD

The outcomes studies discussed above relate to immediate school impacts, not to longer term ones post-school. These are important issues for the theme of this book, as there has been the view that many of those identified as having mild to moderate learning difficulties can later blend into the adult community post-school. Edgerton (1967) used the term 'cloak of competence' in the USA to refer to those considered mildly mentally retarded in school fitting into post-school communities. That young people considered to be 'retarded' during their schooling appear to be more competent post-school has also been noted in the UK (Richardson and Koller, 1992). Despite the importance of the post-school period for evaluating school impacts and for the care and well-being of those who received special educational provision, it has been widely noted that there have been very few longitudinal studies of these longer term outcomes (Crowther *et al.*, 1998; Hornby and Kidd, 2001). The post-school experiences of young people who were designated at school as having moderate learning difficulties have changed considerably since the 1980s. About 20 per cent of 16-year-olds in the UK remained in full-time education a quarter of a century ago, while the rest entered the labour market, sometimes combining this with part-time study (Dee, 2001). However, in the late 1970s and early 1980s concern grew about youth unemployment and low staying-on rates in the UK compared to those in other developed countries. Steps were then taken to increase participation in post-16 education and training opportunities. The Warnock Committee (DES, 1978) noted that young people with special needs were often unemployed or under-employed but that those with MLD were able to hold down a job with minimal extra support. One report following the Warnock Report concluded that school leavers with special educational needs required more education and training opportunities as well as more support in combating the high level of social isolation and psychological problems experienced by many in their late teens and early twenties (Walker, 1982).

Walker (1982) examined the destinations of 393 school leavers with a wide range of special educational needs and compared them with a control group of 115. He found a comparable level of employment at age 18 for the young people with learning difficulties and/or disabilities as those who were non-disabled (66 per cent). The figure for those with ESN(M) (now MLD) was 64 per cent. While the remainder of those without disabilities were in education and training, their disabled peers were unemployed or attending social services day centres. Also, most of those with special needs who were working had semi-skilled or unskilled jobs and had experienced more periods of unemployment. More recent surveys show the significant decrease in those in open employment. For example, Ward *et al.* (1994) found that an increasing number of those with learning difficulties and disabilities remaining in continuing education and training, reflecting a general trend throughout the

1980s in post-16 destinations. They analysed the destinations of 619 school leavers with a range of learning difficulties and/or disabilities up to the age of 20. Over the course of the two-year study, 9 per cent entered open employment, 31 per cent were in continuing education and training (including 65 at school), 22 per cent were lost to the researchers and the remaining 38 per cent were in day centres or unemployed. These authors also reported that the type of disability was loosely linked to young people's most probable route on leaving school, so that those with physical disabilities alone were most likely to enter paid employment.

Several other small-scale studies also show the specific decrease in the numbers of young people with moderate learning difficulties entering open employment (May and Hughes, 1985; Freshwater and Leyden, 1989; Hornby and Kidd, 2001). May and Hughes (1985) followed up 63 young people with MLD in Scotland over two years after leaving school. By this time only three of the 63 (5 per cent) were in open employment. This compares with figures derived by these authors for the period before 1980 of between 50–90 per cent in open employment. Freshwater and Leyden (1989) followed 47 young people who left a MLD special school in the Midlands for between three and ten years. Many could not be traced and this affects the representative nature of their sample, as US studies show that those who are harder to trace are more likely to have employment. Nevertheless, only four of the 47 (9 per cent) were in open employment. A similarly negative view is found in the Hornby and Kidd (2001) study of 24 pupils with moderate learning difficulties who had transferred from special to mainstream school; a large majority were unemployed (71 per cent).

This Hornby and Kidd study was a follow-up of a previous study of 29 young people who were transferred from special schools to mainstream schools ten years before (Kidd and Hornby, 1993). Their views were surveyed one year after the transfer. Most of the parents (65 per cent) and the young people (76 per cent) were happy with the transfer. However, the authors found a notable difference in responses for those transferred to units in the mainstream compared to those who were only in mainstream classes. For those mainly in units, 92 per cent of parents and 92 per cent of young people were happy with the transfer. By contrast, for those only in mainstream classes, only 47 per cent of parents and 64 per cent of young people were happy. This is an interesting difference, but given the small scale of the sample, it is difficult to have confidence in this relationship between placement in mainstream and satisfaction ratings and its wider applicability. Most of these young people (24) were traced between three and nine years after leaving school. They had spent three years on average in the mainstream after being seven years on average in the special school. Their retrospective views about their schooling were also interesting. Most (63 per cent) rated their school experiences as helpful to extremely helpful, the rest as unhelpful to extremely unhelpful. There was also a continuation of differential satisfaction with school provision depending on the kind of transfer. Those who were in units in the mainstream had been mostly satisfied (92 per cent), while only 33 per cent of those only in mainstream classes had been satisfied. However, Hornby and Kidd (2001) also report that though the mainstream unit students were consistent over time in reporting greater satisfaction, they did not have increased employment success after leaving school. What was missing for pupils in both mainstream class only and mainstream unit provision was work-related experience before leaving school. So, despite all the efforts made for these groups to be included prior to leaving school, they had not achieved a similar level of inclusion after leaving school in employment terms. The conclusion they draw from this small-scale study is that provision for pupils with MLD in secondary schools which is more likely to optimise social inclusion will be focused more on location and social aspects rather than curriculum inclusion. Their advice was that these pupils need a curriculum focused on functional skills to support their post-school development of independence and that this requires work experience during their latter school years.

Some of Hornby and Kidd's conclusions are consistent with some key findings from an on-going longitudinal study of the post-16 transition of pupils with SEN (Polat et al., 2001), even though the study was not confined to those who had moderate learning difficulties. In this national study of 2,313 young people who had been identified as having SEN (the range of learning difficulties, EBD and sensory and motor difficulties), their parents, senior teachers and SEN co-ordinators, they found that parents and carers were more satisfied with transition preparation in special than in mainstream schools (64 per cent and 44 per cent respectively). Special school pupils tended to report more positive attitudes towards and experiences of school and their teachers than mainstream pupils. Mainstream pupils appeared to have more restricted social lives and lower aspirations and expectations, and participated more in work experience than their special school peers. However, as these authors recognise, these differences might reflect the greater severity and range of difficulties of those in special schools.

Concluding comments

This chapter has brought together a wide range of recent and relevant literature about aspects of the school education of pupils with MLD within the wider issues of provision for pupils with SEN. Research on those who go to special schools for MLD raises questions about the continuing role for special schools with this designation, as they have become in practice schools which cater for more mixed needs. The conclusion that there has been no serious attempt to develop a curriculum or pedagogy for this group was also considered in relation to the recently developed national guidelines for pupils with learning difficulties. As regards inclusion, we recognised that inclusion for this MLD group cannot be separated from wider issues about this movement in school provision. It was also argued that there is continuity between previous ideas about integration and current concepts of inclusion; forcing issues into false dichotomies is not tenable. Current concepts of inclusion were also shown to operate at a level of generality that can lose contact with operational reality; definitions do not specify, for example, what is meant by participation in local schools. This means that it is hard to identify what makes a school inclusive; lists of factors associated with inclusive schools tend to overlook the ambiguity, tensions and complexity of schooling. Inclusion, it was argued, is at best an 'orienting' term which draws attention to issues and commitments to belonging and participation. These tensions can be considered, as introduced in the previous chapter, in terms of dilemmas of difference. This dilemmatic perspective applies to decision making at various key levels in the system, and calls for resolutions which balance contrary values and factors. That there are no firm general conclusions about the efficacy of inclusion for the MLD group can be understood partly in these terms. The reviews of these outcome studies do indicate, however, that there is no evidence that full-time segregated provision has better academic outcomes than mainstream provision. A more fine-grained US study was examined to show that though inclusive programmes can be effective, there is no evidence of superior inclusive programmes that can yet replace traditional special education services or elements of these services. Finally, some small-scale studies of post-school experience and provision for the MLD group show a significant decline in open employment, despite all the efforts to include these young people before leaving school.

Chapter 4

Children's perspectives on their special provision

Introduction

One relatively neglected facet of the inclusion question is children's own perspective on their special educational provision. In this chapter we report and discuss a study that contributes to this field through examining the perspectives of children and young people who receive special education provision for their moderate learning difficulties. This study examined the assumption that pupils' perspectives will reflect a tension between positive aspects (wanting and appreciating help) and negative aspects (wanting to avoid stigmatising associations), whether in special schools, mainstream withdrawal or in-class supported placements. This assumption was built on the findings from previous studies that focused on the child's perspective. The largest study was conducted some years ago by the Inner London Education Authority (ILEA) as part of a survey of pupils' perspectives on the range of London special schooling (ILEA, 1986). Some studies focused on specific areas of special needs, for example hearing impairment (Lynas, 1986), or moderate learning difficulties (Norwich, 1997), while others covered different areas of special educational needs (Cheston, 1994; Lewis, 1995). Some looked at older students who were in post-school provision (SCPR, 1996) and others were conducted in other countries, for example Greece (Padeliadu and Zigmond, 1996). Following the argument in previous chapters, this tension relates to positive and negative personal evaluations of 'difference', the positive aspects of receiving individually appropriate help with learning, and the negative aspects of experiencing stigma and devaluation. The rationale for this study was, therefore, connected to wider theory and research into 'difference dilemmas', outlined in previous chapters.

Lynas (1986), in her study of the inclusion of children with hearing impairment in mainstream schools, showed that they did not like to be 'shown up' in front of other children, yet overall they did not resent the special attention that they received. She interpreted this as indicating a basic dilemma about inclusion: between treating pupils as 'normal', on one hand, and catering for special needs through providing additional help, on the other. The ILEA study (1986) found pupils to be generally positive about their special schools and appreciative of the help they received. Different groups made some criticisms of special schools for various reasons. These ranged from limitations of the curriculum to being isolated and over-protected. With reference to special schools for MLD, most pupils in two MLD special schools (80 per cent) reported feeling happy in their school, with a majority (60 per cent) liking being at a special school. Less than 1 in 5 thought that inclusion (or integration, the term used then) was a good idea, with just over half seeing it as a bad idea or having mixed feelings about it. The most common reasons against inclusion were the fear of not being able to cope with the work, that there would not be enough help and that they would experience bullying and teasing.

In the smaller scale study of one London MLD special school (Norwich, 1997), the majority of adolescent pupils reported that the school helped them with their learning. Very few had confidence that the mainstream schools could provide adequately for them. Only one of the 19 was in favour of mainstream provision and supported the closing of MLD special schools. This contrasted with the majority who favoured keeping MLD special schools open. These results were consistent with the findings from the larger ILEA study 11 years before. These pupils' personal evaluations of special school were mostly positive (60 per cent), with the main reasons being about the curriculum and the teaching. Most pupils reported that their parents also held positive views about the special school. These positive views contrasted with the mainly negative views of their peers – those in their special school, and those from mainstream schools. The most common negative reports were of critical and shaming comments directed at those going to special schools – 'dumb school' or 'shameful to come here'. Several of those interviewed expressed their anger at this devaluation by their peers. This small-scale study indicated that these pupils recognised the positive benefits of special school, while also appreciating that they share a devalued identity through going to special school. This study illustrated the tensions experienced by the special school pupils.

The original SEN Code of Practice (DfE, 1994), which set out the procedures for identifying, assessing and providing for pupils with SEN in 1994, promoted practices that took account of children's views and feelings about their special provision. In the revised SEN Code (DfES, 2001), these principles have been further emphasised and, as noted previously, recognising the child's voice in education is part of a wider movement across various areas of social provision, for example as recommended in the Children Act 1989. However, it has been noted that the enthusiasm for children and young people to give their views sometimes goes beyond their language and conceptual abilities, especially of those with severe or profound intellectual impairments (Felce, 2002). Policy imperatives can tend to assume the ease of eliciting views and feelings without questioning the adequacy of elicitation methods, which suggest the need for some discussion about interviewing children and young people with learning difficulties and disabilities.

Research in eliciting perspectives

It is now widely recognised that there is a need for varying approaches to enable children and young people to contribute to and participate in decisions about education provision and individual education plans (Lewis and Lindsay, 2000). For instance, various techniques based on pictorial representations are now used to communicate with children whose problems are within the autistic spectrum and with those who have verbal or written communication problems (Kirkbride, 1999). Information technology is also widely used to enable those with difficulties with physical writing to put their thoughts down through word processing (Detheridge and Detheridge, 1997). The growing practical interest in children's perspectives has also generated various methodologies for doing this (Gersch *et al.*, 1993; CDC, 1995; Jelly *et al.*, 2000).

Eliciting perspectives is not just a technical matter; it also involves complex ethical considerations. Seeking children's perspectives has been a growing trend over the 1990s. Several research studies, mostly small scale, have investigated children's perspectives with relevance to special education (for example, Whitaker, 1994; Sheldon, 1991; Caffyn and Millet, 1992; Cooper, 1993; Armstrong *et al.*, 1993; Wade and Moore, 1993; Norwich, 1997). More recently, researchers have been asking more specifically about the dynamics and processes involved in such enterprises (Graue and Walsh, 1998; Christensen and James, 2000; Scott, 2000). Some of the factors that have been considered include:

- the child's and young person's competences and characteristics;
- the questioner's competences and characteristics;
- the purpose and use made of eliciting the child's and young person's views;
- the setting and context: power, relationship and emotional factors;
- ethical and human rights considerations.

Lewis and Lindsay (2000) bring together a range of contributors who examine various facets of these factors in depth. Competences in this field include cognitive, linguistic and physical capabilities, for example what children can understand, their receptive and expressive language abilities and their physical skills to provide adequate responses to questions and assessment tasks (Daniels and Jenkins, 2000).

The issue of eliciting reliable and valid information is crucial, and has long been identified as critical to the research process with children and adults. Two significant issues that have been identified are that of children 'pleasing the interviewer', and 'presenting an ideal self' (Begley, 2000). Stalker (1998) and Grove *et al.* (2000) have also highlighted the related tendency of some children to acquiesce to the suggestions of others. These issues are more complex with children than adults, as children are in situations of even greater power differentials. Further, children may find themselves in situations where the questioner might in fact be part of a problem for them: children may not be in an environment where they can be open in communication, when they are subject to threats or fear.

There is also a growing trend to treat children as participants in the research process, a paradigm approach whose ideal is to empower children and see them as the experts (Warren, 2000; Davis *et al.*, 2000). This is a move to counter the power differential between adults and children, and this is reinforced by the call for children to have a voice as an expression of their human rights (Davie *et al.*, 1996).

Study aims and methods

The study was designed to elicit the perspectives of a representative sample of boys and girls with mild to moderate general learning difficulties in one LEA towards the end of the Key Stage 2 and during the Key Stage 3 of their mainstream or special schooling. The focus was on their perceptions and evaluations of their educational provision, their self-perceptions and self-evaluations, and their responses to the terms and labels relevant to them. In this chapter we report and discuss the findings about how these children saw their educational provision in mainstream and special school settings. Further findings from the study about self-perceptions, perceptions of labels and experiences of bullying will be discussed in more detail in the following two chapters. We report the findings relevant to the following study aims:

1   to examine how children with MLD see their special provision;
2   to find out whether their views include positive and negative aspects;
3   to examine whether any of these perspectives vary according to type of special education placement, age or gender of pupils.

The project took place in a South-West county LEA, which was approached as it had a well-established tradition of inclusive practice. All pupils in the LEA who had Statements of SEN in which mild to moderate general learning difficulties was a main feature were identified from the central Statement database. The term 'general learning difficulty' was taken as synonymous with moderate learning difficulties. The LEA used the broad definition of learning difficulties based on the SEN Code of Practice (DfE, 1994) (see page 141 for details). All pupils in the two age ranges, 10 to 11 years and 13 to 14 years, were then identified. The aim was to identify 50 pupils in each age

Table 4.1 Breakdown of sample: school by age and gender

	10	11	12	13	14	Total
Mainstream school boys	5	8	0	9	5	27
Mainstream school girls	7	5	0	5	7	24
Special school boys	8	5	1	4	8	26
Special school girls	6	6	0	3	9	24
Total	26	24	1	21	29	101

range, with half being drawn from mainstream, and half from the four relevant LEA special schools.

The final study sample of mainstream pupils was distributed amongst 33 schools (51 children altogether), of whom eight had placements in designated resource bases (units) in four of these mainstream schools. For the special school pupils, 24 had placements in two generic special schools, and 26 were in special schools designated for children with MLD. The pupils from each of the four combinations of school and age range were also selected to keep a balance between boys and girls, and between rural and urban settings, as far as was possible (see Tables 4.1 and 4.2).

No attempt was made to match the pupils in the mainstream and special schools in terms of kind and degrees of learning difficulties, for several reasons. Those in special school were expected to have more severe difficulties, which in fact proved to be the case. Details of difficulties were recorded from each pupil's current Statement, and their most recent National Curriculum attainment levels in mathematics and English were also collected. The recency of the issuing of Statements varied, as would be expected given the age range of the pupils. Some Statements were issued when the children were 6 years old, while others had been issued within the last year. Nevertheless, this data enabled a comparison to be made between the nature and severity of difficulties of the samples in each school setting. Table 2.2 (page 14) shows the combination of difficulties additional to MLD. Of the whole sample, more pupils were recorded as having a language and communication difficulty (LCD) with MLD than having MLD alone – 60 per cent in this group. It was clear that pupils in these special schools had more

Table 4.2 Kind of school by setting

	Urban setting	Rural setting
Mainstream schools	22	29
Special schools	26	24

Table 4.3 Number of pupils with MLD only and additional areas of difficulty, by school

	Mainstream school	Special school	Total
MLD only	12 (75%)	4 (25%)	16
MLD + 1	29 (49%)	20 (51%)	49
MLD + 2	10 (29%)	24 (71%)	34
MLD + 3	0 (0%)	2 (100%)	2

additional areas of difficulties, as summarised in Table 4.3. This shows that 75 per cent of pupils with MLD only were in mainstream schools, while 25 per cent were in special schools. On the other hand, of pupils with MLD plus two other areas of difficulties, 71 per cent were in special schools while only 29 per cent were in mainstream schools.

Analysis of National Curriculum attainment levels across schools, as assessed by teachers, again highlighted the differences between school types. For example, pupils in special schools showed greater percentages below Level 1. Conversely, the higher attainment Levels 3 and 4 were found more in the mainstream than special schools sample. For fuller details about research approach and procedures, see Norwich and Kelly (2004).

Findings

A number of key areas are presented, starting with perspectives on present provision in special and mainstream schools, how others respond to learning needs and the kinds and sources of additional help received. The following sections present perspectives on and preferences for learning support in mainstream classes, and pupils' general views and preferences for alternative forms of provision (mainstream pupils about special schools and special school pupils about mainstream schools). Abbreviations used to identify pupils' backgrounds are given below.

MS	mainstream pupil	S	secondary
SS	special school pupil	U	urban
M	male	R	rural
F	female	G	generic provision
P	primary	D	designated provision

Perspectives on present schools and provision

Overall views on current schools varied, with 65 per cent expressing mainly positive evaluations, 31 per cent a combination of mixed perspectives, that is, both positive and negative evaluations, and only 4 per cent reported mainly negative views. There were no overall differences in perspectives between primary and secondary, or mainstream and special school pupils. There was, however, a tendency for mainstream boys to have more positive perspectives and for mainstream girls to have more mixed perspectives. (Where group differences are described as significant, this means that in a statistical test [Chi-square] the difference was statistically significant at the $p < 0.05$ level.) Children gave a mix of reasons for their likes and dislikes of their present schools, and these are specified in the following sections. Provision itself was only one of several important factors that children themselves identified as being influential in their feelings about present schools, and schools generally.

Peers

Peers played a very important part in children's school lives, and relationships with others were described as being a significant source of happiness or unhappiness. Having good friends, or being ignored, picked on, or bullied by others in school, often affected feelings about schools. In relation to provision, friends were valued for helping with work difficulties:

MSFSU4 My friends are really good towards me, they know that I've got difficulties so if ever I need anythin' or spelling they can help me all the time.

MSFPR4 Hum, they're kind, they stand up for me, and they help me, and they tell also the people off not to call me names.

SSMSD1 We've got six in my class and like all of them there are my mates and that, and like two of them are like on my transport and that. Because it's like friends can help out with each other.

The experience of having a friend in school played a part in enjoying class time as well as playtime, because children were able to support each other:

MSFPR2 She's my special friend, we always play together, we sit together and work together, we have dinner together, we always hang around with each other and get in trouble.

SSFSD3 Without our friends we'd be lonely, wouldn't we?

MSFSR5   Someone to hang out with at dinnertime, if I'm lonely or sad I can talk to them.

Though some children described being left out during playtimes, being left out or ignored by others in class was equally difficult, and created a different kind of loneliness:

MSFSU3   Most people in my form don't like me except for [one boy].

SSMSG2   Get on alright sometimes with other children in class. I don't think anyone's really my friend. Sometimes they punch me and that. Don't know why. Perhaps they don't like me. Makes me feel angry. When they beat me up, outside in the playground.

Children described how peer interaction affected their preference for learning support, as withdrawal meant separation from friends, and in-class support could mean teasing or bullying in class:

MSFPR7   I don't like sitting on my own somewhere, 'cos it's really boring, but when your sitting with a friend you can just have a little chat and ask them the answers and things.

MSMPR5   When I come out sort of like for reference we have a little talk, then I go to my next lesson and come out or go to [the teacher] because [my friend] he helps me, then we can talk while we're doing the work an' stuff like that.

Choice of school was also affected by desire to stay with good friends:

MSFSR3   I wanted to go to [one school] because I knew that my best friend was going to go [there] and I know that my mum wanted me to go to [the other school].

Four out of five pupils in mainstream and special schools reported being 'picked on' or bullied in some way, with two-thirds having experienced more than one kind of bullying (details of 'bullying' are described more fully in Chapter 6). A number of children, however, described situations where other children behaved in contradictory ways to them. These children were described as friends, even though they were likely to tease or even be very unkind:

MSFSU4   Girls would just, like, fall out with me for no reason and make my life a misery. I don't like coming to school, I don't like school at all. And I don't, I don't, the only lessons I like is German and science 'cos there's like most of my friends in there, but I'm getting bullied on at the moment. I just, I go home and have a cry sometimes.

MSMSU5   They just, they're funny. They do get on with me sometimes, it's just, they call me names. One, he is my mate but he's got this thing, I don't know why, he just calls me and makes up, it ain't true, he knows it ain't true but he just says it for fun.

Some children, most particularly secondary special school boys, felt they lost out on friends or that they lost friends because they were at a special school, as these two boys described:

SSMSD2   Cause if I knew them as a friend and they didn't know what school I went to, as soon as I told them, their opinion of me changes. 'Cause I've had that happen to me before and it's, you know, well, they don't want to be your friend because you go to a special school.

SSMSG2   Prefer mainstream, because I've got about ten mates there, and I've only got about three here. It's very important having friends. That's what's worse here. I know other children who need help in mainstream. I'd like to go to their school. It's not fair that I have to be here.

Teachers and teaching assistants

Teachers and teaching assistants were important in terms of being active givers of help and a *visible* source of support for learning. In addition, they were also an important adult relationship, and how they related to children was perceived to affect children's sense of well-being and general evaluation of schools.

In terms of evaluating their teachers, the majority (55 per cent) were mainly positive, 45 per cent were mixed (positive and negative), and none were mainly negative. There were no differences between mainstream and special school pupils, boys and girls and primary and secondary aged pupils. Children's descriptions covered a range of characteristics and behaviours, from descriptions about appearance, to general characteristics, to the way teachers/assistants provided support for learning. Pupils were generally able to describe and distinguish between individuals whose attitude and approach made them feel good or bad, and whose company they enjoyed or not.

Commonly used words to describe good qualities were: kind; nice; supportive; understanding; helpful; fair; friendly; funny; happy; and caring. The most commonly appreciated characteristics were those of general kindness, fairness, fun and helpfulness:

MSFPR1 I like it because all the teachers be kind to me and look after me.

MSMPR5 He's umm kind but he's a bit scruffy, his writing is very . . . writing 'cos even [the assistant] an' that thought it was. They said they might even give him special needs lessons!

MSFSR6 Hum she keeps calm, she doesn't let her temper out that much, and she's just a good teacher really.

SSFPG5 She's nice, she's kind, she's friendly and she's a good teacher, I like her.

SSMSD1 He's honest and like umm, he likes to tell jokes like, and basically we get on with him.

SSFSD3 Well, me and [him] always got on [with] each other, you know. We have a laugh, you know, he's nice to talk to, he's understanding person, he's funny, you know.

Characteristics that children found upsetting were: unfair; not understanding; ignoring; being 'stressy'; shouting/'shouty'; angry; blaming; too teasing/winding people up; being rude and/or abusive; physically handling; unpleasant/loud voices/looks; too strict; too bossy; intrusive; and treating the child like a baby. Least favoured and most often referred to characteristics were 'shouty', unfair, 'stressy'/angry and unhelpful:

MSFPR7 He's a bit too, shouts a bit too much about just a little thing. He could just mention it and then say don't do it again otherwise you will get in trouble.

MSFSR6 She just got angry like with most of the people in lessons.

SSFSD6 'Cause she used to boss me around. She used to tell me what to do. Every five minutes when I was doing something, she told me off. Because I was umm, not doing my work.

SSMSG4 She's all right. Sometimes she's strict and she shouts at you and that. The rest of the teachers are strict, some of them, most of them.

Children reported being particularly upset when they felt unfairly blamed for something that they were not responsible for. In many cases children acknowledged when they had 'lost it', or 'gone over the top', but they felt strongly about being blamed on the strength of past behaviours. A particular irritation was when other children were provocative, and the teacher did not take this into account when responding, despite having the circumstances explained to them:

SSFSG4   Because anythin' that went on, and it was them that was pickin' on me and then when I retaliated they'd go 'she's pickin' on me'. When I actually tried saying to, to the teacher, look, I said look, next door is actually pickin' on me and I'm getting fed up with it. She goes, well can't really do anythin' about it but, I'll say somethin' to [another teacher], she did but it didn't really matter because, whatever they did, she thought it was like my fault.

Teasing and 'winding up' by teachers were acceptable to a point, but some children became upset when teachers went too far, or in some respect their comments felt abusive:

SSFSD2   Stop calling me great gallark and sometimes calls me fatty and I hate it. He keeps winding me up saying he goes out with me. I hate it. He teases, that's all. Stop it. He's boring.

MSMSR5   Quite a few of the teachers say I'm a bit stupid.
Q   How does it feel when a teacher says it?
MSMSR5   I just feel a bit angry.

Response to and support for their learning needs

Experience of support for learning varied between mainstream and special schools by the nature of the different types of school. Special school class sizes were relatively small, with usually one teacher and two in-class support assistants present. In the mainstream, however, classes averaged over thirty and classroom assistants were often part-time, placed to support specific children and/or to support a number of children at different times. Children tended to get to know their learning support staff very well, especially in the special schools where there was the potential for very close relationships to develop.

A feature of mainstream schools was that they had different types of support, including, in some cases, special units. Special schools tended to be more like primary schools, though secondary age pupils did have different teachers for different lessons, and moved from class to class. Secondary aged children in mainstream, including middle schools, often had specific units or places where they were withdrawn to for extra or different work in smaller group. It was here that in some schools, pupils and staff were able to develop closer relationships, and where children could have a 'bolt-hole' from busy mainstream life, which some children found difficult especially during break times. Mainstream secondary schools also tended to have subject based ability sets, and most of the SEN children were found in the lower sets where classes were smaller, and learning support assistants would often work.

Children were aware of how teachers and assistants responded to their learning difficulties, including whether individuals seemed to recognise and understand their needs and whether support was adequate and helpful. As with all other categories, children reported a variety of responses, from very supportive and helpful to unkind, punitive or unhelpful.

Children highlighted clarity and confidence building:

SSFSD3   Well, he's good at saying things, you know, like clear, you know like speaking things.

MSFSR6   He's my maths teacher; he explains things, easy to understand for maths questions. Drama teacher, he teaches us like how to act and not be scared to like perform stuff. My history teacher she like helps with us to understand history lesson and the geography teacher, he makes it easier to understand like where the countries are.

They described different ways of helping, highlighting encouragement to work independently before asking for help:

SSFSG4   The way she'll actually help you and that, right, she'll say look just try on your own for 10 to 15 minutes, and then if you go to her, look I've tried, look here's my trying, then she'll help you.

MSMSU4   Say like the teacher has already explained it on the board, then [the assistants] help you with the question, and that they read them through and they explain it in a different way, like on a piece of paper or something. They are not telling me, they are trying to get me to work it out, trying to explain a clue or something.

Or making lessons interesting and informative:

SSFPD3   She does good things like interestin', she tries to make it interestin' the work and that, so quite good.

And spending time with pupils to help them learn from their errors:

SSMSD2   He helps you on the computers and teaches you how to do stuff when you leave school on the computers. He doesn't just give you the computer and leave you to, you know, bugger it up a thousand times. And if you go wrong he tells you where you've gone wrong so you, you can actually, you know, start off where you were, and know what to do next, 'cause he does it in stages like, like, all in a group press this button, and he goes press the red button, or something.

Appropriate responses lead to satisfied pupils:

SSMSD1 I'm pretty happy with what he does.

A further area of support that some children commented on was that of behaviour. Some children acknowledged their own behavioural problems (more details on this, and the link between learning difficulties and behavioural problems, are discussed in Chapter 5), and were aware of and grateful for help in calming them down:

SSFSD3 Well sometimes maths, you know. But they help me with my behaviour though, I know that, they, you know they talk to me, you know. They always say 'calm down', don't have a fight, you know.

In some cases the teachers and assistants were also reported as being aware that children were becoming stressed over schoolwork and sometimes needed help with controlling their behaviour:

MSFSU2 They get really worried an' that lot about me going stressed an' that lot and they sometimes come over and help me an' I take it on at them, take it, yeah.

A common problem for children was in not understanding things the first time round, so approachability and patience in teachers, being willing to explain again and again if necessary, was highly valued:

MSFSR6 The work gets harder an' like you don't understand it, and if you like put your hand up they come over and explain that you need to, like, and they tell you twice so that you can understand it a bit more better.

Many children described positive experiences, though there were also other descriptions that highlighted less satisfactory experiences in terms of receiving help. In some cases children found teachers unapproachable, or were too scared to ask them things:

MSFPU1 [Can't ask] 'cause I'm scared of him. 'Cause he gets angry and I ain't very keen on him. Worrying, scared and all that.

Which contrasted with pupils' experience of other teachers:

MSFPU1   He's a good chap and he's friendly, and he helps us. I just go and ask him 'cause I ain't scared. Can then understand. It just feels natural.

A number of children felt they did not receive any help in the first place:

SSFPG4   'Cause I tried to get the answers and I did and no, she never helped me at all. It used to make me feel sad 'cause I never had any help.

In other cases some pupils found it difficult to ask for help if they did not know the individual and how teacher would respond:

MSMSU4   I find basic skills easy, but I'm scared to tell [the SEN co-ordinator, or SENCo] that. Umm, if I know them really well then I'll ask them, if they are very new I am scared to ask them because I don't know them and I don't know if they will be strict or that.

Q   How easy or how hard do you find it to ask for somebody to help you?

MSMSU4   Umm special needs teachers are ok, but some teachers I'm a bit scared of, yeah. Same reasons, I'm just scared really, because I don't know them.

A number of children referred to times when they felt individuals did not understand their problems, and sometimes behaved in unfair or punitive ways:

MSFSU6   They can be a bit stressy, nag at you. But like if you are not concentrating on your work, or doing something wrong, or you're not supposed to do, like if I'm writing slow. Can be unfair sometimes. Just telling you, like saying, write down this, and I'm a bit slow, and if you haven't finished, they say hurry up then!

MSMSU2   Most of the teachers in [that school] thought I was just lazy. Well it's more just the anger but yeah it was quite upsetting to see that obviously quite intelligent people such as the teachers couldn't grasp that I did have a problem and it was quite saddening yeah.

Some children described problems in understanding teachers' explanations, sometimes because things were not said in a way that the pupil could understand, and sometimes because of other distractions:

MSMSR1   I don't really like it when, hum, they don't explain it right, explain what's going on, because most of the people talk and interrupt, so most people can't understand so she has to read it over again, and gets really shouty.

MSMSU4   I'm not too keen on her. I think she sets us a lot of homework every time, she writes all these words down on the board that I don't understand, even if she says it to me, I won't understand it because it's very hard.

Quality and quantity of help with learning

About half of pupils (53 per cent) thought they had enough help with learning in their present situation, 26 per cent did not, and 21 per cent described mixed experiences. This was an overall judgement, which included different areas of learning and sometimes different teachers. There were no significant differences in these levels of perceived help between category groups, mainstream and special school, boys and girls and older and younger pupils.

Some examples of mainstream children's positive attitudes to receiving help with learning were:

MSFPR3   It's quite good because, because it [the assistant] is kind and she helps me with anything really.

MSFPR7   They try to explain it and read it through lots of times until eventually you do. They are, very patient with everything. Fun and that's it.

MSMPU2   She helps me sometimes as well, yeah. I've got loads of teachers helpin' me.

MSMSR7   I think it's a good thing [to get help]. 'Cos with writing I need help.

Q   What would it be like if people didn't help you and just left you to get on with it?

MSMSR7   Then I wouldn't do the work at all.

Some described mixed experiences:

MSFSU4   Not very much help at all. I've had a lot more help than I did over there.

MSMSR1   I feel like I've got enough help now 'cause I didn't feel like I got enough help in Year 7. Because in Year 7 I couldn't actually quite understand any of it. Now when they explain it more like, when they translate it a bit easier I can understand what's going on.

Others reported not getting sufficient help:

SSMSG2   Would like more help with writing and reading. Makes me feel angry.

MSFSU1   I actually got special needs but I don't go. I actually need help with all my lessons but I don't get it. All the lessons 'cos I can't get on with it.

MSFSU2   I sometimes put my hand up, say their name an' that, but they sometimes come over, but if they are helping someone that is struggling they say wait a minute, I'm just helping this boy or girl. I'd like to get a bit more help than usual. They teach me really good there, they was helping me a lot an' that.

MSFSU3   Have to wait 'cos [the assistants are] helping someone else. A long time. Not that much help.

Some children complained about the way in which help was provided, often identifying various elements within this. The following case highlights this, identifying problems with accents, wanting a different approach to help, and becoming uncomfortable and embarrassed about having to keep asking for help:

MSFSR3   I'm not really good at computers but I am good when, hum, it comes to play, when you can play games but not when it is, hum, when you have to work instructions, 'cause we got this man and I think he's kind of Scottish or Irish and, hum, and I can't really listen really hardly 'cause I don't understand what he's sayin'. I have to keep on going up to him to ask for help. He always comes back and helps but, hum, he, he doesn't show me, he tells me what to do.

Q   So you'd like him to actually show you how to do it?

MSFSR3   A little yes. Hum, sometimes I give up and I just ask a teacher but when I keep on askin' a teacher, hum, and, hum, about two or three times then I don't want to go back up 'cause, hum, 'cause hum, hum, hum, the teacher will have, I feel like the teacher will probably get fed up of me. Hum, I'm worried about.

MSFSR3   Yeah and then I just feel like I can't do the work and then I just try but I can't do it then, hum, I feel, hum, I feel uncomfortable. I'm embarrassed of askin' about four times. Hum, I thi, I thi,

I think other teachers are who think that I get ridiculous asking for help all the time.

Some gave examples of when, from their point of view, the amount of type of help was inappropriate:

MSFPR2   Yeah. I've got too much actually. Well I always askin' for teachers to help me but sometimes I don't ask and I just, just want to get on with my work.

MSFSU4   But one of the ladies would come up to me like every five minutes when I would already know what to do she would just ask me again and I would already knew what I'm doing. And it would get on my nerves so one day I told her to go away and I got in trouble for it and told her to shut up. When they just get at you all the time and like when you don't when the teachers that's teachin' or he's already told you what you're doin' and then the helper comes up to you and says oh you alright and when I already know what I'm doing and he's like stays there for about 20 minutes going through it an' I already knew what I'm doing so I could have been getting on with it.

Waiting for help with learning in class

Though only half the sample indicated their views about waiting, more pupils reported not waiting for help (42 per cent) than having to wait (33 per cent), and a quarter of the sample reported that they sometimes had to wait. There were no significant differences between pupils in mainstream and special schools, nor between boys and girls. However, there were significant differences between primary and secondary boys, with the latter reporting more waiting than the former. This tended to happen more in mainstream than special schools, but differences were not significant.

Mainstream children described their experiences in these ways:

MSMSU5   Help very quickly normally. I get enough.

MSFPR3   Hum, well sometimes I have to wait quite a lot but usually with [the assistant] hum she, she comes fairly quick. I have as much help as I need.

MSFPR4   Wait a bit, 'cause she has to help different children.

MSFSU5   Depends how many people are stuck on it. The more people are stuck on it, the longer. If you put your hand up, when you're stuck on it, they can come straight away. I don't have to wait too long really.

MSMSU6   [Waiting?] It's hardly anything. I just sit there in and if they're seeing somebody else yeah, cos there's only one person in there. I try and do the next thing so I don't sit there doing nothing I wait for somebody to call around and see me. I get enough I get really I get too much, because everybody comes like comes to me and say you're right and that and I go yeah.

MSFSU6   Helpers in most of the groups. Some of them help the children who are in wheelchairs. If she is helping me, she might have to leave to help one of these children. They just say wait a minute, then they come straight to you when they've finished with someone else. Like if someone else wants help, she goes over to them, and like, well, she's meant to be helping me, not them!

Despite the higher staff/pupil ratio, special school children still reported having to wait for help, as staff had others to see to:

SSFSD6   I have to wait 'cause she helps other people.

SSFSG1   I got to wait a little bit 'cause I've got think of the other children.

SSMSG2   I would like some more but I can't. 'Cause there ain't a lot of teachers, and there's a lot of children need help.

SSMSD6   Well for one thing you don't have to wait so long for help, you just go up and ask for help. Put your hand up and ask for help and you'll get it straight away sometimes or we've got to queue for help.

SSMSD2   Yeah, in this school, sometimes it's too long, and what it is they don't help you for long enough. Cause of other children in the class, it's not their fault but they also need help at the same time. It's not their fault but if it was a smaller class and, even if you had the same amount of helpers but it was split up into four groups it would be a different thing 'cause if you was split up into groups then the teachers could manage it but so far you can't manage such a big group.

Sources of help

Pupils reported receiving more help with their learning overall from teaching assistants (45 per cent) than teachers (30 per cent). There were no significant differences in the degree of help from assistants and teachers between mainstream and special schools. However, mainstream boys reported much less help from their teachers than special school boys. This is consistent with the tendency reported above for mainstream boys to report having to wait more for help. Though friends as helpers were also mentioned by 15 per cent of pupils overall, this conceals a significant difference: 25 per cent of mainstream pupils compared to only 4 per cent of special school pupils reported receiving help from friends. These excerpts illustrate the mix of helpers:

SSMSG6   I think it's one of the helpers.

MSFSU4   In between really 'cos they can, teachers can help you and so can the helpers.

MSFSU5   Umm, well, probably the assistants, because they come, well, they usually come first.

MSFSR6   Hum, teachers really, the teachers or my friends, but sometimes they get told off.

Q   What do you do if you are struggling like that?

MSFSR1   Hum, just ask my friends.

For some, their sources of help did not appear to materialise – or disappeared:

MSFSR1   I know it started off well in like the first two years, then I moved up into the second class which was Year 2, 3 and half Year 4, that was when I started going downhill because you could put your hand up and ask for help and she'd be like 'oh I'll come over in a minute' and she never come over, she'd just totally forget about you like you weren't even there.

MSFSU6   Sometimes I can't do maths, and, need help with maths, I think I need a helper with maths, but she keeps disappearing.

Whereas others, as these special school children described, found staff approachable, patient and helpful:

SSFSG4   They actually say if it is complicated, this might be a bit complicated and that, so they try and explain it the best way they can. If you don't actually understand it, they don't mind if you turn round and say, 'sorry, miss but I don't understand it'.

SSMSD5   Just explains it all to you, what to do. I just listen and write all the answers down when he gives it to you.

Q   So if he explained it and you tried it and it still wouldn't work and you had to go back, how would he react if you had to go back because you couldn't quite get it?

SSMSD5   I'd ask him for some more help.

Q   And how does he normally react?

SSMSD5   He'd just help me a bit more. I get all the help I need. Just come over and help. They just sit and work through it.

Mainstream learning support: types and preferences

Mainstream pupils reported a range of learning support, with 80 per cent of children reporting having withdrawal (84 per cent) or in-class support (86 per cent) at some time. Of other forms of support, 66 per cent reported group work, 59 per cent one-to-one, 22 per cent assistant at-table, and 8 per cent support for specific subjects. Secondary-age pupils reported more withdrawal and group work, while primary-age pupils reported more in-class support and the assistants supporting them at the table.

Preferences for support showed a wide variation, with 40 per cent preferring mainly withdrawal, 34 per cent in-class support and 30 per cent a mix of the two. There were no age and gender differences for those preferring a mix. However, withdrawal and in-class support were preferred much less by secondary boys than primary boys. It seemed that secondary boys preferred neither kind of support.

Reasons given for preferring withdrawal were: better quality support (47 per cent); less noise and appropriate and better work (29 per cent); more fun (24 per cent); less distraction (22 per cent); more attention (20 per cent); less bullying (12 per cent); and being with friends (8 per cent). The fewer negatives about withdrawal were: boring without friends (14 per cent); and boring and work too hard (8 per cent). There were fewer reasons given for preferring in-class support: like being with teacher and friends (14 per cent); teaching as good as withdrawal (10 per cent); being with friends (6 per cent); not missing out; and getting the same as everyone else (4 per cent). Some excerpts illustrate some of these preferences:

MSFSR4   Stay in the class. With my friends then.

Having a one-to-one helper in class was not always well received:

MSFPU1   Well people do take the Mickey if you've got someone with you. Just feels terrible.

A number of children alluded to noise and distraction in class:

MSMPR5 In Year 5 there's only, say, you'd have this massive room and you'd be, like, and there'd be a maths lesson in there or an English lesson and you'd have all these kids chatting an all that and you couldn't really think an all that.

MSFSR6   [Prefer] out of the class. Because umm, then you can do more things and not get distracted.

A number of children felt that the help they received in withdrawal was no different from being in class:

MSFSR2   The same, they just teach me how they teach in the classroom.
Q   And what sort of help did you get there?
MSFSR2   Same help that I always get.

Children expressed different feelings about similar support styles, as for withdrawal:

MSFPU2   In the big class they do hard work but in 'ere we do easy work. Good. After, when you've finished your work you like do play with some toys, and when it's time to go we go back to our classroom.

MSFPR7   We had to do handwriting and boring stuff like that, which I could do easily. I felt different to everybody [in the special unit], but here they don't do that – they just normal.

Some felt that they received more help in withdrawal settings, which helped them get more work done, though others felt stupid:

MSFSR4   Good. You get more help down there. Get more work done if you get help.

MSFPU1   Hum, just feels stupid. 'Cause there's four of us and some people take the Mickey out of us.

Some children felt that some forms of support reduced opportunities for involvement:

MSMPR5   [Group work is] kind of annoying because say if it's sort of like speaking then you like you want a chance to speak and they keep on speaking so you never get a chance to speak.

Several pupils expressed mixed views about support, as in this case, illustrating tension between wanting and receiving help, but not liking certain elements of support systems:

MSFSU4   [When assistant comes to give me help] well it makes me feel that it's only just me that needs the help and it's no one else in the room that needs help it's just me – 'cos like she comes up to us, and that lot, it's like why is it me?

Q   So why is that bad for you?

MSFSU4   Because it makes me look bad. 'Cos when she comes up to me and I tell her to go away they start laughin' and they start to taking the Mick out of me and fings like, like tha'. That's when it all starts up when she comes up to me, all the time they start.

Q   It sounds as though it makes you feel different, sticking out?

MSFSU4   All the time. I don't really mind as long as I get a little bit of help I don't really mind. I don't mind outside the class as long as it's not for the whole lessons because I like being in with my mates. I don't like getting taken out because it makes me feel like I'm different towards the others.

As in all categories, children expressed a range of experiences and feelings. Overall, though they valued receiving help and support, some did indicate that receiving help made them feel different, and exposed them to ridicule or 'bullying': this bothered some, but not all.

Children's views and experiences of opposite school types

Only seven of the 51 (14 per cent) of the children who were attending mainstream schools had ever attended a special school, whereas 37 out of the 50 (74 per cent) special school children had attended a mainstream school at some point during their school careers. This was slightly more so for girls than boys, but there was no difference between primary and secondary pupils.

All children were asked their views on the opposite school type, regardless of whether they had attended them or not, whether they knew anyone in them, or anything about them. Few children made comments on special schools unless they had some experience of them, though most children were able to make some comment on mainstream schools, as they had attended them, or had peers or siblings attending them.

Mainstream pupils' views of special school

Though only 14 per cent of mainstream pupils had ever been to a special school, 41 per cent overall knew someone who had been to or was presently attending one. This was significantly more so for secondary (58 per cent) than primary pupils (24 per cent). About two-thirds (63 per cent) of mainstream pupils expressed evaluations of special schools, of which 53 per cent were mostly positive views, 28 per cent were mixed and 19 per cent were negative. There was a tendency for girls and primary pupils to be more positive and boys and secondary pupils to be more negative about special schools, though not significantly so. Peer relationships in general, whether positive or negative, affected children's views, even when they valued other factors, such as good provision. These were also likely to affect school choice, as these excerpts illustrate:

MSFSR5   [I didn't go there] 'cause I want to be with [my friend].

MSMSU2   I feel [special schools] are a brilliant thing because in a mainstream school they would be picked on and bullied quite a lot. I wouldn't go I've got too many friends here already.

Most children's views showed that it was rarely one factor alone that affected feelings and choices. Some descriptions highlighted confusions and fears, which suggested a tension between various feelings, as these excerpts highlight:

MSFSU4   I don't really know because all my mates are here, it's just when they start it makes me upset and some of the teachers down here I don't get on with at all. They like, when like some of the girls are being naughty they point at me straight away and, stop it, and it wasn't even me. Well I don't, I wouldn't like to go there 'cos it'd make, 'cos I'm very close to my friends and I don't want to get taken away from my friends. And make me feel different. I wouldn't wan' to, I don't really wanna, I'm not going to that school. I'd rather stay here.

MSFPR3   Because it helps children with, who can't, with their reading and writing and stuff and it will give more encouragement to them. [I prefer] staying here. Because I won't have [my teacher] to help me, and I just like it here and I'm more safe here. Because people like, people, hum, will, the teachers rather, will treat me like I'm a, like I'm thick, like I'm really thick.

These examples are typical in illustrating two of the major fears that several children expressed: being made to feel 'different' and being stigmatised in some way if attending a special school.

A third major fear was that of being 'bullied' in some way. Several children referred to this, as these cases illustrate:

MSFSR3   'Cause when I went to the shop one time with my friend, I heard someone talk to their other person said, [the special school's] a bit stupid, it's got loads of dumb people there, and all that kind of stuff.

MSFSR4   They might get picked on, you never know.
Q   Who would pick on them?
MSFSR4   By the, this school for instance. My friend calls them brainless –
           you get hurt, even though they're not doing it to you, you do feel
           hurt inside. It's not their fault they need help, is it? 'Cause it's
           hurtin' for them cause it's not their fault you're not good at the
           stuff.

MSMPR1   Might give you a bit more help, but I don't want to go there
           though. Just don't. Might take the Mick out of me.
Q   Who might take the Mickey out of you?
MSMPR1   My friends.
Q   Do you ever hear children say horrid things about schools like
           that?
MSMPR1   They say the people are crippled.

One child who had been to a special school felt that other children at the
special school had held him back:

MSMSR7   We didn't get much help, apart from teachers had too much
           naughty kids and I had two friends. I was upset all the time. The
           changing lessons and said stupid kids. Lots of pains. [My parents]
           were all worried and all that, 'cos of these stupid brats. Because
           of all this stress and that's why my mum wanted me to leave 'cos
           I wasn't having a very good time.
Q   What do you think was stopping you getting that help there?
MSMSR7   All the kids.

Like many children, the girl in the next excerpt describes both good and
bad experiences of her time in a special school, and though she continued to
have very positive feelings for her school overall, she realised that it was time
to move on:

MSFSU2   I would like to have stayed at [the special school] but as I was
           getting older I had to move up years and move schools. Yeah,
           pleased that I've come here. It's that there's loads of nice teachers
           here an' that. I never felt bad at all, I felt really happy, good. I
           was getting help an' that with my learning. [I would like] to be
           at [the special school] again, 'cos there was really good times
           but, and a few bad times there. When I squashed my thumb in
           the taxi, being bit on my ear, yeah an' again cuts and bruises an'
           all that lot.

The most outstanding feature of mainstream pupils' views on special schools was that they perceived them as being very good at providing appropriate help for those with learning difficulties, but some were aware that children might be stigmatised if they were attending them. The only pupil who considered going to a special school was a girl who had previously attended one: most others were generally happy with their present schools, and did not want to leave their friends.

Special school pupils' views of mainstream schools

By contrast, 74 per cent of the special school pupils had had mainstream school experience. This was slightly more so for girls than boys, but there was no difference between primary and secondary pupils. Many of these pupils (62 per cent) expressed evaluations of mainstream schools, mostly a mix of positive and negative views (48 per cent). Some 35 per cent expressed mainly negative views, while only 16 per cent expressed mainly positive views. There were no differences between boys and girls or primary- and secondary-age pupils.

This higher ratio of children who had previously attended mainstream schools meant that they were able to compare their experiences of different types of school directly, and this enabled them to make value judgements based on actual knowledge of difference, rather than hearsay or assumption. In this case, a girl commented on the pace of work in mainstream school, and how this did not fit with her abilities:

SSFSG4   I thought it was quite of a rush, like you had to get it done in their time not your pace in your time – our teacher [here] doesn't actually mind us, takin' our time on it, I don't miss half of it. [It felt] really, really horrible 'cause I thought I was really missin' out on lessons and that, not keepin' up with them all and that. I thought it was quite of a rush [in my other school] like you had to get it done in their time not your pace in your time.

Some remembered that in mainstream schools there were generally fewer learning support assistants around to help, and that there is more support in the special school:

SSFPD2   In this school there's more grown-ups, but in, but in my old school, didn't have very many grown-ups, in class, at the moment I've got three, and then at that time I had one. At me old school there's not very many, I didn't really get very much help. I did not know what I was doing, and I didn't get very much help.

SSFSG1   More help, here than my old school, and teacher's better than there, than the old school. They help you more, the teachers [here].

Some pupils, especially those who were quiet or well-behaved, felt they were left out or ignored. In this case, despite negative experiences, this boy still wanted to return to mainstream:

SSMSD2   [I would prefer to be] in a mainstream school, but I would like people to make an effort, not just to leave me in the back of the class, like they did in the last school. There used to be thirty children in the class and if you were behind or a bit shy you usually got left behind, you just asked for, for some help and no one ever gave you any help they were, they, you know they sort of went up to you and they told you what to do, and then they went off – after a while you give up, at the back of the class, you give up.

It was not uncommon for children to describe multiple issues or problems, as these cases illustrate:

SSFPD5   Can't do choosing, can't do work. Horrible, don't like it. Big children around, children horrible to me, pushed me around. Had a struggle with some of the work. Don't remember anything else. Had problems there.

SSFPG1   [The children] were OK with me. [The work] was a bit too hard for me to do.

Some children described feeling left out and lonely, or bullied in some way, especially in relation to their learning difficulties:

SSFPD2   I felt quite lonely. Because most of the children wanted to play by themselves with other children who've been, who've been in that class for quite a long time, that means that, that I couldn't really get on with any of the other people.

SSFSG1   I was picked on, I think more, because I couldn't read, I'm not sure. They call me thick I think, dumb.

SSFSG6   Getting picked on. I was a bit scared going into [that school] anyway. Because I had no friends in the class. Because I'm different and I couldn't read or spell and they knew. They thought I'd be a bit of a game for teasing. They were calling me thick. I can't remember really. I know I was getting called thick a lot. [I felt] angry and upset really. I just kept it quiet.

Experiences of teachers were mixed. Several children felt that their mainstream teachers did not seem to understand or accept that they had a genuine learning difficulty, and some felt they were 'punished' because they could not do the work, as illustrated here:

SSMSD4   Well she, that, I remember that day, well, I writ a story right, like I did it in my best writing right? And it wasn't very good then but anyway she, do you know what she made me do? She made me spend all lunchtime and the hour and 20 minutes we had in that school writin' this out and I didn't get to have lunch – it wasn't very nice.

SSFSG2   I didn't like her. She was really horrible and she always got hold of you. Didn't get much help there. It was the teachers, they, only one, two teachers I liked there. They just like, like looked at you really horrible.

SSFSG6   I liked it there, but there was one teacher there who wasn't very nice and I don't think he liked me much. He read my stuff out to the whole class and I felt like he was teasing me and I was getting all upset, because I knew that I couldn't read or spell, and he knew that I couldn't and he read it out to the whole class. I didn't like him.

Not all experiences of mainstream were negative, and some children recognised benefits, such as being treated age-appropriately:

SSMSD2   'Cause at my old school, I was a lot younger and you was expected when you go out of the room to behave and everything and you was expected to get on with your work because you were old enough, when you're ten you was expected, you're old enough and you're sensible enough and they treat you like adults. Expected if they asked you to do something on your own, you do it. You don't have a hundred million teachers telling you how to do it and treat you like a baby [as happens here] – it's annoying 'cause just 'cause you go to a special school, this school, teachers think you're more baby than you, just because you have learning difficulties doesn't mean that you're like a baby and that you should be treated like a baby.

This boy, amongst others, felt there were more opportunities to pursue hobbies in bigger mainstream schools:

SSMSD2   When you want to do something and it's your hobby, in other schools they're so big, like [the mainstream secondary], you could get the hobby, so if you wanted to play cricket, 'cause they've probably got their own cricket team, their own football team . . . It had everythink a mainstream school would have, and there was more fields and there wasn't even one football pitch we can even practice on in this school.

Though most children described negative or mixed experiences of their previous or mainstream schools, there were positive experiences as well:

SSFPD4   Nobody was horrible to me there.

SSMPG1   Get on all right with [the children]. Nice teacher.

SSFSG6   [The teachers] were nice.
Q   Do you think they recognised that you had some problems and needed a bit of help with this work?
SSFSG6   Yes, because I used to go to one of the assistants, I think it is, that helps children what can't read or spell, I think it was that has problems.

One of the secondary special school boys recognised that his friends were getting help in mainstream, and felt he would get the same too:

SSMSD1   I reckon that if they can get extra help then I could probably do that.

Comparative preferences for mainstream and special schools

Table 4.4 shows that the majority of pupils prefer their current school, but not a large majority in either type of school. Only one pupil in mainstream

Table 4.4 Preference for present and other schools

	Present school	Mainstream school	Special school	Do not know/mind	Total
Mainstream pupils	33 (65%)	13 (25%)	1 (2%)	4 (8%)	51
Special pupils	27 (54%)	18 (36%)	1* (2%)	4 (8%)	50
All pupils	60 (59%)	31 (31%)	2 (2%)	8 (8%)	101

Key: * prefers mainstream–special school link scheme

preferred a special school, whilst 18 in special school preferred a mainstream school. However, 13 mainstream pupils preferred another mainstream school to their present one. When analysing these overall data in terms of gender and age, there was a significant tendency for secondary compared to primary special school pupils to prefer a mainstream school (54 per cent to 20 per cent) and a similar tendency for special school boys compared to girls to prefer mainstream (54 per cent to 21 per cent).

Summary and discussion

This chapter has summarised and illustrated pupils' perspectives on various elements of provision for their special educational needs. It has described their feelings about the teaching they experienced and other aspects which were found to be important to them. The most notable of these were their relationships with peers, and the effects of staff attitudes and behaviours on their general sense of well-being and happiness in school. As expected, pupils presented a mix of contrary views in all categories, indicating either positive or negative perspectives, or a mix of both. Though there were some differences between groups based on age, gender and school type, few of these were significant, though there were notable exceptions.

Pupils had differing experiences of school type, with about three-quarters of special school pupils having attended mainstream at some stage in comparison to less than a sixth of mainstream pupils having ever attended a special school. These differing experiences may have had some effects on their evaluations generally. Mainstream pupils were generally more positive than special school pupils, held fewer mixed views and fewer mainly negative perceptions. Further, amongst mainstream pupils, there was a tendency for girls and primary pupils in general to be more positive about special schools, and boys and secondary pupils in general to be more negative, though not significantly so.

Mainstream pupils identified stigmatisation and/or bullying as a major factor for negative feelings about special schools, though they also tended to perceive these schools as offering good support. Special school pupils were more likely to make judgements based on personal experience of mainstream schools, and negative judgements were made on inadequate or inappropriate provision, no provision, insensitive reactions from teachers/assistants, and 'bullying' by peers, either inside or outside of school.

Overall, there were few significant differences in perceptions of learning support between mainstream and special school pupils as described in this sample. The most outstanding difference was that mainstream pupils perceived that they were more likely to receive help from friends than special school pupils. Positive relationships with peers were important, and this extra dimension within mainstream may have contributed to a greater sense of belonging and engagement, despite perceived difference in academic ability.

Where special school pupils commented on waiting, they were aware that this was often due to teachers/assistants needing to help others. This observation highlighted the fact that though, on average, special school pupils were exposed to more direct sources of help within their classes and schools than mainstream pupils, the greater needs of *all* pupils within these drew on those sources of help, and reduced actual help available to individuals.

Preference for type of help in mainstream schools generated a mix of responses and views; quality of help, belonging or being left out, and being with friends or being stigmatised or bullied as a result of receiving help were identified as particularly important elements for preferred choice: secondary boys did not have a preferred type of help.

Notable differences were evident in attitudes and preferences, especially for secondary boys. Secondary boys overall seemed least satisfied with elements of provision than other groups, and special school secondary boys were most dissatisfied with being in their present school. Further, despite the fact that mainstream secondary boys were dissatisfied with elements of their provision, they still preferred remaining in their schools, or staying within the mainstream system. As previously observed, peer relationships were a considerable factor in choices and preferences, but they were not the only factors that mattered. Though pupils referred to quality and appropriateness of provision, and often valued these, the factors that seemed to most influence their *feelings* about provision and school preference were around stigmatisation and 'bullying'. These factors suggest issues around identity, and that acceptance of provision may be more strongly linked with the way pupils experience provision within the wider setting, that is, not only within their classes, but also within and outside their schools, than the actual fact of help itself: children's comments substantiate this view. For this sample, the fact that secondary school boys in particular were unhappy about being in special schools raises questions about the suitability of such placements for this special needs age group, and why this group in particular should be most affected by feelings of stigma. Though secondary school boys were most unanimous in this view, others expressed similar feelings. These issues are analysed and discussed more fully in the following two chapters.

Though around half were generally satisfied with the help they received, a substantial number were not, and over half reported having to wait for help at times. That there were no differences in perceptions between school type suggests no specific advantage to being in a special school in this respect. Further, the importance of help from classroom assistants was highlighted across both school types, emphasising their importance in their own right as providers of help, regardless of setting. As expected, children presented mixed views and reported mixed experiences across schools. This variance suggests differences in quality of support, and children's accounts also indicated that the ethos of individual schools was important. The fact that individual children were able to identify the qualities of provision and providers, and distinguish between positive and negative experiences and relationships suggests that there are differences, rather than that children perceive the quality of their provision in blanket terms. Clearly, individual pupils' area of SEN and other characteristics might also contribute to the way individual children perceive their environment, and how others perceive them.

In addition to having varying special needs, age may have had some influence on perceptions, even though there were few significant differences across groups overall. Some children commented on changes and growing maturity, and improvements in their learning over time, as well as attitudinal change. Further, children's accounts covered their whole school careers to date, and differing levels of awareness accounted for some variance in responses, and especially *feelings* around issues of provision.

This research adopted a naturalistic approach in eliciting the views of pupils, and took a broader view that enabled a holistic perspective to be obtained, which highlighted that evaluation of provision goes beyond formal elements alone. Children's accounts show that experience of provision is varied and does not remain static, and that numerous factors appear to interact with the basic elements. The following two chapters continue this exploration, building towards a greater understanding of children's views, and how these views affect the inclusion argument.

Chapter 5

Perceptions of self and of labels

Relevant and related studies

The primary focus of this chapter is the relationship between self-perceptions and stigma. It examines the tensions associated with 'difference dilemmas' in relation to self-perceptions. It examines, on one hand, whether pupils with MLD experience a contrary sense of self and, on the other, how pupils with MLD respond to various labels and how they evaluate them. Previous studies show that the exposure of children and young people with mild intellectual impairments to negative attitudes is not necessarily reflected in negative self-perceptions (Coleman, 1985; Jahoda et al., 1988; Chapman, 1988; Wade and Moore, 1993; Norwich, 1997). Jahoda *et al.* (1988), for example, found in a Scottish study that all the young people in their sample had insight into being stigmatised and had experience of abuse and rejection. However, few of them saw themselves as essentially different from others and did not internalise a negative view of themselves. In a previous study of 19 secondary-age pupils at a London school for MLD (Norwich, 1997), it was found that most had mixed positive and negative views of their special schooling and also did not internalise the negative views to which they were exposed. Positive self-perceptions predominated over negative ones. In this and the Jahoda study the findings were inconsistent with the reflected appraisal theory, a social constructionist perspective. This is the theory that self-perceptions are formed from internalising others' attitudes and communications (Blumer, 1969; Gergen, 1977). What the Jahoda and Norwich studies indicated was that the young people with disabilities actively interpret and select from the views of others in contributing to the formation of their self-perceptions.

In a recent series of English studies, Crabtree (2002) found that pupils with MLD were aware of their learning difficulties and that those with MLD in special schools had significantly higher self-concepts of their general intellectual and mathematics abilities than those with MLD in mainstream schools. Crabtree also found that MLD pupils in special schools made social comparisons with other MLD pupils. Those with MLD in the mainstream, by contrast, made comparisons with those without MLD. This is consistent with social comparison theory (Festinger, 1954), which assumes that comparisons with those of similar abilities will result in positive self-perceptions, while comparisons with those of high abilities will lead to less positive self-perceptions.

Crabtree and Rutland (2001), using similar ways of assessing self-perceptions as in the previous study (Harter Self-Perception Profile, which covers scholastic, social, athletic, behavioural, physical and global dimensions), examined why previous studies had shown no difference in self-worth or self-evaluation between stigmatised and non-stigmatised groups (for example, Chapman, 1988; Heath and Ross, 2000). They referred to mechanisms, proposed by Crocker and Major (1989), by which stigmatised individuals may protect their self-evaluation by: (1) attributing negative feedback to discrimination against the group; (2) selectively comparing outcomes with those of the in-group rather than relatively advantaged out-group; and (3) devaluing dimensions of comparison on which their group typically performs poorly and valuing those at which the group excels. Crabtree and Rutland found that children attending MLD special schools, compared to those without learning difficulties attending mainstream schools, did not differ in their levels of scholastic self-perception or global self-worth or evaluation. However, unlike the mainstream group, the MLD group's scholastic self-perceptions did not relate to their overall self-evaluation. Also, the MLD group assigned less importance to the scholastic area, while the non-learning difficulty group assigned more importance to this dimension. In a second related study these authors also showed that changing the comparison group from MLD to non-MLD pupils influenced self-perceptions and evaluations. These two studies are consistent with a social comparison theory of self-evaluations and illustrate two strategies that teenagers with MLD may use to protect their self-evaluations, devaluing the dimensions of social comparison and selecting a comparison group to enable positive self-evaluations. The authors also suggest that these conclusions have relevance to inclusive practice in schools. Placing pupils with MLD in mainstream schools presents them with a comparison group of those with higher attainments and without learning difficulties, which can hinder their capacity to protect their self-evaluations. They suggest that this can be countered if pupils with MLD were placed with a group of others with MLD. This would provide an alternative group for social comparison, which may help them to preserve their self-evaluations. The other implication for supporting pupils' self-evaluation would be for schools and teachers to emphasise areas where the MLD pupils perform at a higher level. This may help them protect their self-evaluations to some extent, but it cannot compensate in cases where there is no relative high performance.

In a recent Canadian study of teenagers who had experienced school failure and were placed in separate 'specialised' educational settings (Maieano *et al.*, 2003), self-perceptions were also assessed using the Harter scales. Self-perceptions across a range of areas were assessed for pupils with 'mental retardation' and 'conduct difficulties' and compared to groups with and without difficulties in a mainstream school setting. Their main finding was that the female students who experienced failure in special settings had higher scores on scholastic and athletic self-perceptions than their counterparts in the mainstream settings. Though this difference was only for females, not males, and it related to a group wider than that corresponding to the MLD group in this country, their interpretation of the commonly found higher self-perceptions in special settings is interesting. The higher self-perceptions in special settings were seen as an over-estimation, which was defensive and reflected the protective environment and educational methods used in these settings. This is a different explanation of the raised levels of self-perceptions compared to the social comparison approach used by Crabtree and others. However, it is possible that both explanations may be relevant to this pervasive and persistent finding, as they are connected. What Maieano *et al.* refer to as a protective environment may also be seen as one where non-academic activities and outcomes are valued. In such an environment, pupils can protect their self-evaluation by basing it on valued dimensions other than academic outcomes, as Crabtree and Rutland suggest.

Much of the research on the self-perceptions of pupils with learning difficulties in mainstream and separate settings is focused on those with learning disabilities in the USA (the US category of 'learning disability', or LD, corresponds to specific learning difficulties in the UK), not on those with difficulties related to MLD. Nevertheless, some of this research is relevant to the MLD group, if only to illustrate a contrast. For example, Bear *et al.* (2002) found in a meta-analysis of 61 studies of self-concept that children with learning disabilities perceived their academic ability less favourably than their peers without learning disabilities. This difference was less evident for other areas of self-perception, nor did they find, contrary to previous reviews, that self-perceptions were different in separate compared to mainstream settings. This contrasts with findings from an Israeli study (Butler and Marinov-Glassman, 1995), which compared the perceived competence of students in grades 3, 5 and 7 (ages 9, 11 and 13) of those with learning disabilities in special schools, those with learning disabilities in special classes in the mainstream and lower achievers in mainstream classes. They found that perceived competence was higher in the special school LD group than the special class LD or mainstream class groups for grade 5. In the younger groups no differences in perceived competence were found across settings, nor were there clear difference in the oldest group. A study like this shows how generalisations may not always apply, even though the study is not specifically about MLD. It is also interesting to contrast the conclusions from the Bear *et al.* (2002) review with an earlier study by Bear *et al.* (1991), which did show in a group of 9-year-old children with learning disabilities that the academic and behaviour self-perceptions and general self-evaluations of those with LD were lower than those without LD in integrated classes. However, the self-perceptions of those without LD in integrated settings were higher than those without LD in non-integrated settings. The authors interpret their findings as indicating that though integration/inclusion may not enhance the self-perceptions of those with LD, it may enhance the self-perceptions of those without learning disabilities.

Some studies in the learning disabilities area examine how self-perceptions and self-understanding are related to self-evaluation. These studies are interesting as they have connections with some of the studies, discussed above, about how pupils with MLD who have low academic self-perceptions manage to protect their self-evaluations. Cosden *et al.* (1999) examined how students with learning disabilities came to know that they had learning difficulties and whether increased knowledge was associated with higher self-evaluations. In a sample of elementary and junior high students they found that these students found out about their learning problems through being told by parents or teachers; some had not been told by anyone. However, they found no relationship between general self-evaluations and students' knowledge about their learning disabilities. Students' knowledge about their learning disabilities was related instead to their academic attainments and their academic self-perceptions. General self-evaluation was related to attainments in non-academic areas. Research into the knowledge that students have of their learning disabilities is concerned with finding ways for students with learning disabilities to maintain positive self-evaluation. An earlier study by Kloomak and Cosden (1994) aimed to examine how those with LD managed to maintain positive self-perceptions despite experiencing academic difficulties. In a sample of 9- to 12-year-old students with learning disabilities they assessed self-perceptions in a range of areas as well as perceived social support. Those who had higher general self-evaluation were found to see themselves as more intelligent, to be more competent in other non-academic areas and saw themselves as receiving more social support. However, these students did not maintain high general self-evaluation by discounting the value of academic work. This last finding indicates that one of the mechanisms to protect self-evaluation identified by Crocker and Major (1989) was not used by this group. They had other ways of doing so.

Much of the above research on the self has assumed that there are different dimensions to self-perceptions (Harter, 1983; Marsh and Shavelson, 1985). Most of the research on the self, especially from a psychological perspective, also uses general constructs, such as academic self-concept or self-perception, which are assumed to apply to all children in similar ways. These constructs with their constituent sub-domains are used to design standard inventories, which enable quantitative comparisons between individuals and groups. Finlay and Lyons (2001) have reviewed some of the methodological issues that arise when using self-report measures with people with what they call 'mental retardation'. Some of their points clearly relate to those with moderate learning difficulties. Specifically, they raise questions about the statements used in inventories, the format provided for responses and the psychometric properties (reliability and validity) of such measures. They recommend that more attention needs to be paid to establishing the validity of such measures and being clear about those for whom they are useful.

The measure used by Crabtree (2002), for example, used a modified version of the Self-Perception Profile (Renick and Harter, 1989). This particular inventory was designed for children and young people with learning difficulties in the USA, based on other measures designed by Harter for those without learning difficulties. It has been further modified and shown to have good psychometric characteristics (reliability and validity) for similar groups in the UK. Like other such inventories it also has the benefit of covering a range of predefined areas. However, its response format, like other similar inventories, channels responses into a linear scale. This leads to scaling which is interpreted as low to high on a dimension, in this case along several predefined domains of self-perceptions. As valuable as such an approach can be for certain purposes, its design does not enable children to express how they think and feel about themselves in their own idiosyncratic ways. This calls for a more naturalistic and idiographic approach to eliciting self-perceptions which would also enable respondents to express a mix of self-perceptions and self-evaluations without constraining them into a linear scale. A more naturalistic approach is called for for this kind of study, one exemplified in the Jahoda study, which uses semi-structured interviews to explore the young peoples' sense of stigma and their conceptions of being different from others. Oliver (1986) and Fox and Norwich (1992) have also shown that the self-perceptions of those with intellectual difficulties can be assessed reliably using semi-structured interviews based on elicitation methods derived from Personal Construct Theory (Kelly, 1955). This discussion provides a rationale for the study of self-perception reported in this chapter.

The other focus of this chapter is pupil perceptions of labels that are used to refer to them. Labelling has long been a focus of interest and concern in special education and disability circles. Labels which are used to refer to people with intellectual impairments, such as special educational needs, have come to be criticised for marking out some individuals as different in negative ways, as devaluing them and therefore as discriminating against them (Solity, 1991), or as 'the language of sentimentality and prejudice' (Corbett, 1996). Labels can be used in negative ways when they have negative connotations and are used to stigmatise someone. They can also operate as stereotypes and lead to negative first impressions, and limit peoples' expectations and judgements about those with impairments. But it has also been argued that labels can provide the means to identify certain groups of people who require additional help with their education (Norwich, 1993). These negative and positive aspects of labelling and identification can be seen to reflect the dilemmas of difference discussed above.

Hastings and Remington (1993) have argued that we need to examine who is affected by labels (the individuals labelled, their families, professionals, etc.) and the factors that influence these effects. Assertions that labels only have negative aspects need to be tested against experiences and this involves examining the connotations of labels and any changes in connotation over time. Norwich (1999) studied the evaluation of several well-known labels in the field (abnormality, deficit, disability, impairment, learning difficulties, special educational needs) by trainee and experienced teachers. It was found that the Warnock terms (SEN and learning difficulties) were evaluated positively, while the labels with medical associations (such as abnormality and impairment) were evaluated negatively. The label 'disability' was evaluated less positively than SEN, despite encouragement from advocates of the social model of disability to abandon the SEN notion and replace it by the disability term. However, this study was limited to the use of a rating scale method of assessing label evaluation and was confined only to a group of professionals. There was a clear need to examine evaluations of labels by pupils with MLD themselves using a more naturalistic research approach.

Aims and methodology of the study

The preceding review of literature shows that there have been no large-scale UK studies of the self-perceptions of school-age children identified as having moderate learning difficulties using more naturalistic methods. Neither has there been a study of the tensions between positive and negative aspects of self-perceptions, nor of how these children evaluate the different labels used about them. The study therefore had several aims relating to the self-perceptions of children who had been identified as having moderate learning difficulties using a more naturalistic qualitative approach:

1 to investigate the balance between positive, negative and mixed self-perceptions;
2 to examine these children's evaluations of terms and labels used by others to describe them;
3 whether these perceptions and evaluations vary according to special educational placement, gender and/or age.

The data relevant to these aims were collected as part of the project described more fully in Chapter 4. For full details about the semi-structured interviewing and transcript analysis methods see Kelly and Norwich (2004).

Educational self-perceptions

Awareness and acknowledgement of learning difficulties

Over 90 per cent of children expressed an awareness of their learning difficulties, with the only differences being between older and younger pupils, in that older ones expressed slightly more awareness than younger ones (98 per cent to 82 per cent).

SSFSG5   I realised that all along.

SSFSG6   I think I recognised it in Year 3 or Year 4.

Awareness of having learning difficulties was particularly apparent to children when they were comparing themselves with others. Numerous cases of this were described, illustrating where children were aware that others were better at things than they were, that sometimes they were the better ones, or more likely, that there was a mix of differences across and within individuals:

MSMPR1   [He's] better, or the same, he doesn't need special help, I do.

SSFSG1   She's better than me. She can read better than I can, write and I can't, she's brainier.

SSFPD3   I'd like to be like clever like drawing like he is, 'cause he's really good at drawing and like, making up stories and poems and that. I feel like a bit jealous when he like does the things that I'm not good at.

SSFSD3   Well [my younger sister] actually is clever than me, she is, she's good at reading, maths, I wish I was like her really, you know.

MSMSU5   I don't see why everybody else should be better than me. [Friend's] brainier than me. [Other boy is] better than me at schoolwork. I can't handle these questions . . .

MSFPR8   He needs help with his spellings and stuff, just like me. Umm, she's good at doing homework and I'm not good, I need help. I'm a bit better at spelling and reading and [she's] not very good reading. Also she's not very good at writing words from her spelling book. I am [better].

Children were specifically asked what they found difficult or easy, and some significant differences between mainstream and special school pupils were found. Mainstream pupils report experiencing more difficulties than special school pupils in English/literacy – mainstream (94 per cent) to special school

(76 per cent), a difference of 18 per cent; in maths/numeracy – mainstream (61 per cent) to special school (46 per cent), a difference of 15 per cent; and other subjects – mainstream (55 per cent) to special school (26 per cent), a difference of 29 per cent.

Though mainstream children made more references to difficult-to-learn subjects than special school pupils, English/literacy and maths/numeracy were identified as the most difficult for both groups. This difference could be a condition of the 'cushioning' effect of special schools where children may have easier work, better support, or are given a false sense of their own abilities (see below). Other subjects were generally found to be easier than mathematics and English for both school groups. Children made fewer references to subjects they found easy to learn, and there were smaller differences in percentages across groups and subjects.

Minimising or denial of learning difficulties

There was also a low overall level (15 per cent) of pupils minimising or denying their learning difficulties. No significant differences were found between groups, though secondary aged pupils tended to minimise or deny their difficulties more than primary aged pupils (18 per cent compared with 10 per cent).

SSMSD6   Well he thought the other school was too good for me so he had to give me something a little bit more harder. Well it sounds like my other school was too easy and stuff and everybody at my old school found it hard. Me, I used to found it easy. Yeah and it isn't. Well it can be sometimes but, on the whole, it is quite easy.

But as some commented, they were not fully aware of their position when they were younger, as they did not have the understanding:

MSMSU2   I didn't really feel much about it because I was quite young at that stage and I hadn't figured out many of my views or anything, and I didn't quite understand the problem.

Self-perceptions of educational abilities

Overall 65 per cent of the sample expressed feelings about their educational abilities, with more from mainstream than special schools doing so.

There was a significantly different pattern of reported feelings in mainstream and special schools (see Figure 5.1), with mainstream pupils displaying more mixed self-perceptions (73 per cent) than special school pupils (34 per cent), and slightly more negative self-perceptions than their special

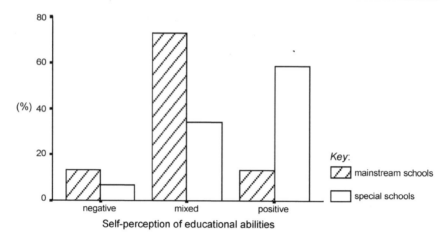

Figure 5.1 Self-perception of educational abilities for mainstream and special school pupils

school counterparts: both groups reported relatively low negative self-perceptions (13 per cent and 7 per cent respectively). There was a marked difference, however, in positive self-perceptions between the two groups, with special school pupils presenting higher levels than mainstream children (59 per cent to 14 per cent). The proportions of positive, negative and mixed educational self-perceptions were similar across age and gender.

These figures need careful consideration, as the 'mixed' category represents having both positive and negative self-perceptions, which suggests that these pupils may be having different thoughts and feelings at different times. This further suggests that something may be triggering these responses, a factor that needs further investigation.

Children used a variety of words and expressions to describe their feelings about their learning difficulties in the three main category areas of positive, negative and neutral, 'not bothered'. Overall 44 per cent of children expressed some negative feelings, and these included being upset, feeling hurt or sad, being lonely, or feeling frustration and anger; 23 per cent intimated in various ways that they were 'not bothered', whilst 33 per cent expressed a mix of views which included negative feelings as well as 'not bothered'. No child suggested being happy about having learning difficulties.

An example of mixed self-perceptions of educational abilities is described here:

SSMSD2   I'm normal in the sense that I can act my age and can have a conversation and I know what I'm talking about, like most words and all that lot, and can have a conversation, I know what words mean. I don't have to, you know, ask people what this word is and what this word means and all that on words, but when you look at a poster, normal people look at a poster and they look at it and it's like, um, it's like they look at that, that [matter], that CD box and they know exactly what it says, first off, just one glance of it, and then you have to look, go right up close to it and read every single word and it's, over and over again before you get, you know . . . the complete . . .

Which contrasts with a positive self-evaluation:

MSMSU2   I would probably describe myself as an intelligent boy and probably, hum, grown up a lot more and sometimes getting on with my work and mainly, hum . . . mainly I need to just a little bit, just to listen a little bit more and then I'll get probably a good job when I'm older.

Many negative evaluations covered a range of concerns, fears and feelings:

MSFPU1   [I found out I had learning difficulties] when I was about seven or eight. Felt terrible, worried. 'Cause I thought people would take the Mickey out of me. [They] sometimes [said] 'you're thick and backward, you need to go to a handicapped school'. My, hum, my, friends what I don't like [said this].

MSMPU6   Handwriting, copying. A bit sad inside. It's hard and you can't do it. Still a struggle.

MSMSU4   Feeling bad because I can't understand it, and I want to get it done so I can read it at home and that.

Feelings around learning difficulties did not necessarily remain static, and pupils often recognised and were pleased when they felt they were making progress and improvements:

SSMPD3   Umm, about my eyes, and I got glasses now. Problems with my eyes, it keeps on hurting when I read, umm lots of readin' like and words to take home, to umm, practice. And I'm getting series 10 now on my reading book. I'm feeling pleased.

A number of children who expressed mixed feelings indicated some of the reasons why their feelings fluctuated or changed, and their reactions, as these excerpts illustrate:

SSFSG2   Because I'm weren't very good at my readin', and writin' before, and now I've got good at it. Yeah, I get a bit angry with my work when I can't do it, I slam the pen down. Feel really cross. Got cross with myself.

SSMSD7   Stop working. Quite nervous.

Anger and frustration were commonly expressed emotions, but it was note-worthy that there were differences related to experiences of anger. Some children were angry/frustrated at themselves because they could not do the work:

MSMSR6   [Angry at] myself. Because I can't get it.

MSMSU2   Anger. The fact that I can't, that what my mind is thinking, my hand won't write down neat or fast enough.

MSFSR4   [Get angry at] my work, feel like screwing it up. But I get over it in the end.

For others, anger came about as a result of teasing or bullying by others, and loss of temper as a result of this:

MSMPR5   Because sometimes in lessons I get something wrong and I get another wrong I just screw up the paper, throw it at someone's head and then I get told off. It just, I don't mind, but when people tease me I sort of like get angry.

Others, though perhaps experiencing some frustration at their own difficul-ties, were more likely to be angry because they were not getting help:

MSMSR6   Angry. That they won't help me.

SSMSG2   Would like more help with writing and reading. Makes me feel angry.

These descriptions highlight *distinctive* reasons for children's reactions, and that expressed emotions could reflect various feelings relating to a mix of factors.

General self-perceptions

Responses relevant to this question were categorised into traits (such as being friendly, helpful, kind, funny) and general descriptions about self and of own abilities (such as appearance, being good at sports, etc.). These were distin-guished from responses that referred directly to educational abilities in school, such as those relating to literacy, numeracy and other academic and cognitive abilities. Responses were further categorised as mainly positive or mainly negative self-descriptors, and those expressing a mix of both. Overall 84 per cent of the sample expressed self-perceptions of general non-academic characteristics, with views being largely mixed (47 per cent) or mainly positive (46 per cent), and only a few being mainly negative (7 per cent). There were no significant variations between school, age or gender groups.

Views of how others see them

An important part of this investigation was to see how children felt others saw them. Almost all children (98 per cent) were able to do this to some degree. In terms of general descriptions, 79 per cent described others as presenting mixed views or described a mix of views by different people, 19 per cent reported mainly positive views and 2 per cent mainly negative views. There were no significant differences between groups.

Overall 79 per cent of the sample gave accounts of others' views of them in terms of educational abilities. Examples of positive accounts were given:

SSMPG6   My mum thinks I'm clever.

SSMPD3   He's been a good boy, an' doin' nice work at school.

Negative accounts by others are illustrated by the following:

MSFSU3   'Cos, umm, like my sister once when we were up at the pool she kept on saying that I had a mind of a 6-year-old and even my mum said that to us, I don't mind a 6-year-old. [People] don't really like say it, but I can tell that they laugh and are very horrible.

SSMPD1   [Mum] says a bit stupid and that. [Feel] sad, sad, sad . . . Dad feels the same. So does my sister.

Others were perceived as giving mixed accounts:

MSMSR3   Good work most of the time, and silly and mess up the work.

MSMSR4   Bit untidy in my writin', good worker, listens well, does what he's told and bit bossy.

There was a significant tendency for mainstream school boys' perceptions of others' accounts of their educational abilities to be mixed (41 per cent) or negative (31 per cent) but for special school boys' perceptions to be mainly positive (86 per cent) (see Figure 5.2). However, there were no differences between mainstream and special school girls. The overall balance was: 80 per cent positive, 16 per cent mixed and 3 per cent negative. Nor were there

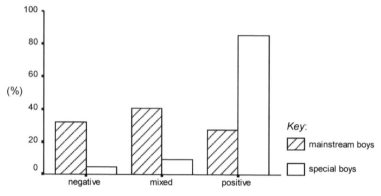

Others' accounts of self in terms of educational abilities

Figure 5.2 Others' description of self in terms of educational abilities (boys)

differences between all primary and secondary pupils, the overall balance being 68 per cent positive, 21 per cent mixed and 11 per cent negative.

Responses to labels

Children were presented with 15 different labels to represent current formal terms ('SEN', 'special needs' [SN], 'SN', 'learning difficulties', 'learning disabilities', 'disability'), more historic formal terms ('abnormal', 'retarded', 'handicapped', 'backward') and current everyday lay terms ('slow', 'stupid', 'thick', 'spas', 'spastic', 'has help'). They were asked to identify the ones they had heard of. The most commonly identified labels were: 'stupid' 78 per cent; 'thick' 76 per cent; 'has help' 65 per cent; 'disabled' 57 per cent; 'spastic' 57 per cent; 'slow' 55 per cent; 'learning difficulty' 40 per cent; and 'spas' 38 per cent.

Children also identified words that had been applied to them by others. 'Stupid', 'thick', 'has help', 'spastic', 'slow' and 'spas' were reported as used by 51 per cent, 49 per cent, 46 per cent, 30 per cent, 26 per cent and 17 per cent respectively. It is notable that the current terms 'SEN' and 'learning difficulty' were used to describe themselves or used by others about them by only 1 in 8 of the pupils.

The level of using these labels to describe self was reported as very low. The most commonly used labels were 'slow', 'thick' and 'stupid' and were referred to by 16 per cent, 12 per cent and 11 per cent respectively: only 9 per cent reported that they described themselves as 'having help', even though this was the most positively evaluated label.

Not surprisingly, children did not like words that were insulting or abusive in some way (thick 71 per cent, stupid 58 per cent, slow 44 per cent, and spastic 44 per cent). The label 'has help' was the only one that most children evaluated as positive or neutral (36 per cent and 32 per cent respectively), though 20 per cent perceived it negatively, especially if it was connected to 'special'. Children generally had not heard of less currently used labels such as 'abnormal', 'retarded' or 'backward', but equally, only a few had heard 'SEN' (12 per cent). 'Learning difficulty', a currently used label, had been heard of by 40 per cent of children, and was the only label where the balance of evaluation was towards neutral (27 per cent).

There were few significant differences in pupils' responses to labels between groups, with most differences being age related (12 per cent). Secondary-age pupils had more negative evaluations of certain labels ('learning difficulties', 'learning disability', 'disability', 'spastic' and 'backward'), had heard of more labels and reported more labels applied to them than primary pupils (including 'spas' and 'thick').

There were several notable school differences. Although the label 'has help' was the most positively evaluated term overall, it was evaluated much more positively by mainstream (49 per cent) than special school pupils (22 per cent). Interestingly, it was the special school pupils who described themselves more as 'having help' (16 per cent) than the mainstream pupils (2 per cent). Further, 'thick' was used by 24 per cent of mainstream pupils but by none in special schools as a self-descriptor. This was the label that was most negatively evaluated and second most widely known overall.

Feelings about labels

Children's reactions to labels varied considerably not only across individuals, but also within individuals themselves. Reactions to labels seemed to be personal: some children being relatively sanguine in their responses, others were 'not bothered' by some, but very strongly bothered by others, and yet others were likely to react strongly to many labels. The following sections look particularly at the words that were heard of and used about children most frequently, and that generated the strongest and most diverse feelings and reactions.

Stupid and thick

'Stupid' and 'thick' were not only reported as the most commonly heard words; they were also the two words most commonly used by others to describe children. Generally children did not use words to describe themselves as frequently as others did, but 'stupid' and 'thick' were two of the words children were most likely to use to describe themselves (12 per cent and 11 per cent), though they were more likely to refer to themselves as slow (16 per cent).

A number of children, mainly older, were not bothered about such words, and some readily admitted that everyone could be stupid sometimes. Others said they were not bothered when they knew it was being done in fun, and diverse feelings were expressed when children felt they were not stupid. For some the name calling highlighted to them that they did, in fact, feel stupid:

MSFSR4   They say it to me only in a jokerly way though. [If not said in a jokey way] hurt inside and sad.

SSFSG6   Stupid? I don't really listen to that, because I know I'm not. I just push it off my shoulders. Just take no notice of them.

MSFSU6   What do you call me that for?! I'm not exactly stupid.

MSFPU1   Make me feel stupid.

SSFSD3   I just ignore them, you know. Deep down, you know . . . I think deep down I do sometimes feel a bit stupid, you know . . . she keeps calling me names. Well if people call me stupid, you know, I sometimes be stupid.

For some, name-calling became a normal part of life which they just accepted, whereas for others even discussing it upset them:

SSMSD2   Well, you don't feel over the moon but you have, after a while, with people keep saying it you get used to it. It's just the normal thing. It's just the normal thing.

SSMPG5   Upset me and make me angry, make me real angry. Like that. I start doing that now. Upset.

SSMPD1   Oh, I don't want to talk about this bit.

Some children were able to distinguish between name calling and positive 'labelling':

MSFSR3   When I need help I get help, I need a little bit more help at things than other people don't and they say that I'm thick, hum, instead of saying that I need more help.

The following excerpts show one girl's feelings about being called names and its effects on her. Her story is not atypical:

MSFSU4   They would just call me, they would call me stupid and thick and things like that. And they just like push me and make me, make my life a misery. Umm, it affects me because people think I'm bad and – people say nasty things about me and things like that. Call me stupid and things like that an'.

MSFSU4   Well it's a bit, a bit in between, sometimes I feel bad about myself and sometimes it's just . . . It makes me feel stupid if you know what I mean, 'cos they're calling me stupid and then I think to myself well am I actually stupid?

MSFSU4   But now I've come, it feels like it's just me with the problem, because everybody else can do all the work and I have to have help and it makes me feel well, like I'm stupid or something because I need help and they don't really need it.

MSFSU4   It can be upsetting but I've just got to a stage where I can ignore it and just walk away from it but if it was about a year ago I would start throwing a tantrum and crying and things like that but now if anybody calls me stupid I would just walk away.

MSFSU4   [I think I am stupid] because of the way I am, spelling and things like that, 'cos like I do some spellings at home and times tables and things like that and when I don't get it right I just think to myself, like sometimes I'll go to myself oh I'm thick, and my mum will just turn around and looks at me 'cos I call myself thick all the time, because I've got used to people calling me it so I just call myself it.

Receiving help

This study focuses on whether children experienced tension between wanting and receiving help, and stigma attached to it. For this reason, it was not entirely surprising that some children expressed negative or mixed feelings about receiving help:

SSMSD2   No, they just need a little bit of help once in a while. They make out it's such a major thing if you're a bit behind, it's quite a common thing and they make out that you're stupid. It's like, like one in three and that's pretty a lot, innit. Saying, saying that they need learning help and that they need extra help and stuff like that. The special one, no, I don't like 'special help'.

However, a good number were positive about receiving help, and happy to acknowledge that they needed help:

MSFSR6   Because sometimes I do need help in lessons, and it's not difficult to ask for help.

SSMSD4   Feels OK, at the end of the day I need help, and it's good to have help.

MSMSR7   Bit of help reading, bit of help writing, spellings. I don't mind.

For some, receiving help was not a problem as others were in the same position, whereas for others it was as bad as name-calling:

MSFPR7   Alright because it doesn't make any different to me 'cos there's other people doing it as well.

MSFPR8   I just don't like the word and I don't know why people keep doing this to me. Saying horrible things to me.

SSMPG3   Oh, hum, very, not very nice thing to say. 'Cause I don't really like it if people call me names.

MSMSR3   I'd just tell them to shut up. 'Cause, 'cause I know I don't need help or anythink like that.

SSFSD6   Grumpy. Because they keep on tellin' me that I need special help.

Finally, some could distinguish its meaning depending on who was saying it, and why:

SSFSG4   Quite happy. Because if a child said it, I'd feel sad but, if a teacher said it, I would think they would be right, 'cause I do need quite a lot of help with most things.

Special needs

The terms 'special needs' and 'SEN', as official current terms, were not widely recognised, and generated a mix of responses, from positive or neutral to causing distress:

SSFPD2   I have special needs anyway. Umm, everybody really calls me that, but not everybody. Uh, happy, again.

MSMPU5   Don't really bother me 'cos it's for helping me.

SSMPG5   That's what I am! You're going to start me crying now. They're stupid words. They don't even call me any name!

For some, any labels that highlighted having learning difficulties generated a response of wishing to distance themselves from and deny these facts:

SSMSG3   My sister says and my brother says I'm a bit backwards. So I've got special needs, have I? I don't want to.

SSFPD5   Make me run away, it's horrible. I do need some help, it's not OK. I don't understand sometimes. Upsets me a bit.

SSFSG5   Angry. Because I know it isn't true.

Several children found it hard to come to terms with their learning difficulties, as this case illustrates:

MSFSU4   I wish I could be a little more like [my sister] with the brains because I feel, she's quite brainy as well all my three younger sister, two younger sisters and [she's] quite brainy and there's only me an' her that needs special needs. They've said it to me, 'cos my mum went to the doctor thing because I'm under special needs at the moment, so I know I'm on special needs at the moment. I'm getting used to it now because I'm getting used to it as I go along really.

For others, labelling was perceived as an unnecessary way of making them 'stand out' from others:

SSMSD2   You don't need special needs. It's when you're walking along the road, you don't see people going 'He needs special needs.' Like if you were in a wheelchair, you don't need to be reminded that you're not the same as everyone else, that you can't walk. Nothing. Nothing's good about that 'cause it's not fair to rate someone by the way they, if they can't read and write. It's like they need special needs so they're different.

As with other 'labels' children were able to recognise when the words were meant in a positive way and were helpful, and when there was a negative connotation to their use:

MSFSR3   When someone knows I need special needs, that they'll know that I need – I feel a bit embarrassed. [That], hum, that I'm not good at work.

MSMSR1   Hum, I'd just like, run to a different place and go with my other friends. If it was [said] in a nice way then no, but if it was in a horrible way, then yes.

MSMSR4   Unkind, miserable. Because it depends what people sayin' it and it's the spite in the way they say it some of the time. Just thinking I don't want to know 'em, they are just being unkind. You feel sad.

What is 'bad' and 'good' about using 'labelling' words?

Children were asked what they felt might be 'bad' or 'good' in using 'labelling' words. Despite many 'don't knows', replies indicated that labels were 'bad' when they were used in a rude, nasty or hurtful way. Some saw labelling words as swear words:

MSFPR6   It's rude.

SSFPD6   Some of them are swear words and they're not good words.

SSMSD4   Well, the swear words. Well it makes me feel very unhappy that you shouldn't be using the words anyway really.

Many children found it hard to say what was good about using labelling words, though most understood that some 'labels' meant that they would get help, and that this was a good thing:

MSFSU4   I don't really know, all I know is that it is there to sort of help you so.

SSFSD4   Because you'll get a lot of help.

MSFSU2   If they say they need special help then they go ahead and say oh they go to the teacher and say, 'can I take out to help 'em with extra, more help?'

MSFSR4   Good thing really, allowed to say that he needs more help 'n' that.

Others could see that the labelling words explained special needs, and that this led to help:

MSMPR5   They understand that you got it, that you need the help.

SSFSG6   Yes, because that person knows that they need it, that they need to think about giving the person more help.

But labels were always liable to make some feel sensitive, as was evident in mainstream and special school children:

SSMSD2   Yeah, I do think that's good saying they need a little bit help, but they shouldn't put actually, actually label them as something, they shouldn't actually label them, like that. They label them 'Your child needs special needs'.

MSMSR8   It's not saying like they're thick, it's just like you've got needs, special needs. If you say they're thick they take it the wrong way. May get help? Yes, 'cos once they get help they can slowly progress. Or if they are good enough they can quickly progress.

Summary and discussion

Our aim in this project was to take a broader view of children's learning difficulties and the support that they receive than has usually been adopted. By using a naturalistic approach, we aimed to gain a holistic view of their experiences, relationships within schools, and feelings about these, and this took our knowledge beyond linear dimensions. By doing this, we have been able to show that children's experiences are diverse, that they do not remain static, rather that they are dynamic. Children described changes over time, including fluctuations between positive and negative experiences and relationships and, often, a mix of the two at any given time. Their accounts highlighted diverse experiences running in parallel to each other, and interactions between these.

The previous chapter looked specifically at children's perceptions of the support networks available for their learning difficulties, and their feelings around aspects of these. This chapter has taken the analysis further, by examining and describing children's views of themselves, how others see them, and their perceptions of the labels used to describe them. This highlights the diversity and contrariness of children's self-perceptions, paralleling their experiences, and the mix of views they have as to how others see them. Further, their accounts indicate how they try to make sense of these differing experiences – not always successfully – and which factors seem to play the strongest roles in influencing their self-perceptions.

Some significant differences were found between mainstream and special school pupils. The majority of children acknowledged that they had learning difficulties, but mainstream pupils not only identified more, they also expressed more mixed and negative feelings about them than special school pupils did: special school pupils tended to have very high educational self-perceptions. This may have been an effect of two aspects: the fact that special school pupils may be more 'cushioned' against the reality of their learning difficulties by being isolated from those of differing abilities; and the fact that mainstream pupils cannot hide from these differences, as they are constantly mixing with and comparing themselves with others of differing abilities. Further, their need for support is more open to view than special school pupils, as all children in special schools receive help. Mainstream children's accounts in particular highlighted the reality of these experiences as described here.

There were some age and gender differences, in that older pupils were slightly more likely to be aware of learning difficulties than younger ones, and secondary boys were slightly more likely to deny or minimise their difficulties. These findings are not surprising in that it would be expected that older pupils have more awareness, but equally, that they might be more sensitive to stigma than younger pupils. Children's accounts certainly support this view, as many pupils were articulate in describing and expressing their experiences and negative feelings around any forms of stigmatisation, though this was also evident across all groups.

A difference was found between children's academic self-perceptions, and their general self-perceptions, in that there were no significant differences between pupils in mainstream and special schools in the general compared to the academic category: children tended to have mixed or positive general self-perceptions overall. Secondary-age boys' views on how others see their academic abilities also showed some variation, in that mainstream school boys tended to have mixed and negative perceptions, whereas special school boys again showed high levels of positive self-perceptions. These views again might be a reflection of status in schools, where special school boys are 'top dogs' in relatively small schools, whereas mainstream school boys are most likely to be in bottom sets of very large schools. Interestingly, despite a preponderance of negative or mixed feelings in several areas, secondary boys still preferred to remain in the mainstream schools, and special school boys preferred to be in the mainstream as well.

Children's views of labels supported other findings, in that they highlighted the issues of stigma attached to these, and helped to clarify why children were sensitive to issues around learning difficulties. What was significant was that children were aware that people used labels in different contexts, and that the same labels could be used in either positive or negative ways, and thus have different meanings. Though some children were aware of this difference, there were others, as illustrated in this chapter, for whom this distinction was not always clear: even when this distinction was clear, some pupils still found it difficult to perceive labels positively. The fact that labels used in a positive manner to help with learning difficulties could also be used to insult, belittle or bully children, was confusing for them. Further, the fact that sometimes teachers used these words in a way that was, or was perceived to be, abusive, added to the confusion. A further notable area was the extent to which children were exposed to negative connotations of labels, as in the form of name-calling. In addition, name-calling was often associated with learning difficulties, which adds to the issue of influences on self-perceptions.

Children recognised more labelling words that were used about them than they used to describe themselves. They often expressed strong feelings about individual words, and showed a variation and mix of feelings. Most interestingly, feelings around words about helping with work generated some mixed reactions, and though 'helping' words were some of the few receiving most positive or neutral evaluations, few pupils acknowledged actually having help.

It seemed, from this sample, that many pupils had significant issues with labelling words, regardless of type or context, and that this played a role in influencing their views on having learning difficulties, their self-perceptions and receiving support for these. Though many valued support, and a number could see that some labels were instrumental in instigating support, other factors were in place which played a role in creating tensions about this. The next chapter on bullying will point to some of the possible reasons for this.

Chapter 6

Social interaction, acceptance and bullying of pupils with MLD

Introduction

We examine in this chapter the social interactions and bullying of pupils with MLD in mainstream and special schools. Although social acceptance and bullying were not part of the explicit aims of the study of pupils' perspective, which we introduced in Chapter 4, they emerged as very significant issues, especially bullying, in the qualitative data that we collected. Before presenting some of the detailed findings from our analysis we discuss some of the relevant literature on these themes. It is notable that there is a much more substantial research into the social interactions of children with learning disability in the USA, than those with MLD-like difficulties. LD is the US term, which broadly corresponds to the term specific learning difficulties in the UK (SpLD). These findings have some relevance to the MLD group, the focus of this book, as they illustrate the responses of those without learning difficulties to a group with learning difficulties.

More than a quarter of a century ago, Bryan (1974) documented in the USA that children identified as having learning disabilities were less well accepted and more frequently rejected by their classmates than children without LD. This kind of finding has persisted since then in different contexts of schooling. For example, Vaughn *et al.* (1996) found in another small-scale US study that students with LD, age 8 to 10 years old, were less liked and more frequently rejected than non-LD pupils in inclusive classrooms, where learning support was in the mainstream class and not by withdrawal teaching. Despite being less liked and more often rejected, the LD group did not report more feelings of loneliness than the non-LD group, while they showed an increased number of within-class reciprocal friendships from the autumn to spring terms. These authors conclude, but with some caution, that the study indicates that those with LD in the inclusive class fared as well as similar students in withdrawal settings ('resource rooms' in US terminology). The finding that children with learning disabilities have reduced social status has been shown in other US studies, such as in the review of 17 studies using sociometric ratings compared to 'non-disabled' children (Ochoa and

Olvarez, 1995). In a more recent US study, Pavri and Luftig (2000) found that 11-year-old students with learning disabilities were less popular, experienced more loneliness and were less socially acceptable than those without learning disabilities. Similar findings have also been found in other countries, such as Spain (Camabra and Silvestre, 2003) and Israel (Tur-Kaspa et al., 1999).

There are similarities between the Vaughn study, described above, and the Tur-Kaspa one, in that both were of children with learning disabilities who were in inclusive classrooms (not withdrawn for support). In the study by Tur-Kaspa et al., over the period of one year, the LD group showed fewer reciprocal friendships and more reciprocal rejections, with the non-LD group showing the opposite trend. This finding seemed to contradict the Vaughn study finding discussed above, which showed increased reciprocal friendships. Tur-Kaspa explains the difference in terms of the starting levels of reciprocal friendships in both studies. In the Vaughn study the rise in reciprocal friendships was from 26 per cent to 53 per cent of the sample, while in the Tur-Kaspa study it started at 67 per cent and reduced to 61 per cent. Tur-Kaspa et al. concluded on the basis of these two studies that about 60 per cent of students with LD form and maintain at least one reciprocal friendship over the school year. The implication is that despite their lower social status, these children had some positive social relationships, a conclusion supported by other US studies (Juvonen and Bear, 1992; Pavri and Monda-Amaya, 2001). For example, in the study by Pavri and Monda-Amaya, students aged between 8 and 10 years old with learning disabilities were interviewed, as were their mainstream class teachers. This study indicated that the students with learning disabilities felt lonely, while still feeling part of a social network. The study also showed that they and their teachers disagreed about their preferred strategies for support. Farmer and Farmer (1996), in a slightly earlier US study, also showed how those with learning, emotional or behavioural difficulties fitted into the class social structure. This study examined the social affiliations in three US primary schools, focusing in particular on the academically 'gifted' and those with difficulties. They found that students formed distinct peer clusters based on their shared characteristics and that those with exceptionalities were well integrated through their peer clusters in the overall social structure of their classes.

The tentative pattern emerging from this disparate collection of studies is that despite having low social status, these children with learning disabilities still managed to form and maintain some positive social relationships in inclusive settings. This conclusion is consistent with the US study reported by Meyer (2001) of the impact of inclusion on the social lives and friendship of children with 'severe disabilities'. In this five-year study 20 children with severe disabilities, aged from 6 to 19 years, in inclusive settings, were matched with comparable children in segregated settings. Meyer reports that those in inclusive settings had significantly out-performed those in segregated settings on all measures, though she did not specify what these measures were. In an earlier study she did find that those with disabilities in mainstream classes were nominated less often than those without disabilities as 'best friend', 'regular friend', 'someone to work with', 'out of school companion' and 'someone to invite to a party'. Meyer raised the important point that despite receiving fewer nominations, the disabled children still received some nominations, which parents and children themselves might still value. The significance of such findings, therefore, calls for more interpretive studies of social relationships. This is where Meyer introduces a model of friendship called 'frames of friendship' to distinguish between different kinds of friendships – 'best friend', 'regular friend', 'just another child', 'I'll help', 'inclusion child', and 'ghost' or 'guest'. The model assumes that people experience all six frames of friendship in different circumstances and with different people. They are appropriate for different circumstances and there will be a balance across the frames. Difficulties are assumed to arise when a child's experiences all fall within certain frames that exclude positive social relationships with peers. Meyer discusses situations in 'inclusive classrooms' where children with disabilities were 'ghosts'; everyone went about their activities and treated the child as not existing in the classroom. She also discusses the 'inclusion child' frame, in which the child with disability was treated as different, for example through peers talking in baby talk to the child. In terms of children with disabilities having 'regular' or 'best friends', they identified cases where this was and was not found. When children with disabilities were 'regular friends', this was associated with adults supporting the children's social contacts. They identified on the bases of their studies four variables associated with children's social relationships:

1   the child's repertoire of social skills;
2   the social ecology that supports or hinders social relationships;
3   adult mediation that can facilitate or block opportunities for social interactions;
4   peer skills, support and expectations that support positive interactions with children with disabilities.

She comments that there has been too much focus on the child's repertoire rather than also focusing on the ecology, and the roles of adults and non-disabled peers and interactions.

Some of these 'frames of friendship' distinctions are evident in a rare UK paper based on recent studies into the inclusion of children with Down Syndrome (Cuckle et al., 2002). They concluded that though children aged 8 to 11 years were popular as regards choosing work partners in class, they were not often identified as 'best friends' or invited home. They also reported that secondary teachers saw the children with DS as needing more support and guidance in forming friendships than their non-DS peers. Some of these children would be identified as having moderate learning difficulties, so this study is more directly related to the focus of this book than the US studies of children with learning disabilities. More directly related to the focus of the book is a US study of students identified as having 'mild mental retardation' (MMR), a group more similar to the UK MLD group (Siperstein *et al.*, 1997). In this study they examined the quality of relationships in pairs of children with and without MMR. Compared with relationships where both children in the pair did not have MMR, they found less collaboration and more limited shared decision-making. There was less cooperative play and shared laughter and less symmetry in lead role taking. In a larger scale Israeli study, Heiman and Margalit (1998) examined the experiences of loneliness and depression, and peer perceptions of social status, in 11- to 16-year-old students identified with MMR in different settings. MMR students in special schools and in self-contained classes in mainstream schools reported more experiences of loneliness and depression than students without MMR. However, the significance of the setting for these experiences was influenced by the age of the students. Pre-adolescent students with MMR in mainstream schools reported more depression and feelings of loneliness and were perceived as having lower social status than their counterparts in special schools. The reverse was found for older adolescent students: those in special schools experienced more loneliness and depression. These authors attribute this difference to development changes between the younger and older students.

There has only been one large-scale UK study about the social status and relationships of children with MLD (Nabuzoka and Smith, 1993). This found that children identified as having moderate learning difficulties were less popular and more rejected than non-MLD children. This study focused on 179 children with MLD aged 8 to 12 years from six classes in two mainstream schools which had special needs resource units. Though less popular and more rejected than non-MLD children, the MLD children were not nominated as more disruptive or bullying. This indicates, according to the authors, that their lower social status was not due to aggressiveness or disruptiveness. What did seem to distinguish the MLD and non-MLD groups in terms of their rejection were differences in the peer perceptions of their cooperativeness, seeking help and being victims of bullying. The authors interpreted these factors as significant, as they were the ones in which the MLD children were over-represented. The authors concluded that the social problems faced in inclusive settings by those with MLD do not arise from behavioural factors (disruptiveness and aggressiveness), but from difficulties in handling interpersonal demands and situations (needing help, being victims of bullying and being less cooperative). This is a notable study, not only for its UK origins, but because it is one of few studies which attempts to analyse the lower social status of children with learning difficulties. It probably has relevance not only to the MLD groups, the focus of this book, but to those with specific learning difficulties, the focus of the US studies on children with learning disabilities.

There has been a strong research tradition that has examined the incidence, nature and prevention of school bullying in the UK (Smith and Sharp, 1994; Glover *et al.*, 2000) and more widely in Europe (Olweus, 1993; Roland, 2002) and North America (Ma, 2002). Name-calling has also been the focus of recent research (Lines, 2001; Crozier and Dimock, 1999; Crozier and Sklipidou, 2002). These studies have shown name-calling to be hurtful both when examined during and in retrospect after schooling. These studies refer to hurtful names being associated with physical appearance and racist name-calling. It is relevant to this book that there has been little reference to characteristics associated with learning difficulties in these studies. However, there has been consistent UK research showing that children with learning and other difficulties are more susceptible to bullying (O'Moore and Hilary, 1989; Martlew and Hodson, 1991; Whitney *et al.*, 1994; Hugh-Jones and Smith, 1999).

The most systematic and comprehensive study was conducted as part of the Sheffield Project by Whitney *et al.* (1994), which was associated with the study discussed above by Nabuzoka and Smith (1993). It involved 186 children aged between 6 and 15 years in eight schools. Three were middle and five were secondary schools, all with additional resource units for SEN. The 99 children with SEN had Statements or were in the process of receiving a Statement. They were matched with children without SEN in the same schools for age, gender, ethnicity and year group. A range of SEN was represented in the sample, including those with sensory and physical disabilities as well as those with varying levels of learning difficulties, including some with MLD. The sample included children from the two mainstream schools with units for MLD amongst the eight schools. Another important feature of this sample of children was that in most of the schools the children spent more than 40 per cent of their time in mainstream classes. In one school this was only 20 per cent of their time, while in another it was 100 per cent of their time. The study showed that the children with SEN were significantly more at risk of being bullied than children without SEN: two-thirds, compared to a quarter of children respectively. SEN children also reported being bullied more often than those without SEN. However, the study also showed that children with SEN also reported bullying others slightly more frequently than children without SEN: one-third compared to one-sixth respectively. Interviews showed that the bullying was related to their special educational needs.

The breakdown in the reports of bullying showed that those with moderate learning difficulties were at greater risk of being bullied than those with lesser learning difficulties. However, the number of children in the different SEN areas made systematic comparisons difficult. The study also examined the impact of anti-bullying interventions in these eight schools. These interventions included the development of a whole school policy on bullying, curriculum programmes, (such as drama, use of videos, and relevant literature), playground programmes (such as training lunchtime supervisors) and working with victims (such as assertiveness training). After eight months it was found that there was a reduction in the reported frequency of bullying in the schools as reported by pupils with SEN and their teachers. Judgements about whether the overall incidence of bullying had changed showed a balance towards improvement amongst the 76 children and 11 teachers. The authors concluded that their findings have considerable relevance to those with responsibilities for children with SEN in inclusive settings.

Name-calling and 'bullying'

Incidence and form

Children in our study reported different types of negative interactions from peers, which we categorised as 'bullying' (bullying is in inverted commas as it was reported rather than observed directly or reported by others; it is used as an umbrella term to cover experiences from 'teasing' to physical attacks). We separated these into three main types – physical, verbal (name calling and labelling), and teasing (similar to verbal but presented as fun or humorous). 'Teasing' was identified as a separate category, and presented here as a form of 'bullying' as children's descriptions usually presented these 'just in fun' experiences as distressing ones. Verbal bullying was mostly in the form of name-calling, and for many children was perceived as being akin to being labelled (see pages 110–13).

We found that overall 83 per cent of the sample experienced some form of 'bullying', with a mixture of types having been experienced by 68 per cent, mainly verbal by 24 per cent, mainly physical by 5 per cent and mainly teasing only by 3 per cent. There were no significant differences overall for any groups.

Targets for 'bullying': appearance and family members

Children reported various 'targets' for verbal bullying, which included comments about appearance, or members of their families. Some of these comments were made about physical disabilities, as these cases illustrate:

MSFSR5   Callin' me names. Takin' the Mick out of my speech. [I feel] angry.

MSFPR1   They call me a pig and a slowcoach, because I walk very slow, because with my legs I can twist it and it hurts when I twist it. [I feel] quite upset. I go in the corner and cry. I think no one likes me cause I'm ugly. [I feel] quite like a special needs girl. Not a good thing 'cause people says I'm special needs and I don't like it.

MSMSR4   Ah you're fat, you're another fat bee and everyfink else and they callin' my mum a cripple and everything. Then I get upset. It's because she's been in a wheelchair [from] when she was about thirty. [I get upset], turn round and hit them. Sometimes I have fits. [Afterwards I feel] miserable, thinking no, I haven't done that again.

Targets for 'bullying': learning difficulties and receiving help

Of particular relevance to this research, we found that 49 per cent of children reported 'bullying' relating in some way to their learning difficulties, which was common to all groups. Comments were often directed at the difficulty itself, or were made with reference to going to a special school:

SSFSD1   [My neighbours] always call me [special school] dunce. I don't take no notice of them.

SSFSG1   I was picked on I think more, because I couldn't read, I'm not sure. They call me thick, I think, umm, dumb.

MSFPR1   A bit scared [of neighbours]. Because everyone was picking on me, saying 'special needs girl'.

MSFSU2   It's like I get upset that things I can't do an' all that, but things like that other people can do, but I can't. Just that I can't do the work. They usually laugh at me an' that lot 'cos I can't do the work an' that. [I feel a] little bit upset an' that lot. They sometimes take the Mickey, saying your having special help an' that. Makes me feel a little bit upset an' that.

Some children were aware of getting picked on for receiving extra help in the classroom:

MSFPU1   Well people do take the Mickey if you've got someone with you. Just feels terrible. [Getting help in a group], hum, just feels stupid. 'Cause there's four of us and some people take the Mickey out of us. Hum, just feel like lonely and all that. 'Cause usually they break up with me and then go off with someone else. They just call me names and go off with their friend.

MSFSU4   [Getting help in class] makes me look bad. 'Cos when she comes up to me and I tell her to go away they start laughin' and they start to taking the Mick out of me and fings like, like tha'. That's when it all starts up when she comes up to me all the time they start. Sometimes it's just the way I am toward people, and then they react and things like that 'cos I can have a go if I wan' a go I can have a go. But sometimes it's them just like coming up to me and believing other people when I 'aven't said nothing.

Some felt that having special needs, and/or receiving help, affected friendships, as this girl described:

MSFPR1   Saying, 'I don't know what she's on about,' and all that. Quite upset, cause I can't change what I'm talking about and all that. They call me 'special needs' again. They go, [*mocking voice*] 'special needs!' [I feel] sad and grotty. 'Cause it makes me, I haven't got any more friends. Like [my friend], we fall out sometimes and I haven't got any friends if we fall out.

Source of 'bullying': pupils in own school

About half of the pupils (52 per cent) in the whole sample reported some 'bullying' by pupils in their own school. Differences were found when taking account of gender, age and school together. Mainstream primary girls reported significantly more in-school 'bullying' than special school primary girls (83 per cent to 42 per cent), while there were no differences between primary mainstream and special school boys. By contrast, for secondary boys, mainstream school pupils reported less in-school 'bullying' than special school boys (17 per cent to 70 per cent), while there were no such differences between mainstream secondary and special secondary girls.

SSFPD3   [Being called names] I don't find that funny, well I don't find it very funny at all. I just go and play with my friends who, like, take care of me and all that, so.

SSFSG6   Getting picked on. I was a bit scared going into [school] anyway. Because I had no friends in the class. [I was being picked on] because I'm different and I couldn't read or spell and they knew. They thought I'd be a bit of a game for teasing. They were calling me thick. I can't remember really. I know I was getting called thick a lot. [I felt] angry and upset really. I just kept it quiet.

SSFSD2   [Get bullied here made me] sad. Want to leave but I can't. 'Cause I'm not old enough. This boy calls me a fatty.

SSFSG4   Well I quite like it here and that, in, when I get picked on an' that I think – I don't really wanna come here anymore, like that, so.

As many children's descriptions highlighted, some of the 'bullying' was in the form of teasing in school or class. Children seemed to try and minimise it, but their extended descriptions suggest that even 'teasing' can 'get' to them – eventually – and lead to an explosion of some kind:

MSMPR7   Like you have to get used to it, like, when someone is teasing you about you can't read and write, you just have to annoy them and get used to it. [I feel] a little bit cross 'cos, umm, like and then umm, 'cos I bang the table and I say shut up to this boy because he keeps talking and talking and talking and that's it. In my old school, yeah, there's this girl, she says like, 'You can't read and write' and then I just annoy her and just go out the room. [I feel] sad really. Walk away. It's not my fault.

Sources of 'bullying': neighbours and outside school

Children in both mainstream and special school reported 'bullying' by pupils from other mainstream schools, or by children in their neighbourhoods. Special school pupils reported significantly more 'bullying' overall in this setting than mainstream (30 per cent compared to 12 per cent), and this was significantly greater for special school children in their neighbourhoods (48 per cent to 4 per cent), and particularly for primary-age children. Some examples illustrate these experiences:

MSFPR1   Because sometimes I don't really want to go to school, because some people pick on me and all that. In the school, and some out of the school.

SSFPG2   'Cause my other school is horrible. Because they's all pickin' on me. Beatin' me up, calling me names. Swearing words, umm, sad. Because they didn't like me.

Special school pupils in particular were bullied about going to their schools:

SSMPG3   'Cause when I came to this school, when I went home, they would laugh at me and say 'Oh [he] goes to [the special school]', like [our mainstream] school's betta than [that special school], 'cause that school is even worser. This school's fun and that school down there, 'cause they were horrible when I went down there, they say 'you smell' and that.

SSFPD3   Umm, well, umm, there's a girl down my way and she always says that she likes take the Mickey. She goes ha, ha, [she's] going to a dumb school, and I don't think they know this. I just say, well, if she was at this school I would take the Mickey out of her, but she don't need to do that because I haven't done nothin' wrong, to her at all. It's like this; she gets everybody else on my back and starts bullying an' all that. I get really, really angry, I feel like thumping her one.

Though children did not like personal insults, there were a number who became particularly upset when they thought their school or the disabled children within the school were being attacked, as this case shows:

SSFSG4   [Neighbours], they call me 'spastic, stupid' and I do like, you're takin' like the Mick out of the disabled basically, the ones with disabilities. [It makes me feel] really down and that, so. It just upsets me because they're being horrible to me, they go, 'you go to a spastic school, you go to a spastic school' and I go, 'it's not a spastic school, it just a disability school and also you're taking the Mick out of the disabled children'. Cause, umm, she goes, 'you're a spassy, you go to a special school'. Mostly [I get upset because she's] attacking the school, like where they've got special needs here. I don't like the Mick being took out of them. Like one day somebody called, turned round and said, umm, when you take the Mick out the handicapped children, it makes me think of, that like you're taking the Mick out of [children who can't help it].

Some children experienced bullying about their schools at home:

SSFSD3   I do know they just think [special school children are] thick or somethin'. [My sister, who goes to mainstream] sometimes, she's in the right mood, she say nice things about my school. If somebody winds her up, you know, she says horrible things about my school.

SSFPG5   My cousins pick on me. Oh, why you going to [the special school], I say it's not up to you, it's up to me what I do.

Feelings about and consequences of 'bullying'

Feelings about 'bullying' were expressed by 77 per cent of those reporting 'bullying'. Most of these pupils (56 per cent) reported some kind of mixed negative response (sad, upset, hurt or withdrawn, or occasionally angry or confused, 36 per cent) and neutral response (ignoring it, not being bothered, keeping calm, or telling the teacher, 5 per cent). Only 3 per cent reported mainly neutral responses. There were no significant differences in feelings about 'bullying' for differences in gender, age or kind of school.

Feeling were expressed in different ways, with some children being able to contain their feelings quite well, despite being upset by the bullying, whereas others were more liable to lose control. The following descriptions illustrate the levels of reaction to bullying, as described by the children.

When being asked to describe their bullying experiences, some children found it hard to even talk about it, and had to be persuaded to give any detail:

MSMSR7   Calling names, about anything really. Don't want to tell about it.

MSFPU1   Half of 'em I get on with and half of 'em I don't. Hum, they just call me names and I can't stand being called names. I don't want to say all these names. Smelly and swearing words. [I feel] sad.

Children described diverse feelings that arose from bullying, including embarrassment and withdrawal:

MSFSR5   Hum, [this girl] yesterday was pickin' on me for a long, long time, and I've sorted it out now. Callin' me names. Takin' the Mick out of my speech. [I feel] angry. Hide all day. [In my previous school], hum, they were like mostly the year above me in Year 8. I said they picked on me but my form teacher didn't believe me. It makes me hide.

MSFPU4   I get very upset when some people bully me. I'm so upset because if they bully you, you're just afraid because you think if you want to be at home and then tell your mum and dad. When you tell your mum and dad you feel too embarrassed.

Feelings of being upset were not exclusive to any group, and secondary boys were as liable to react like this as any other group. Expressing mixed feelings and reactions was not uncommon, as this case illustrates:

MSMSU4   I try not to, umm, cry about it. [I have cried] occasionally at home, yeah, yeah. [I've been kept back a year]. I feel, umm, bit sad sort of in my mind, 'cos I don't like them asking me [about that]. I feel a bit upset. [I feel] sad, yeah. 'Cos [bullying] makes me a bit aggressive and that. Umm, umm, because, umm, because I just don't like them calling me names, I might go tell a teacher or just ignore them.

Extensive or multiple experiences of bullying were likely to make some children doubt themselves, as these cases illustrate:

MSFSU4   People say nasty things about me and things like that. It makes me feel stupid if you know what I mean, 'cos they're calling me stupid and then I think to myself, well am I actually stupid?

SSFSG4   I just literally turned round and said, 'look, I've done nothing.' They were saying, 'You're horrible and smelly, two-faced' and all that. Pretty upset. I felt like really upset. I felt like lashin' out but I didn't. If it's a boy with disabilities, I don't mind, but if he hasn't got disabilities I do mind because it really hurts. I feel really angry inside. Sometimes I actually think it's me, I, I think it is like me, it's encouraging them to say it.

The latter excerpt illustrates retaliation, which was evident in some cases, though for this girl it did not lessen her self-doubt. Other children either 'exploded' or retaliated in some way:

MSMSU5   One day I'll lose it.

MSFSU1   [I feel] upset. I just bottle it up and then it just comes out. Name-calling.

MSFPR7   I call them names, 'cos they call me names.

MSMSU6   Well at first it's nothin' but then afterwards it keeps on building up and then building up and then I just lash out.

MSMSU2   Well, I generally feel very angry, and there are times where I get so angry and I'll just bottle it up, and I just don't want to walk behind them and hit them in the head. That is what happened at my old school, I ended up hurting someone who was not anything to do with the problem, who just happened to get in the way accidentally. So that's what I am scared of happening here, so I generally bottle it up, and I get sometimes visions when I'm sleeping of, umm, me doing quite horrific things to them.

SSFSG3   Just the school [neighbours] are nasty about, and me. That I'm disabled and handicapped and all this lot. [I feel] cross. Well I'll just start on 'em and start beating hell out of 'em. Can't calm my temper down.

A particular consequence of bullying was that of the links between learning difficulty, sometimes with receiving help, and 'bullying', and how this might lead to behavioural problems, as some excerpts illustrate:

MSMSD2 The fact that I can't, that what my mind is thinking, my hand won't write down neat or fast enough. It doesn't really bother me that my writing isn't as neat or organised as anyone else, but it does sometimes get to me when I've just been bullied and I write something I can get – it's really frustrating. It's sometimes almost as bad as the bullying. When I feel I can just snap my pencil in half because it is just so frustrating.

MSFSU4 Umm, it affects me because people think I'm bad and, people say nasty things about me and things like that. Call me stupid and things like that an'.

MSMPR1 If anybody kicks me, I kick them back. Sometimes kick people first. Get on me nerves. They annoy me. When they start tantalising me and making fun of me. They just get up and they just get in my way all the time and have a go at me. But when they make fun of me they call me stupid and they say this is you making stupid impressions of me.

A few children felt that they were changing in their reactions to bullying. Some felt that they were maturing, and therefore reacting more calmly, others had actually begun to retaliate more as they got older:

MSFSU6 Did not take any notice [now]. I used to get a bit upset.

SSFSG1 [I did] nothin', didn't do nothin' 'cause too young. Hmm, fight now cause I'm older.

Some continued to be puzzled as to why they were the targets of bullying:

SSFSG I dunno, it makes me angry I just don't know why they doin' it to me.

Others recognised the value of friends in helping to deal with bullying or being supported and therefore being stronger in dealing with it:

MSMSR1 [Friends] probably, like, mostly stick up for me. It makes me, like, feel a little bit happier.

MSMPR4 When I get beat up [my friends] tell the teacher.

Bullying sometimes had serious consequences for children, as these cases highlight, though they illustrate radically different outcomes:

MSFSU6 OK, but I used to get a lot of picked on in primary school, but where I'm getting older, and in secondary schools, they are going to different schools. They used to call me, because I used to pull my hair out, used to get stressed, and, umm, they used to call me baldy. I tried to cover it up with hair bands and that. I was in foster care then. I didn't do it at school; I used to do it at home. Don't pull my hair out no more. Feel better now. That was also where they called me fleabag, because I used to hang out with a girl who had something wrong with her [in a wheelchair], helping her. Because the only reason why I don't like coming to school is because of the bullying. I don't like it because of nothin' else. Just because of the bullying.

MSFSU1   [I was taken out of school], I weren't really allowed back but I wanted to come back. 'Cos I was bullied and it was going on since Year 7. Got fed up with staying at home. Yeah, we were going to find me another school but they had three weeks before the six weeks holiday and all the three six weeks holidays and three weeks after the six weeks holiday so they said they would definitely find me a school, social services, but they didn't.

MSFSU4   I've locked myself in the bathroom and sometimes it makes me feel suicidal but I won't actually do it because [someone in my family] committed suicide so when I do like feel suicidal it just reminds me of [that], so . . .

Three important features of bullying were whether children felt able to disclose to anyone, whether they actually did disclose, and what happened after disclosure. As in all categories, children displayed a mix of personal responses, but also a mix of responses from others. There seemed some evidence that bullying as a whole was *not*, from the child's point of view, being treated effectively, as these cases illustrated:

MSMSU4   [I'm sure] they will [take me seriously] but I'm just scared of saying. [Mum] comes in, definitely, she'll come in and have a word with a teacher. If you would have a problem with bullying that's one thing, they would sort out. Bullying, and over here they don't, I find they don't do that or they say they'll sort it out and they don't.

SSFSG4   Well, I quite like it here and that, in, when I get picked on an' that I think, I don't really want to come here anymore, like that, so. Children, not actually live near me but they actually live in [the area] and they actually come to this school. They go 'I don't want you on this table', 'I don't want you nowhere near me, you scabby, an' smelly and all that'. Down, really down.

[Teachers don't really do anything], they just tell 'em off, give 'em a warnin'.

MSFSU4   Getting bullied, like beaten up, 'cos I've had quite a bit of bullying lately. Umm, girls would just, like, fall out with me for no reason and make my life a misery. I don't, I don't like coming to school, I don't like school at all. And I don't, I don't, the only lessons I like is German and science 'cos there's like most of my friends in there but I'm getting bullied on at the moment.

Social in-groups/out-groups

The literature at the beginning of this chapter includes a discussion on friendship groups, belonging and isolation, and the likelihood of differing levels of interpersonal inclusion or acceptance experienced by those with learning difficulties. Social inclusion/exclusion was not specifically researched for this project, but relationships with peers were included by way of discovering how children felt about themselves (Chapter 5). It was found that friends were very important, as described in Chapter 4, and Chapters 5 and 6 highlight the negative experiences of bullying and name-calling, which frequently reflect children's difference: learning difficulties and/or need for support were commonly identified targets of difference. Children's experiences of friendships and social isolation/exclusion did, in fact, support some of the findings from the literature, in that a good number of these children described themselves as, at least, sometimes being left out or isolated. Some examples of these are described here.

Referring to the previous chapter on self and labels, it was found that few described themselves as having special needs. Though most acknowledged learning difficulties and receiving help, there were some tensions around this, as was reflected in their self-descriptions and feelings about themselves, and labels used to describe them. Interestingly, a number of children referred to others as having special needs, and being sympathetic to this, but not seeing themselves in this way. Children made a distinction between themselves and others as *different*, but sometimes these differences were in their 'favour'. Some described others who in some way were less 'advantaged' than they were, for example being physically disabled, or having learning difficulties, but identified these children as different from *them*, and disassociated themselves in some way from the similarity:

Q   When you're getting help in class, do you ever find that children say anything to you about it?
MSMPU6   They might take the Mickey out of them.

SSFSG4   [Neighbours] go, 'you go to a spastic school, you got to a spastic school' and I go, 'it's not a spastic school, it just a disability school and also you're taking the Mick out of the disabled children'. Cause, umm, she goes you're a spassy; you go to a special school. Mostly [I get upset because she's] attacking the school, like where they've got special needs here. I don't like the Mick being took out of them. Like one day somebody called, turned round and said, umm, when you take the Mick out the handicapped children, it makes me think of, that like you're taking the Mick out of [children who can't help it].

A number of children described friendships with children who were disadvantaged themselves in some way, but it was not always clear who was initiating the friendship, and how 'equal' these friendships were:

MSMPU5   'Cos we've got a boy in our class who can bleed to death so he just comes and plays with me, and sometimes he don't want to play our games, so I just say let's play a new game with him. [He gets picked on.] They don't say anything 'cos we are different, I dish them afterwards. It makes me feel angry. Because I don't like my friends getting picked on.

SSFPG3   [Neighbours] call me four eyes, I'm cross-eyed. They kick me and that. Some friends do but no, none of them, some of them don't, some people make funny faces at me. That girl with the bad leg, she's, she's my, she likes me. I tell my mum. Makes me sad.

Children's accounts suggest that belonging was important to them, as previous chapters illustrate, and linked strongly with higher self-esteem and identity. Friends were seen as a protective factor, as well as contributing to increased well-being:

MSMSR1   I find it hard to say [what they call me] actually. They sometimes call me like queer boy and that but then again I respond back. I usually tell them to go away or something. It makes me like a little bit upset. [Friends] probably like mostly stick up for me. Makes me like feel a little bit happier.

MSFPR4   They're really, really horrible. And a lot of them in the classroom. Boys and girls. Smelly and all that stuff. [I feel] sad. Well, I tell, I tell my teacher sometimes when they're really, really horrible in the playground. She, they'll go in and she'll just tell 'em off. She does enough. [Friends], hum, they're kind, they stand up for me, and they help me, and they tell, also, the people off not to call me names. [Makes me feel] happy.

Some children simply felt that they were not wanted, a feeling that was particularly noted amongst mainstream primary girls:

MSFPR4   Children in my class, it's just the children in my class, they, they, it happens quite often. If they, they say they're not my friends. Well, well when we are having dinner people kick me under the table. Sad. It hurts. Kick me down there. They've been horrible to me since I came.

MSFPR8   [*Sighs*] I feel much better but I'm still having a lot of problems with my, umm, friends in Year 8 who is bullying me. They're mates [three of them]. They say swear words and push me in the cupboard with these two doors, one either side and they shut me in and they laugh through the window that I was trying to get out because I was banging on the window. I just don't understand it. I just don't know why that they keep on doing it for. Upset me and me ang', make me angry because they are getting angry about me because they don't want me here. None of my friends are good to me.

MSFPU1   You're thick and backward, you need to go to a handicapped school. My, hum, my friends what I don't like [say these things]. Hum, just feel like lonely and all that. 'Cause usually they break up with me and then go off with someone else. They just call me names and go off with their friend.

Summary and discussion

This chapter has highlighted and described children's experiences of 'bullying' and interpersonal social inclusion/exclusion. Though we had not specifically set out to look at these areas, bullying in particular was discovered to be a significant experience in the lives of these children, and through seeking children's perspectives on themselves in relation to provision, factors around interpersonal inclusion/exclusion were brought to light.

In line with the literature described above, it was clear that a number of children did experience elements of interpersonal exclusion and isolation, often had few friends, and had friends who also had learning or other difficulties, or who were even more 'disadvantaged' than they were. Most older children seemed to have better circles of friends, but some of the younger ones, or when they were younger, seemed more likely to have problems with friendships: notably, in this sample, mainstream primary girls described significant amounts of bullying. It is not possible to say exactly why this was. Behavioural and language difficulties may have been a contributing factor in some cases. However, a substantial number made reference to bullying and learning difficulty status, which did seem to isolate them, especially mainstream pupils, as this was a notable difference. Primary school children's experience was mixed across schools, suggesting that the ethos of individual schools may have played a contributing role in how they were accepted by others in their schools. Further, primary schools were less likely to have children with Statements than secondary schools, where there would be more children from a wider geographical area, therefore presenting children with greater resources for friends like themselves. The fact that most schools had special SEN units/resource rooms also gave older pupils a meeting point with others similar to themselves.

Pupils from all groups were exposed to bullying, and some individuals described more pervasive experiences than others. All children were liable to be subjected to bullying in their own schools, though special school pupils were more likely to be targeted outside of school as well: these children were targeted both for having learning difficulties and for being in special schools. Bullying was strongly linked to learning difficulties and was described as being distressing for most who experienced it.

This chapter links with the previous chapters on perceptions of provision and self, and increases our understanding, most importantly, as to why children feel as they do. Children's accounts strongly implied that bullying, especially of a verbal nature, could affect the way they saw themselves. A good number presented mixed views about all aspects of themselves, suggesting struggles with perceptions of self and experience. In terms of provision, as expected, there was evidence of tension and difference, and these seemed most strongly linked with the attitudes of others, rather than the intrinsic nature of their difficulties alone. The significance of these findings is to implicate wider interpersonal relationships in how pupils perceive themselves and their schooling.

Chapter 7

Survey of LEA policy and practice for moderate learning difficulties

Introduction

In this chapter we summarise the findings from a national survey which was conducted during the first part of 2003 of all LEAs in England and Wales. The aim of the survey was to find out from an LEA perspective about provision for children designated as having moderate learning difficulties. The survey was conducted using a short five-page questionnaire, containing 12 questions on the following areas:

1 whether the term MLD is used in the LEA;
2 how the term or any other related one is used, if used;
3 how the LEA defines MLD;
4 how their definition differs from current proposed in early 2003 by the DfES for SEN classification;
5 general views in the LEA about the term MLD;
6 number of special schools with MLD or related designation;
7 numbers of units for MLD or including MLD in general units;
8 three years' data on the numbers of pupils with Statements for MLD, in special schools for MLD and total number with Statements;
9 changes in trends of these data;
10 LEA criteria for identifying MLD-like difficulties;
11 summary of key changes in provision over the last five years in the LEA;
12 plans for future change (whether in the LEA's educational development plans).

The draft questionnaire was tried out with a group of officers from one LEA and amendments were made before it was sent out to all educational officers with SEN responsibilities.

Table 7.1 Distribution survey LEAs and all LEAs in English regions

	No. and % of survey LEAs	No. and % of all LEAs
East Midlands	3	9
	6%	6%
East England	4	10
	8%	7%
North East	5	12
	10%	8%
North West	9	22
	19%	15%
London	4	32
	8%	22%
South East	9	19
	18%	13%
South West	7	15
	14%	10%
West Midland	3	14
	6%	9%
Yorkshire/Humberside	5	15
	10%	10%
Total	49	148

Background information about responding LEAs

A total of 58 LEAs responded to the survey, 49 English LEAs and nine Welsh LEAs, representing 33 per cent of English and 56 per cent of Welsh LEAs. As Table 7.1 shows, these English LEAs were from all of the nine listed regions. In East Midlands, East England, North East and Yorkshire/Humberside, the percentage of responding LEAs was within 2 per cent points of the actual percentage of LEAs in these regions. There was a higher percentage of responding LEAs from the North West, South East and South West than the actual proportion of all LEAs in these regions. However, London LEAs were the least represented amongst responding LEAs; 8 per cent of the sample but 22 per cent of all LEAs. As regards type of LEA, Table 7.2 also shows the under-representation of London in the sample, and the over-representation of county LEAs. These county LEAs are mainly in the North West, South East and South West. A similar percentage of Metropolitan and Unitary LEAs were found in the sample as in the national breakdown.

The survey questionnaire was completed by LEA officers who had several different role titles. For example, the most common titles were Education Officer, Advisor, Advisory Teacher, Head of SEN Service, Head of SEN and Inclusion Service, Head of Inclusion Service, SEN Manager, Pupil Services Manager and Principal Educational Psychologist.

Table 7.2 Distribution of types of English LEAs

	No. and % of survey LEAs	No. and % of all LEAs
County	17	33
	34%	22%
London	4	33
	8%	22%
Metropolitan	12	36
	24%	24%
Unitary	16	46
	33%	31%
Total	49	148

The term MLD

When asked what term is used by the LEA in policy and practice for pupils who are often referred to as having moderate learning difficulties, 46 LEAs (79 per cent) reported that they used the term MLD, while seven LEAs (12 per cent) did not (there were missing data for five LEAs). When asked, if they used a more general term, to specify what this was, a variety of terms were reported (see Table 7.3). The more common terms were 'learning difficulty' and 'general learning difficulty'. These correspond with terms used in the first SEN Code of Practice, as does 'cognition and learning', which derives from the revised Code.

In most LEAs the term MLD is used to refer to pupils' area of difficulty (55 LEAs, 95 per cent). In a majority of LEAs the term was also used to refer to the type of provision, for example the type of special school or type of learning support (35 LEAs, 60 per cent).

Understanding and defining the term MLD

When asked to say what the term MLD means in their LEA, there were many varied and complex answers, which were analysed thematically for

Table 7.3 Other terms also used

	N = 21
Learning difficulty	6
General learning difficulty	5
Complex learning difficulty	2
Developmental or learning delay	2
Cognition and learning	2
Other	4

key terms and phrases. In this analysis each response might be analysed in terms of several themes. Table 7.4, which summarises these themes, shows that the most frequent aspects of these definitions relate to the distinction between low all-round attainments and low cognitive ability. One-third of the responding LEAs used some measure of cognitive abilities in their defini-tion of MLD (for example, IQ 50–70 or general cognitive ability 60–70); this was the most frequent theme in the definitions. However, only six LEAs (13 per cent) made reference to cognitive abilities and not to attainments in their definition. Many more referred to slow progress across all or a number of curriculum areas (23 per cent). Of these, five LEAs referred to cut-offs for identifying low attainments, for example 2–5 per cent or 1–2 per cent (11 per cent). Almost as many LEAs defined MLD in terms of both attainment and ability (20 per cent). The next most frequent theme was the association with other areas of difficulties, for example behaviour, confidence, speech and language, sensory, physical and social skills (19 per cent). Another fairly fre-quent theme in these definitions was that the delay or difficulties were not of a specific nor severe kind (11 per cent). This was to mark out the differentia-tion between moderate general learning difficulties and specific and severe difficulties. It is interesting that only six LEAs (13 per cent) stated that they did not use the term MLD for a variety of reasons. These LEAs found some other term more useful, for example 'complex needs' or the revised SEN Code's dimension 'cognition and learning', or they focused on pupils' 'actual learning needs' along a 'continuum of difficulties'.

When asked in what ways their LEA definition was similar to and different from what was at that stage (early 2003) the proposed DfES definition of MLD, most responded that it was broadly similar (60 per cent). The pro-posed DfES definition was as follows:

> MLD is used to describe developmental delay across a number of areas. Pupils with moderate learning difficulties will have academic attain-ment below expected levels in most subjects of the curriculum. Pupils will have difficulty in acquiring basic literacy and numeracy skills and many will have speech and language difficulties associated with intel-lectual delay. A few may also have low self esteem, low levels of concen-tration, under-developed social skills and have behavioural, emotional and social difficulty and/or physical disability that affect their learning abilities.
>
> (DfES, 2002)

Ten LEAs (24 per cent) commented that their definition was similar to this one, but had some key difference, for example they did not refer to any asso-ciated difficulties, or they had some additional aspect, including specific cognitive ability score cut-off levels.

Table 7.4 Definitions of and positions about the term MLD

N = 47 responses	Frequency	% of total LEAs (and rank)
Slow progress, delay all/range/number of curriculum areas	11	23% (2nd)
Low ability and low general attainment	9	20% (3rd)
No reference to attainments, only cognitive abilities	6	13% (5th)
NOT USED; more useful term 'complex needs', focus on 'actual learning needs', 'continuum of difficulties', use Code's 4 dimensions (complex LD + communication/interaction or learning and behaviour)	6	13% (5th)
General difficulties across curriculum (2–5%, 1–2%)	5	11% (6th)
Attainments significantly below peers	4	
Difficulty in learning, learning disability, delay	3	
Significant LDs where general attainments low	2	
Main difficulty in National Curriculum (NC) terms	1	
Significant and persistent difficulty in language, literacy and numeracy (tests specified but not level above KS1)	1	
LD in terms of two areas of NC, several dimensions (educational, economic, ecological, clinical); attainment levels and/or cognitive abilities <2nd centile	1	
2 conditions of 5 (significant developmental delay, language delay, accessing NC, handwriting, tasks not understood)	1	
3 elements significantly below peers in NC attainments + slower progress than peers +IQ 55–70	1	
Reference to learning skills, strategies, memory, processing and generalisation difficulties	1	
Can attain functional academic levels and adult independence	1	
Moderate mismatch between skills/abilities and demands of learning environment	1	
Difficulties accessing curriculum due to learning and other difficulties	1	
Other aspects		
Cognitive ability test scores (IQ 50–70, GCA 60–70, below 2nd centile)	15	33% (1st)
Associated immaturity, behaviour, confidence difficulties, speech/language, difficulty with concepts, physical, sensory, social skills difficulties (some combination)	9	19% (4th)
Not severe and/or not specific	5	11% (6th)
Reference to specific subject areas/core subjects	3	
Specific attainment levels for different ages	3	
Reference to the provided questionnaire DfES definition	3	
No formal definition	2	
Outside key stage	2	
Have or might have a Statement	2	
Not have Statement	2	
In mainstream unless significant and additional needs in special schools	1	
Not met in mainstream schools	1	

General view in LEA about validity and usefulness of MLD or related term

When asked if there is a general view in their LEA about the validity and use-fulness of terms like MLD or other similar terms, not quite half the respon-dents said that there was a general view (48 per cent). A significant minority said they could not identify a view (28 per cent) and less said there was not a general view (19 per cent), with five responses missing. For those who said there was a general view, there was a clear tension between positive and negative views (Table 7.5). The most frequent comment was that the MLD term was increasingly a questioned term with limited value. Despite this, almost the same percentage considered the term positively, as providing a common term of reference and useful for planning provision. Other positive comments were that the term is a starting point for defining learning diffi-culties, a shorthand for professionals and parents and useful for statis-tical purposes. The other negative comments highlighted that the term was vague and general and gave little indication of presenting difficulties, nor approaches to be used with the child. There were single comments that were even more critical – moving away from the use of the term because it reflected a medical model and ignored a continuum of need, and towards definitions that focused on areas of learning or 'complex learning difficulties' as this blurred the distinction between severe and moderate learning difficul-ties. There were five LEAs where the response was explicitly mixed, picking out the tensions between the above positive and negative aspects.

The mixed response to the MLD term is exemplified in the following quote from one LEA:

> To label a pupil as having MLD at a given time within their school career can serve to limit expectations of the teaching staff. The LEA tries not to categorise children, but to meet their needs in an inclusive environment wherever possible. Categories used only for data collection and analysis.

By contrast, another LEA exemplified the position which abandoned this particular term:

> The validity of the term is increasingly questioned, e.g. where is the dividing line between MLD and SLD. The main value has been historical and in the way provision has been structured. However, as an LEA we are fast moving towards a more inclusive approach: most 'MLD' children are in mainstream education and we are re-organising our special schools to provide for the whole range of learning difficulties, whilst recognising the fact that most MLD children do not need these kinds of facilities.

Table 7.5 Positive, negative and mixed comments about the validity and value of the term MLD

N = 44	Frequency	%
Positive		
Planning provision/purpose of provision	5	12%
Common vocabulary	4	10%
For starting process of defining level of learning difficulty	2	
Shorthand of use to professionals and parents	2	
Statistical purposes	2	
Negative		
Global term is vague/too general – risks guessing	3	
Gives no indication of presenting difficulties, and approaches best for child	3	
Not allow flexibility of provision	1	
Increasingly dubious/questioned term/limited value	11	26%
Moved to definitions of learning difficulties in terms of areas of difficulties, e.g language	1	
Implies medical rather than preferred social model	1	
Use complex LD to avoid differentiating between MLD and SLD	1	
Refer to continuum of need and general learning difficulties	1	
Mixed		
Useful shorthand, but lacks specificity, not overuse labels	2	
Consensus amongst officers but not teachers	1	
Useful for data management, planning provision, not useful in determining response to needs	2	
Not discussed	2	
LEA reviewing criteria, etc.	2	

Special schools and units designated for MLD or including MLD

Overall 107 special schools were identified by the 58 LEAs for pupils with MLD or as including pupils with MLD. Most of these special schools had a MLD designation (87 per cent), with only 7 per cent designated as mixed, while there were no details about designations for 5 per cent of the identified special schools. This represented an average of 1.6 special schools per LEA, where the designation was for MLD. These special schools represented considerable variation of the age ranges for the special schools.

Table 7.6 shows that the most frequent age range for all these special schools is from Key Stage 1 to Key Stage 4. The next most frequent are similar but extend to the Foundation and post-Key Stage 4 ages. So the most frequent pattern is for full age range MLD special schools. Only 12 per cent of special schools were for pupils at Key Stage 2 and below, the primary phases, while only one special school was for Key Stages 3 and 4, secondary phases.

Table 7.6 Age ranges reported in sample MLD special schools

Key Stage range	Frequency
KS1 to KS4	31
Foundation to KS4	12
Foundation to post-KS4	11
Foundation to KS2	8
KS2 to KS4	8
KS1 to KS2	5
KS1 to post-K4	3
KS2 to post-KS4	3
KS3 to KS4	1
KS2 to KS3	1
KS2	1
KS4	1

Table 7.7 shows the distribution of mainstream units designated for MLD. There were slightly more LEAs with MLD units in the primary Key Stages (36 per cent) than in the secondary Stages (30 per cent), with fewer in the Key Stage 2 and 3 phases. Of those LEAs with MLD units, most had one or two units in both primary and secondary stages. Far fewer LEAs reported general mainstream units which included pupils with MLD (Table 7.8), 16 per cent for the primary stages and 5 per cent for the secondary stages. Some Welsh LEAs had 10 to 13 mainstream schools with units.

Percentages of pupils with Statements for learning difficulties designated as MLD

Table 7.9 shows the data over the last three years in the sample LEAs of the proportion of pupils with MLD of all pupils with Statements. This shows that just over a quarter of all pupils with Statements had an MLD designation and this did not vary over the period of time. It is to be noted

Table 7.7 Frequency of mainstream schools with units or resource centres with a MLD or general designation

	MLD units										
	0	1	2	3	4	5	6	7	8	9	>9
KS1 + 2	37	6	7	2	1	2	2	0	1	0	>0
KS2 + 3	50	2	2	1	0	0	0	0	0	0	>1
KS3 + 4	39	6	7	2	1	1	0	0	0	0	>1

Table 7.8 Frequency of mainstream schools with units or resource centres with a general designation including MLD

	General units including MLD									
	0	*1*	*2*	*3*	*4*	*5*	*7/8*	*10*	*12*	*13*
KS1 + 2	48	3	1	0	0	0	2	1	1	1
KS2 + 3	56	0	0	0	0	0	0	0	0	0
KS3 + 4	53	1	1	0	1	0	0	0	0	0

that these averages are based on between 50 and 65 per cent of the total survey sample. However, they do show a considerable variation in this percentage across LEAs. In some LEAs, where the term MLD is less frequently used, this percentage is well below the sample average, as low as 8 per cent; in other LEAs where the term is widely used it is well above the average, as high as 73 per cent. This table does, however, show a trend away from special school for pupils with Statements for MLD. The sample average has decreased from 54 per cent in 2000–01, to 47 per cent in 2001–02, to 43 per cent in 2002–03. This indicator also shows considerable variation across LEAs. In some LEAs, no pupils with learning difficulties are issued with Statements for MLD; in other LEAs, 100 per cent of pupils with Statements for MLD are in special schools.

LEAs' assessments of these trends

Table 7.10 shows that more LEAs (46 per cent) believed that there had been a decrease over the last five years in the total number of pupils with Statements for MLD-like difficulties, than an increase (16 per cent) or no change

Table 7.9 Percentages of MLD pupils with Statements

	% of MLD pupils of all with Statements	% pupils with Statements for MLD in special schools
In 2000–01	Mean = 28% Range 11–28% N = 29	Mean = 54% Range 0–88% N = 25
In 2001–02	Mean = 28% Range 10–69 N = 31	Mean = 47% Range 0–92 N = 28
In 2002–03	Mean = 27% Range 8–73% N = 38	Mean = 43% Range 0–100% N = 38

Table 7.10 Trends in the LEA over the last five years

	Increase	No notable change	Decrease	Comments
Total number of pupils with Statements for MLD-like difficulties (n = 48)	9 16%	13 22%	26 46%	Cannot say (n = 2) Not available (n = 8) 18%
Total number of pupils with Statements for MLD-like difficulties in special schools (n = 45)	4 7%	12 21%	29 52%	Not available (n = 13) 23%
Total number of pupils with Statements for MLD-like difficulties in mainstream schools (n = 43)	18 31%	5 9%	20 36%	Increase in children with MLD but decrease in Statements; Cannot say (n = 2) Not available (n = 15) 27%

(22 per cent). This finding is inconsistent with the trend shown in Table 7.9, and can be used to discount that finding, because it is based on a larger proportion of the total sample. Analysis of the written comments on this decreasing trend shows that LEAs attribute it to increasing delegation of resources to schools and improving inclusive mainstream provision.

Table 7.10 also shows that over half the LEAs report a decrease in the percentage of pupils with Statements for MLD-like difficulties in special schools over the last five years. This is consistent with the decreasing trend shown in Table 7.9. However, this trend was not reported by 16 LEAs; 7 per cent reported an increase and 21 per cent no notable change.

Table 7.10 shows that a similar percentage of LEAs reporting an increase (31 per cent) or a decrease (36 per cent) in the proportion of pupils with Statements for MLD-like difficulties in mainstream schools. Only 9 per cent report no notable change. This indicates that despite the decreasing proportions in special schools, these pupils do not necessarily have Statements in the mainstream school. This was explained in the written comments linked to the question, that there was an increase in the number of children with learning difficulties in the mainstream, but they did not all have Statements.

LEA criteria for identifying MLD

Two-thirds of the sample LEAs reported that they issued specific criteria to identify pupils with MLD-like difficulties, while the rest did not. When asked how they issued and monitored the use of the criteria, more than half of the responding LEAs (59 per cent) referred to guidance documents for schools and professional use. Some LEAs also referred to having SEN statutory assessment panels which monitored the use of criteria (20 per cent), moderation panels, some of which were multi-professional (17 per cent) and the use of an SEN or additional educational need (AEN) audit (12 per cent). Fewer LEAs referred to an annual review system for monitoring, perhaps by a SEN assessment team or group of officers.

An example of LEA practice is reflected in the following account:

> General guidance is given in the LEA's SEN policy and procedures for the identification and assessment of pupils with SEN. 1. The pupils' general cognitive abilities fall within the range of the lowest 2 per cent, 2. Attainments in literacy and often numeracy will fall within the lowest 1 per cent, and 3. The pupils' difficulties are not linked to poor attendance. Scores are gathered through the Educational Psychology Service and LEA's SEN services, mainstream records, Education Support staff (teachers) visit schools on an allocation basis to advise on the application of criteria.

Changes and plans in organisation of SEN provision

LEAs outlined broad changes in their provision over the last five years in terms of several different dimensions. Fewer LEAs responded to this open-ended question than the previous questions. The responses will be summarised in broad terms. As regards changes in the Key Stages covered in their special schooling for pupils with MLD difficulties, most responding reported no changes, though some referred to a move to secondary KS3–4 provision. There were more references to this phase than were recorded in the details of their special schools. This indicates some inconsistency in their responses. Other LEAs referred to extending the early years provision, fewer primary MLD schools and more all-through schools (nursery to post-KS4). Most responding LEAs reported no change in the number of special schools, with fewer having closed or planning to close special schools. As regards changes in additionally resourced units or support centres in mainstream schools, most reported no change, though almost as many reported opening units. However, it was interesting that almost as many reported closing them down. LEAs reported a wide range of types of learning support in mainstream schools. Most reference was to the resource base for learning support, more delegation to mainstream schools. There were also several references to more schools buying in central advisory services. Other changes included: the flexible use of additional resources (not as a unit); smaller groups and programme differentiation; preventive and pro-active support; increased training; working through the National Strategies; outreach support special schools and a move from generic to specialist support services.

As regards links between MLD special schools and mainstream schools, a few reported no such links, and a couple referred to an increase in links. Most responding reported established links and almost as many were currently developing these links. When asked to comment on any other notable features of changes over the last five years, a similar picture emerged as from previous responses: a move away from Statements, special schools under review, more special school outreach, more delegated resources for mainstream schools (leading to fewer Statements) establishing special units and fewer pupils going to special schools

Half the LEA sample reported that future plans for pupils with MLD were set out in the LEAs' Educational Development Plan. Plans for changes in the phases of schooling were to reduce the number of special schools, have generic primary special schools and to review phases. There were plans to reduce the number of MLD special schools, the number of pupils in the MLD special schools, diversify the role of the special schools, for example develop outreach, and reorganise provision for pupils with MLD, by placing those with lesser degrees of MLD in mainstream, while placing the remaining pupils with MLD with those with SLD into newly designated special schools. Plans for additionally resourced units continued the pattern of recent changes: more general units, for some LEAs, while closing units to promote more inclusion, for others. The same was found for learning support plans: better training, more differentiation, smaller groups and more delegation to mainstream. As regards plans for links between mainstream and special schools, some plans continued past kinds of changes: special school outreach, re-organising special to match mainstream phases to enable better links and all special schools having mainstream links. Other plans were different: more two-way links, rebuild special school in mainstream setting, more dual placements and more comprehensive support services. When asked about other features of future plans, several approaches not raised before were reported: developing an inclusive network, more use of school self-review to raise attainments for the lowest 20 per cent of attainers (comparing attainments of pupils at School Action and School Action Plus to non-SEN pupils) and building inclusive schools to coincide with other school buildings programmes.

Summary and discussion of the findings

About a third of LEAs responded to the survey questionnaire, though it was higher for Welsh than English LEAs. This represented the range of the LEAs according to region and type of LEA found nationally. However, there were relatively few London LEAs and more county LEAs. This indicates that the overall findings might apply less in London than to the rest of the country. A large majority of responding LEAs reported using the term MLD, while many fewer did not, only seven LEAs. The alternative terms which they reported using instead were more general terms, such as, learning difficulty,

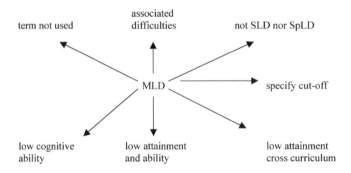

Figure 7.1 Concept map of themes in LEA definitions of the term MLD

complex learning difficulty or cognition and learning difficulty. The most common use of the term was to refer to an area of pupil difficulty, with fewer LEAs reporting its use to refer to a type of provision.

Analysis of the LEAs' definition of the term MLD showed a wide range of themes. These are summarised in the concept map in Figure 7.1. The key distinction is between LEAs that define MLD in terms of only low attainment across the curriculum and those LEAs that also refer to low cognitive ability. Some LEAs only referred to cognitive ability and not low curriculum attainment, but this could be implicit in how they reported their definition. Some of those referring to cognitive ability and/or low attainment also specified cut-offs for these. Some LEAs also referred to associated difficulties, though the list of these varied across LEAs. Some were also explicit that MLD was a differential term from severe learning difficulties, on one hand, and specific learning difficulties, on the other. A minority did not use the term at all.

From the analysis of LEA definitions, it is possible to identify three prototypes, kinds of definitions that represent the range found:

1   low attainments across the curriculum, cut-offs sometimes specified, and associated with other difficulties;
2   low attainment, with low cognitive ability levels, sometimes cut-offs specified, associated difficulties and distinct from severe and specific learning difficulties;
3   do not use the term, reject its value.

The second prototype represents a more traditional approach, where cognitive ability cut-offs are used and there is differential identification from other kinds of learning difficulties. The first prototype represents a rejection of cognitive ability in the definition, relying on a curriculum basis for identifying low attainment. It reflects the kind of definition presented in the first SEN Code of Practice in the early 1990s. What is interesting is that the current DfES definition of MLD goes beyond the first prototype in referring to 'difficulties in . . . understanding concepts' (DfES, 2003a, page 5), but does not refer to cognitive ability with its links to traditional IQ testing, nor does it specify a cut-off. There are two other major differences between the two prototypes arising from the LEA survey and the DfES definition. The DfES emphasises that MLD identification depends on additional provision being made. This reinforces the point that the difficulties exist despite interventions. It also states that the needs of pupils with MLD will not be met by the 'normal differentiation and the flexibilities of the National Curriculum'.

About half of the responding LEA officers reported that there was a general view in their LEA about the validity and usefulness of the term. However, about a quarter said they could not say and almost one in five said there was not. Taken with the comments which explained the general view, it was clear that there was a tension between the case for and against the value of the term. The positive points were that the MLD term provided a common reference point, useful for planning provision, for statistical purposes and as a starting point for assessing learning difficulties. These were countered with the negatives about its vagueness, its limited use in defining the specific presenting difficulties and teaching approaches to be used and its inconsistency with assumptions about a continuum of need.

The survey also showed these survey LEAs still retained MLD as the predominant designation for their special schools, with only a small minority of LEAs having some mixed difficulty designation. Similarly, most of these special schools were reported as all age, not phase-based as in mainstream schools. The majority of LEAs in the survey also did not report having units or resource centres at either primary or secondary phases designated for MLD pupils or general units which covered MLD. The MLD units were also more common than general units.

Data provided by the sample LEAs, though not by all of them, indicated that about a quarter of all pupils with Statements were in the MLD area. This did not appear to decrease over the last three years, which contradicted what officers reported elsewhere in the survey. Their reports of an overall decrease represented a larger proportion of the survey sample and cover a slightly longer period of time. The overall MLD proportion of all Statements was also lower than the figures quoted in the Audit Commission (2002b) Report for Scotland (33 per cent) and Wales (34 per cent). This difference was found for English and not Welsh LEAs. An average of 35 per cent of Statements in the MLD area were found for the Welsh LEAs in the survey, which corresponds to the Audit Commission figures. It was also found that the Welsh LEAs reported using a cognitive ability cut-off much more frequently than English LEAs in the sample (67 per cent compared to 18 per cent). This might account for their greater identification of MLD and the higher proportion of MLD pupils of their total number of pupils with Statements. As discussed above, this national average difference conceals a wide variation in this indicator within England and Wales. The data does, however, show a decrease from 2000 for three years overall in the proportion of pupils with Statements for MLD in special schools, by about 11 per cent. This downward trend is corroborated by officer reports later in the survey.

Though fewer LEAs provided an overview of recent changes in their provision for pupils with MLD, the overall picture was a mixed one. More LEAs reported no change in the phasing of special schools (for instance, from all age to primary/secondary) than reported such changes (for example, fewer primary MLD schools and more all age special schools). There were reports of units opening and units closing, with the flexible use of resources not in a unit. Other notable changes included greater delegation of resources to mainstream schools, schools buying in more central advisory services, more specialist support services, more preventive work, continuing professional development and greater special school outreach work. One area where there was a clear trend was the enhancement of the already developed systems of special–mainstream schools links. As regards future plans, these showed a continuation of these trends with no particular shift in focus or strategy.

In concluding this chapter it is important to note that the general picture that arose from the survey is based on a sample which was not representative of London LEAs. What was found from this sample, which represents the other regions, may not apply to London to the same degree. Not all the responding LEAs gave answers to all the questions, thus reducing the sample size for some questions. Nevertheless, this survey provides a unique perspective on how LEAs conceptualise learning difficulties that are described as MLD, their patterns of provision and recent and likely future developments.

Chapter 8

The future for children with MLD

As a special educational need or not?

The position so far

The main conclusions from the preceding chapters will be summarised in this final chapter. The overview of the relevant literature and the findings from the two studies are integrated into a position that can address whether there is a future for MLD as a category and area of special educational needs and provision. It will be clear as the chapter unfolds that this is not just a question of terms and labels, but one of considerable relevance to how the school system regards and responds to the variation in children's and young people's learning abilities and attainments. It has significance for how schools in general respond to those who have difficulties in learning, for the commitment to inclusion and for the funding and management of the overall system.

Categories, history and current issues

In the second chapter we addressed questions about the nature and existence of children with moderate learning difficulties, or whether they are a product or construction of the social and school system. This involved an examination of the current category of MLD and previous ones from an historical perspective. One of the features of the present system is the confusion over the term 'learning difficulties'. It is used to refer to all children with all kinds of special educational needs, as well as to refer to those with cognitive difficulties with varying degrees of severity. It was suggested that this ambiguity has enabled the system of SEN to avoid being built on a system of classifying kinds and degrees of intellectual difficulties. It did this by switching focus onto additional provision and away from the nature of the child's difficulties or disabilities. This provided a way of side-stepping the very contentious issues surrounding the measurement of cognitive abilities. The SEN system was advocated as having abandoned categories of child difficulties, but in fact continued them in more positively framed terms. The system that operates currently therefore continues this ambivalence towards categories.

The critique of categories has been influential in current Government formulations of the areas of SEN. In the latest version of the SEN Code of Practice the case is made against hard and fast categories and the emphasis is put on the child's unique circumstances and needs. Four dimensions of special educational needs are presented so that a child may have needs along more than one dimension. Categories are then referenced within these dimensions. We also show that there have been attempts to grapple with the complexity of the category of MLD itself in terms of a three-dimensional model which identifies variations in terms of (1) the severity of the learning difficulties, (2) the presence of sensory and motor difficulties and (3) the presence of emotional and behavioural difficulties. Although this approach deals with complexity, it does not deal with the definition of learning difficulties, whether in terms of curriculum attainments only or attainments and cognitive abilities. Nor does it address the specificity issues concerned with having specific operational criteria for identifying those having MLD.

We showed in Chapter 2 how the sample in our first study illustrates the degree of association between moderate learning difficulties and other areas of difficulties. We found that more children were recorded as having language and communication difficulties with MLD than having MLD alone. We also found that 52 per cent of those with MLD in special schools had two or three associated difficulties compared to only 20 per cent of those with MLD in mainstream schools. The high incidence of associated difficulties has also been documented in the literature going back to the classic Isle of Wight epidemiological study and the well-known National Child Development study as well as a recent study of who goes to MLD special schools. All this sets the scene for a critical discussion of the formal re-introduction of a SEN classification similar in many respects to the pre-Warnock system of educational handicap categories. Consultations about this classification resulted in many criticisms of the initial MLD definition as either unclear or inaccurate. The Government line was that this was one of the hardest areas to define. In response to criticisms that the MLD definition was too broad, the revised and final version, now in operation, was to introduce two limiting conditions. One was to specify more clearly that needs could not be met by normal differentiation and National Curriculum flexibilities, the other was to introduce a reference to greater difficulties than peers in understanding concepts. The first condition can be welcomed for referring to the general learning environment, but still lacks specificity about what counts as normal differentiation. The second condition is interesting in re-introducing the historic reference to limited intellectual abilities, without addressing the historic question of its operational specificity.

The UK system of SEN was then discussed in terms of the recent OECD study of international systems of classification. National classification systems can be analysed in terms of four basic patterns: (1) whether they use disability categories only, (2) whether they use disability categories and include disadvantaged students, (3) whether they use disability categories and include disadvantaged students and gifted children, and (4) whether they are based on needed provision in response to exceptionalities (not student characteristics). The UK SEN system was identified in 2000 as like the fourth pattern, being provision based and previously having no formal categories. It might now be more like pattern 1, based on disability categories. However, we question this because there is another important dimension not identified in the OECD scheme – how the classifications are used. The UK SEN system is committed in policy and practice to a focus on individual needs analysis, for example in individual educational plans and in Statements. Categories have been introduced for general monitoring and planning purposes. This is different from a system where categories of educationally relevant disabilities impact directly on individual educational needs analysis. However, there is a risk that the new classification may be transferred into the needs analysis system and so undermine the assessment and decision making which is supposed to be focused on the individual child in their educational context.

The OECD scheme also seems to make a clear-cut distinction between child characteristic-based classifications and provision-based classifications (patterns 1, 2 and 3 versus 4). If the UK system was meant to be an example of pattern 4 or a provision-based classification, analysis shows that this is not an either–or difference. Though SEN is defined in terms of additional or different provision, it cannot avoid saying who this provision is for. Some child characteristics have to be used. In the UK legislation, the broad reference is to those with learning difficulties, which is only defined in terms of difficulties not arising from English being an additional language. With the SEN classification, learning difficulties are now referenced against the new categories. However, the OECD scheme is useful in highlighting that the current UK SEN system does not include other areas of SEN covered in other countries, such as 'disadvantaged' and 'gifted' children. It does not go beyond the disability field and in that sense does not fulfil the potential of the SEN model. This is relevant to the criticisms of SEN in terms of inclusive education, where inclusion is said to be a broader notion relating to students who are at risk of exclusion or vulnerable. If the UK SEN system adopted the full meaning of the SEN model, this would be less associated with disability and be less different in principle from the coverage of inclusive education. The OECD scheme and its three-part category system, in terms of disability (category A), social-economic (category C) and uncertain causality (category B) are also useful in illustrating the variations between countries in their reported percentages of students with MLD difficulties. The international comparison also shows that many countries use the term 'mental', while some use the term 'intellectual', in referring to students with these kinds of difficulties. These terms are combined with terms like disabilities, retardation or handicap. No other country in this study has constructed a term that combines learning, on one hand, with difficulties, on the other, to make a term like MLD. Some countries refer to learning in conjunction with handicap or disability, but these are used for what are called specific learning difficulties in this country. The other interesting feature of the OECD study is that the three-part category system shows that the group of students with MLD difficulties were judged in some countries to be in the normatively agreed disability category A, while in other countries to be in causally uncertain category B.

Chapter 2 continued with a historical perspective that showed that the current issues about the MLD category have continued over many decades and can be identified in policy deliberations of over a century ago. The historical analysis of Copeland (2002) was drawn on to illustrate how the issues were formulated in that period and the role and influence of different professional advisors and Government commissions and committees. We discussed Copeland's point that the question of the 'feeble-minded' in the late nineteenth century could have been handled as part of deliberations about the general school or as akin to deliberations about special schooling for those with sensory impairments. By dealing with the question as akin to the latter system, the field came to be divided from general school issues. We also show in Chapter 2 that throughout the twentieth century, policy makers grappled with definitional matters, sometimes making distinctions and looking for criteria on which to ground these. For example, a distinction was made between the 'weak-minded' and the 'imbecile' on the supposed basis that the former 'could earn a living'. By 1913 it was officially acknowledged that there was no recognised standard for the various categories and considerable variation in local use. The survey reported in Chapter 7 shows the continuation of this problem in current LEA practices.

The historical perspective also showed that new terms come to be introduced to redefine and sometimes enlarge groups recognised as having difficulties in learning. For example, in the 1920s the Wood Committee introduced the term 'educable defectives' to distinguish between this and a group of 'ineducable defectives', with the former group coming to include not only those previously termed as being 'feeble-minded' but those termed 'dull' and 'backward'. This has similarities to the more recent move by the Warnock Report (1978) to replace the term ESN with the term learning difficulties and to qualify this with moderate and mild as a way of bringing in those seen as 'slow learners'. Historical analysis also shows that Government responses to the looseness of definitions can take the form of tightening up the identification and assessment procedures rather than the criteria. This has continued to the present, as shown in the orientation of the SEN Code of Practice to specify identification and assessment procedures rather than also deal directly with definitional uncertainty. The current uncertainty about the relationship between MLD and intellectual difficulties also has historical precedents. Government regulations in 1945, for example, defined ESN(M) in terms of low educational attainment, but educationalists identify that in practice the term came to be associated with low intellectual abilities.

Chapter 2 also addressed the historic question about the concept of intelligence and assumptions about its general, innate and testable characteristics. Various contemporary positions with their precursors in the early development of intelligence testing and theory were related to questions about identifying and assessing what we now call moderate learning difficulties. It is proposed that this history indicates that there is a social need for concepts and theories about intelligence and for practical means of assessment in school systems. Achieving general agreement about these concepts and techniques confronts social and political value commitments leading to contention and debate. General cognitive ability measures have no formal place in the current official UK SEN position. However, they continue to be used by LEAs in their SEN identification procedures for MLD, as the national survey in Chapter 7 indicated.

The category of SEN and specific categories like MLD have continued to draw criticism. In Chapter 2 we followed the position that treats all functional 'problems' as based on social norms, though there may be more consensus about norms for some 'problem' areas than others. There is more agreement when the 'problem' is more severe or different from the average, and when biological causes can be identified. The chapter focused specifically on Tomlinson's initial study of decision making about ESN(M), which treats the category as socially constructed rather than being an 'innate quality within the child'. Further analyses of the reported data and findings, on which she based her conclusions, showed that, despite some professional differences about concepts of the ESN(M) child, there were still significant agreements about the kinds of accounts used. Some of the differences between professional accounts could be attributed to expected professional differences of training and background. The similarities across professional groups were about functional learning and ability difficulties.

This discussion led to the question of whether categories like SEN and MLD had outlived their usefulness. Attention needs to be given to the persistent and now historic contradiction between the Warnock Report's abandonment of categories alongside recommendations for more positive-sounding categories, like MLD. We also exposed an overly environmental interpretation of the interactive model of special educational needs, a model which is supposed to involve the interaction of child and environmental processes and factors. In practice it makes sense to focus on environmental or systems change, as this is where change comes more easily, but this does not detract from the significance of child factors in understanding the causal origins of SEN. The term 'need' in SEN has also been subject to criticism for its paternalism and implications of professional control. A third challenge to the SEN concept has come from a management perspective, which emphasises planning, effectiveness and efficiency of resource use. The case for and against national categories was examined in terms of their validity, desirability and necessity. It was argued that there is a difference between the validity of categories in principle and their use in practice, which might be dealt with by more specific category systems, better training and moderation. In terms of necessity, it is not clear that those suggesting alternatives actually mean to abandon all categories in their resource allocation function for individual children and replace them by school level allocation systems. Increasing additional resource allocations at school level does not necessarily do away with individual allocation systems, like Statements; the category question does not go away, just the number of children covered is reduced.

Underlying the question of categories is the assertion that SEN and MLD are social constructions fabricated for social institutions by professionals to serve particular purposes and interests not always beneficial to those receiving the categorisations. Chapter 2 introduced an approach to the social construction of low intellectual functioning which does not deny the reality of this phenomenon or the possibility of examining it in systematic empirical ways. This approach denies a version of social constructionism that assumes that difficulties in learning come into existence through a process of social labelling and that a non-labelling approach is an option.

Chapter 2 concluded with an account of the features of an educational classification of SEN. To be relevant to education the classification has to be in curriculum and teaching terms; in terms of broad and balanced learning goals, access and adaptations in teaching methods and their context. It was argued that any adequate classification of this kind would be multi-dimensional as well as be in terms of the learning impact of additional or different educational provision. To justify a category such as MLD, it would be necessary to show that those categorised benefited more from this additional or different provision than those not categorised. Such provision has also to be specified in curriculum, teaching and learning context terms, as distinctive or specialised. It was also suggested that the different social identity conferred by the category may have been important in the continued use of the MLD category. The MLD identity differentiates from identities associated with other allied categories of difficulties in learning – those with more severe learning difficulties, those with specific learning difficulties and those with low general attainments. The social identity benefits would be for parents, in distancing their MLD children from those with SLD, and for teachers, in distancing MLD pupils as different from those with below average functioning. Identity in this sense is based on locating a group along continua of intellectual and social functioning as different from neighbouring groups in terms of functional rather than educational intervention terms. The continued use of the MLD category was also explained in terms of its role in compensatory resource allocation, as a group worthy of additional resources. Differential allocations, it was argued, require decisions about whether to identify a difference as resource-worthy or not, which involves hard decisions or dilemmas of difference. This introduced the dilemmatic theoretical perspective that has been used in the book to understand issues in the MLD field. These dilemmas arise from the tensions between positive and negative conceptions of difference; difference as inequality versus difference as individuality. The chapter concluded with an account of the different areas (identification, curriculum and location of provision) in which difference presents dilemmas. It is concluded that resolving dilemmas implies some negative implications and trading-off.

Curriculum, teaching and inclusion issues

The relative scarcity of research in this field was noted in Chapter 3. Key studies were reviewed, such as a national survey from the mid 1990s on who goes to MLD special schools, which indicated that one in four schools had been re-organised recently along primary and secondary lines. There was a predominance of boys to girls, in line with previous findings. However, there was no over-representation of children from minority ethnic backgrounds, a change from the position in the 1970s. Head teachers estimated that about one in twelve children would better placed elsewhere. The study was concluded with the argument that if special schools are appropriate for this group, then the intake would be defined in more generic terms than just MLD. The scarcity of research was also evident in the curriculum and teaching aspects of MLD provision. A couple of studies in the mid 1990s highlighted the tensions between commonality, as required by the National Curriculum framework of that period, and adaptations required for the pupils' learning difficulties. These two studies illustrated how the dilemmatic perspective helped in understanding the tensions in planning school curricula for pupils with MLD (and others) and the way in which the national curriculum changes in the mid 1990s moved away from tight common curriculum programmes towards greater flexibility of content and the timing of specific programmes with ages.

The latest version of the National Curriculum, with its inclusive commitment and the introduction of guidelines for the curriculum and teaching of those with learning difficulties in 2001, has eased these tensions even further. However, it was also noted that there is some uncertainty about how these guidelines apply to those with MLD, as their construction and relevance are clearer for those with severe and profound and multiple learning difficulties. There has therefore been no serious attempt to develop a curriculum and pedagogy for those identified as having MLD. This was the conclusion of a recent review of international literature. There was no evidence of a distinct or specialised pedagogy for those identified as having MLD, although there is some research which show some groups (for example those with Down Syndrome) have distinctive styles and approaches to learning. The concept of *continua of common pedagogic strategies* was introduced to distinguish between more commonly found adaptations for most pupils and less frequent and more specialised adaptations for those with learning difficulties. The key point is that specialisation of pedagogy is not one of kind, but one of degree along dimensions of intensity and explicitness. A recent review of a pedagogy for MLD, in terms of this framework of specialisation as intensification of common pedagogic strategies, calls the MLD category into question as it has no pedagogic significance.

Chapter 3 also dealt with questions and issues related to inclusion. It was argued that there is greater continuity and connection between the concepts of integration current in the 1980s and the more recent concept of inclusion. Integration has come to be represented as being about placement in mainstream schools and more about assimilation into schools than about schools accommodating pupils with SEN. However, proponents of integration did also focus on changing schools and represented integration as part of the development of community oriented comprehensive schools. The term inclusion came into current use through association with progressive political discourse in terms of social inclusion. However, social inclusion has its roots in 'third way' thinking as an alternative to traditional radical commitments to equality. It was noted in this chapter that it is interesting that those looking for a more radical educational term than integration looked to social inclusion. Where inclusion does go beyond integration is in applying to all those considered to be vulnerable, not just those with disabilities/SEN, and in putting a clearer focus on school change to accommodate disability. However, this moved the inclusion discourse to a level of greater generality, with looser links to operational reality. This is evident in the diverse understandings about what is involved in the commitment to inclusion. Current definitions in terms of participation, for example, do not specify what is meant by participation in local mainstream schools and this introduces significant uncertainty into the inclusion planning process.

Data collected from the LEA survey, reported in Chapter 7, indicated that for the 29 LEAs there had been a decrease in the number of pupils with MLD difficulties in special schools. This also confirmed that there has been a significant proportion of these pupils in mainstream schools over some period of time. These data for MLD correspond with national trends towards lower proportions of pupils in special schools over recent decades, as would be expected, as MLD represents the largest sub-group of all children identified as having SEN. Whether these trends will continue depends on continued planning along inclusive lines. But, as noted in Chapter 3, despite inclusive aspirations it has been hard to specify what makes a school inclusive. Lists of factors that make for inclusive schools can be criticised for their generality, their overlap with other school characteristics, such as school effectiveness, the relative lack of learner outcome studies and their contradiction with research and professional experience of the complexity, ambiguity and tensions in school life. The chapter illustrated these points with a discussion of a recent international literature review on actions to promote school inclusive policies and practices. On the basis of this analysis it is argued that questions of inclusion cannot avoid having to deal with the inter-connections between value, conceptual and empirical matters. At best, inclusion is useful as an 'orienting' term, one which draws attention to issues of belonging and participation in schooling. Beyond that other considerations are relevant – such as, the focus of inclusion and the connection between inclusion in different social sectors.

Assertions of rights as the basis for inclusion were also questioned. This is partly in terms of fundamental rights being to education and not an inclusive education, and partly in terms of the complexity and uncertainty introduced by multiple rights. These potential tensions arise from the fact that we hold multiple values in our society which lead to policy and practice dilemmas, especially in relation to learner differences; dilemmas of difference. The basic dilemma is about recognising differences or not, as either decision can have negative implications and risks – such as setting up lower status provision or not providing adequately for individual needs. This basic dilemma is evident in hard decisions about identification, curriculum design and locational and organisational aspects of provision and teaching programmes. The chapter then summarised and analysed research which illustrates how this dilemmatic perspective helps to understand the nature of inclusive practices. For example, case studies show how schools identified as inclusive encounter difficulties and tensions when the inclusive vision is translated into practice. These tensions can be understood to reflect the interaction of interest groups and power relations within schools, and between schools and external agencies. Other internal research also illustrates that professionals at different levels in the school system do recognise tensions over questions of identification, curriculum and location of provision. These professionals also suggested ways of resolving these dilemmas which tried to combine the values of meeting individual needs in inclusive ways, while trying to minimise the negative implications. The section concludes with a discussion of what is involved in resolving dilemmas; that something valuable might have to be given up and the ideological impurity acknowledged.

Questions about the efficacy and learning outcomes of inclusion with the MLD group were also discussed in Chapter 3. Research reviews indicate that no definitive conclusions can be drawn. Not only is there is a scarcity of quality research in this country about these questions and many research methodological difficulties, there are doubts in some quarters about the value of research in informing questions about inclusive practices. It is argued that these different positions relate to whether research is informed or not by an ideologically pluralist commitment. When it is not, then inclusive values are taken as predominant. In this sceptical position empirical generalisations about learner outcomes are not seen as impacting on this value commitment, but calling for action to remove learner outcome differences. As concluded in

Chapter 3, empirical facts are relevant to the weight given to the various value commitments relevant to decision making. US research over two decades indicates that there is no clear evidence showing better outcomes in separate settings for the MLD group. On the contrary, there is a slight advantage in outcome terms for those in mainstream settings, though placement is not the same as provision. Outcomes can differ according to the kind of programme in mainstream settings. Nevertheless, some of the recent US studies show the sophistication needed in examining model inclusion programmes. Examples of these models show the degree of structuring and adapting of teaching, including individual teaching in mainstream settings. Special education services were not eliminated, rather they were re-conceptualised and distributed. One study illustrated that even when special education resource teachers were required to teach in inclusive settings, more than half continued to use withdrawal services for some of the time.

Longer term outcomes of MLD provision in the post-school years is also an important area for consideration. Though there has been the view that many of those identified as having MLD can later blend into the adult community post-school, the circumstances have changed recently. Before the 1980s most of these students would have entered the labour market, but situation has changed with the growth of youth unemployment after the 1980s. Since then the proportion in open employment has decreased significantly according to several small-scale studies. As in evaluation studies of the impact of MLD provision during the school years, post-school follow-up studies are scarce. However, one small-scale study of transfer from special to mainstream provision suggested that students and their parents were more satisfied with transfer to a mainstream unit than to mainstream class provision. This differential satisfaction persisted in retrospective accounts of their experience in mainstream settings. This study also indicated a significant decline in open employment, despite all the efforts to include these young people before they leave school.

Pupil perspectives on provision, themselves, labels and 'bullying'

The next three chapters summarised key findings from the study of MLD pupils' perspectives and gave examples of these perspectives through direct quotes. Chapter 4 focused on perspectives on special provision in special and mainstream schools. As anticipated from the initial assumptions, the findings showed a notable degree of contrary evaluations. The majority expressed mainly positive evaluations of their present schools and teachers in mainstream and special schools, while a significant minority expressed mixed evaluations. Mainly negative evaluations were low or nonexistent. Pupils' perspectives on receiving help with their learning were consistent with their perceptions about waiting for help. Though most believed that they received enough help and did not have to wait for help, a quarter believed that they did not receive enough help, while a third felt that they had to wait for help with learning. A slightly lower proportion held mixed views about receiving enough help and having to wait for help. Pupils also reported receiving more help from teaching assistants than from their teachers, and more from these adults than from their peers. The central role of teaching assistants reinforces inspection and other observations about the critical role of assistants in the development of more inclusive schooling (Balshaw, 1999).

Mainstream pupils, few of whom had special school experiences, had mostly positive views about special schools. Mainly negative views were held by about one in five, with slightly more, about a quarter, holding mixed views. This was different for special school pupils, where the majority had had mainstream school experiences. For them, only about one in six had mainly positive views of mainstream schools, whereas about half had mixed views, with about a third having mainly negative views. This difference could be due to special school pupils' 'bad' experiences in the mainstream, and mainstream pupils' lack of experience of special schools.

Mainstream pupils reported receiving learning support mostly in withdrawal settings and in-class. Small group and individual support were also reported by more than half the sample. Their preferences were roughly similar across the three options of withdrawal, in-class and a mix. However, more reasons were given for preferring withdrawal than other forms. The quality of teaching, less distraction and less 'bullying' were notable reasons for withdrawal, as were the few references to missing opportunities through withdrawal. These findings are consistent with what has been found in other countries (Padeliadu and Zigmond, 1996). They indicate that taking account of the pupils' voice on learning support does not necessarily support a system which has abandoned withdrawal teaching. This underlies the distinction between inclusive schools and inclusive classrooms. If inclusive schooling and teaching is taken to mean full-time mainstream class placement, then this was inconsistent with many expressed preferences. This point could also be relevant to including special school pupils who have more severe and mixed difficulties into the mainstream. They might also be expected to prefer some learning support in withdrawal settings; perhaps even more so than already included mainstream pupils.

As shown in previous research (Lewis, 1995), most pupils (about three in five overall) preferred their current school to any other. However, only one of the 51 mainstream pupils preferred to go to a special school, while 18 of the 50 special school pupils preferred to go to a mainstream school. Many of those preferring the mainstream were secondary-age special school boys.

Another important finding was that perspectives on provision showed few differences between those in special and those in mainstream schools, boys and girls and older and younger pupils. However, one finding suggested that *mainstream boys* felt they were getting less *help in class* with their learning than those in special schools. Yet, they felt more positive about being in a mainstream school than mainstream girls. This differential evaluation of class and school by mainstream boys is interesting in the context of more *special school boys* preferring to be in the mainstream than special school girls. It could reflect boys being more sensitive and concerned about *where* they are at school than about their learning and teaching in class. Another finding was consistent with this interpretation when applied to secondary boys. Secondary boys in mainstream schools expressed more reluctance to accept the available forms of learning support (withdrawal and in-class support) than primary boys. This reluctance was consistent with another finding, that secondary pupils tended to deny or minimise their learning difficulties more than primary pupils.

Chapter 5 focused on pupils' perceptions of self and labels. It linked the findings to previous studies which indicated that children and young people with learning difficulties actively interpret and select from the views of others in forming their own self-perceptions. The reported study of self-perceptions went further than previous studies in using a more naturalistic approach to examining self-perceptions. Most of the pupils were aware of their learning difficulties and were able to express their feelings about these difficulties. The study confirmed previous studies that the educational self-perceptions of pupils identified as MLD were more positive in special than mainstream school settings. However, it showed the prevalence of mixed self-perceptions in both the educational and non-educational areas and this enabled a more fine-grained interpretation of the mainstream versus special school comparison. Those in special schools had mainly positive educational self-perceptions, while most in mainstream schools had mixed self-perceptions, not mainly negative self-perceptions. This could be interpreted as indicating that mainstream experiences and contact with pupils without MLD leads them to be more realistic about their educational abilities and challenges them to develop an educational identity which addresses their differences in positive ways. Tensions or dilemmas about difference have relevance to personal experiences about themselves too.

Chapter 5 also reported findings which indicated the sensitivity of pupils in both mainstream and special schools to the negative connotations associated with labels and terms applied to them. Perspectives to these labels also expressed the tensions experienced by these pupils over their learning difficulties. The pejorative terms, like 'thick' and 'stupid', were rejected, but some terms were more acceptable if they implied help and support for learning. The chapter reflected the individual ways in which these pupils balanced the positive and negative experiences associated with their learning difficulties.

Chapter 6 examined the social relationships and bullying of pupils identified as having MLD. Reference was made to historical US studies of peer interactions that go back over a quarter of a century, particularly in the allied area of specific learning difficulties. These have shown that children with learning difficulties are less well accepted and more frequently rejected by their classmates than those without learning difficulties. Similar conclusions have also been drawn from studies of children receiving learning support in mainstream class settings. However, despite these general tendencies, other studies show that children with learning difficulties can still manage to form and maintain some positive social relationships in inclusive settings. Like the findings about educational self-perceptions it is not an all-or-nothing situation. Peer relationships can take several forms (for example, best friend, regular friend or guest) and those with learning difficulties, as for those without learning difficulties, can experience a mix of these forms. Fine-grained interpretations and concepts are needed to make sense of these aspects of personal development, relationships and experiences. Factors that can impact on peer relationships involve the child's repertoire of social skills, the social ecology that supports or inhibits social relationships, adult interventions and peer skills and support for positive interactions.

Understanding the lower social acceptability of pupils with MLD in inclusive settings has been attributed to how the MLD children handle interpersonal demands and situations, in particular their need for help, being victims of bullying and being less cooperative. It has not been attributed to behavioural disruptiveness or aggression. Name-calling is a phenomenon which emerged as central to the perspective study reported in Chapters 4, 5 and 6. However, though studies report the hurtful nature of name-calling experiences, the object of name-calling had not been learning difficulties. Studies also show that those with learning difficulties, including those with MLD, are susceptible to more bullying than those without learning difficulties. This has also been shown in schools with units for MLD where children with learning difficulties spend significant periods of time in inclusive settings.

The pupil perspectives study confirmed and extended the findings from these previous studies by examining perceptions of the kinds of bullying experienced, feelings about bullying, the targets and sources of bullying across mainstream and special schools. Overall levels and kinds of bullying were not different across mainstream and special school settings. Much of the reported bullying was aimed at these children's learning difficulties or the learning support available to them. Bullying was attributed to pupils in their own school, with some differences between mainstream and special school pupils depending on gender. Bullying was also attributed to children from other mainstream schools and to others in their neighbourhood. This is where special school pupils attributed consistently more bullying to these sources than mainstream pupils. The feelings expressed about their bullying experiences were mostly a mixture of negative and neutral responses. These experiences were reported to lead to self-doubt, with implications for self-perceptions, withdrawing, or retaliating by name-calling or lashing out. Although we have not reported specific evidence of school differences in the incidence of bullying, there was data indicating that schools in the study did differ in their ethos and commitment to accepting differences and their toleration of bullying related to learning difficulties. School policies and practices with regard to bullying were an issue for both mainstream and special schools.

These findings can be interpreted as supportive, on balance, of the move towards greater mainstream school inclusion for those pupils identified as having MLD in special schools. The conclusion is on balance (there are some contrary indications) as would be expected from the dilemmatic perspective. The findings show a clear preference by a significant number of the special school pupils, though not all, for mainstream school. Those in mainstream schools perceive that they receive as much support as those in special schools and the benefits of more help from their peers and friends than their counterparts in special schools. Mainstream pupils did not report more in-school bullying overall than special school pupils and significantly less bullying than special school pupils from other mainstream school pupils or from neighbours and outsiders. In drawing these conclusions from this study, we need to be aware that those in the special school sample had more severe and multiple needs and that perceptions of support may not correspond with the actual provision of support.

LEA policies and practices for children designated as MLD

Chapter 7 sets out the findings and conclusions from a national survey of a fairly representative sample of about a third of English and Welsh LEAs. With the exception of seven of the 58 responding LEAs, all used the term MLD, though more as a pupil difficulty than as a type of educational provision. LEAs tended to take up Government concepts and definitions in this area, but as there has been variation in the Government's position over the years, so LEAs have selected those aspects which suit their own policy positions. LEA definitions of MLD can be separated into those which refer to low functioning in curriculum attainment terms only and those that refer to low functioning in attainment but also cognitive ability terms. Some, but not all, LEAs also refer to operational cut-offs for low functioning, for both attainment and cognitive abilities. Others include in their definition that MLD is distinct from severe learning difficulties and specific learning difficulties. Many also refer to associated areas of difficulties, while a minority do not use the term at all. From this analysis three prototypes were inferred:

1   low attainments across the cut-offs sometimes specified, and associated with other difficulties;

2   low attainment, with low cognitive ability levels, sometimes cut-offs
    specified, associated difficulties and distinct from severe and specific
    learning difficulties;
3   do not use the term, reject its value.

The second prototype resembles the traditional and current medical style
definitions of mild mental retardation and will be discussed further in the
next section. The first prototype follows recent Government positions as set
out in Codes of Practice. However, as pointed out in Chapter 7, LEAs have
not incorporated two key aspects of the current DfES classification of MLD.
One is the reference to 'difficulties in understanding concepts'; the other is
that identification of MLD depends on the normal differentiations and flexibilities of provision having been made.

   Though half of the LEAs in the survey reported that there was a general
view about the value of the MLD term in their policy and practices, this view
was one which reflected tensions between the positive and negative aspects of
the term. The predominant view seemed to be that the positive aspects
of having a common reference point for planning were countered by the
term's vagueness, its inconsistency with the continuum concept and its
limited value in informing teaching practices. Despite these uncertainties,
LEAs reported that MLD continued as the main designation for special
schools, with few special schools having some other designation, such as
'mixed difficulties'. There is clear evidence indicating the trend towards the
greater inclusion of children with MLD-like difficulties in mainstream
schools – a reduction in numbers and percentages of children with Statements for MLD in special schools over the last five years. However, based on
responses from 38 LEAs, about two in five children with Statements for
MLD are on average still in special schools, though there are enormous
variations between LEAs. The survey also confirms that MLD represents the
largest area of SEN, but more so for Welsh than English LEAs. This might
reflect different MLD identification practices, with Welsh LEAs using cognitive ability cut-offs more than English LEAs.

   Despite the trend away from special school provision, the evidence indicates that when these pupils receive provision in mainstream schools, they do
not necessarily do so with a Statement of SEN – where LEAs had data to
respond, slightly more LEAs reported a decrease in the numbers with Statements for MLD in mainstream schools. This reflects the recent moves to provide additional provision for those with SEN in mainstream schools without
Statements. These trends were corroborated by reports of recent changes in
policy and practice, and plans for continuing changes in the near future by
these LEAs. LEAs reported greater delegation of additional resources to
mainstream schools and greater trends towards special school–mainstream
school links, including more outreach services from special schools. Mainstream units were reported to be opening and closing in different LEAs, with

those closing in order to have more flexible use of additional resources across the mainstream schools. Some LEAs reported reviews of the future of special schools, including those for MLD, rebuilding programmes to locate special schools in mainstream school sites and school reviews to raise attainments for the lowest 20 per cent of attainers. All these developments were in response to inclusive policy commitments, but as we discuss in the next section they do not grapple with basic question of whether there is a future for the MLD category in a more inclusive era.

The end of a category?

The policy and practice survey shows that LEAs follow broadly the Government lead on the concepts they use and the development of special educational provision in this area. There is no evidence of LEAs questioning whether MLD is an area of SEN in the sense in which we now identify special educational needs and disabilities. The Government Department for Education and Skills (DfES) similarly has continued the practices, though in different terms, which were started over a hundred years ago as outlined in Chapter 2. The commitment to inclusive values in the landmark Warnock Report (1978) and in the more recent Green Paper on SEN (DfEE, 1997) and SEN Action Programme (1998) did not lead to any questioning of whether the largest sub-group of pupils identified as having SEN should continue to be identified in this way. There has been an historical unease about this area, a kind of border region between 'disordered' and 'not disordered'.

Inclusion has many dimensions (locational, social and curriculum participation), including a terminological dimension. The current official position, expressed clearly in the Warnock Report, is that there is an underlying continuum of learning and attainment where no clear-cut distinction can be made between those with and those without difficulties in learning. Yet the official position is then to use the MLD category, which identifies a minority as different from those without MLD. Categories can be seen as a form of terminological exclusion. This tension between continua and categories reflects the dilemma of difference over the question of MLD identification: do we identify MLD as an area of SEN or do we not identify? That is the question. As explained in previous chapters, the tension is between providing appropriate and individually relevant provision without stigma and devaluation. This is the tension between commonality and differentiation, calling for a balance between the values of inclusion and of individuality. With reference to the largest sub-group of SEN, do we continue to identify those with significantly low attainments within the SEN system? Is MLD more like low attainment or is it more like disability? It is important to be clear that these basic questions are not about whether to have Statements for MLD or not. This is a question about the meaning of the terms SEN and MLD, as shown by DfES classification (DfES, 2003a), where categories are used for pupils with Statements as well as those receiving additional provision through individual educational plans at the School Action Plus stage of identification.

These kinds of questions could be asked of other areas of SEN, especially of emotional and behaviour difficulties, an area which co-occurs with MLD, as discussed in Chapter 2. They will not be addressed in this book for the pragmatic reason that the main focus of the book is MLD. As these questions for MLD arise from addressing a dilemma to which there is no clear-cut solution, we will examine three options for resolving the dilemma about MLD identification:

1   retain and specify MLD category as an area of SEN;
2   abandon MLD as a SEN category: provide in terms of a social inclusion framework;
3   abandon MLD for the majority, redefine a new, tighter category of mild mixed difficulties for the minority.

I Retain and specify MLD category as an area of SEN

In this option greater weight is given to the values of differentiation and to the need for adapted and protected provision. This is the option which has been in operation internationally in one form or another for over a century with the development of mass democratic systems of schooling. It has associations with medical classifications in assuming that MLD or its terminological equivalent is more like a disability than a variation of the range of 'normal' or typical learning and attainments. However, MLD is represented as a mild disability, as can be seen in the classification of the American Psychiatric Association's *Diagnostic and Statistical Manual* (DSMIV) (APA, 2000). The language in this medical classification is about 'mental retardation', which is presented as a 'disorder' with four degrees of severity: 'This disorder is characterised by significantly sub-average intellectual functioning (approximately IQ 70 or below) with onset below 18 years and concurrent deficits/impairments in adaptive functioning' (APA, 2000, page 347).

What DSMIV classifies as 'mild mental retardation' (MMR) corresponds to some interpretations of MLD in UK terms, as this is where IQ levels are between 50/55 and 70. What characterises this classification is greater specificity and consideration of operational and background aspects of the category. Some detail is provided about the three core criteria: IQ below 70, adaptive functioning and onset before 18 years of age. The known error in IQ tests is recognised as +/− 5 IQ points on the Wechsler scales and this needs to be taken into account. Deficits in adaptive functioning have to be in at least two of eight specified areas (for example, communication, self-care, home living, work, etc.) and have to be assessed in relation to the person's age and own cultural group. The DSMIV definition is similar to the American Association of Mental Retardation's (AAMR, 2002) definition except in terms of severity levels. The AAMR distinguishes between 'pattern and intensity of supports needed' as 'intermittent', 'limited', 'extensive' and 'pervasive'. This is a definition which focuses on both person characteristics and required provision, which has similarities to the OECD (2000) orientation. The DSM background information is also interesting in reporting that 30–40 per cent of individuals identified with MR are seen as having no clear causation, with this applying mostly to those with mild MR (MMR). This is in the context of MMR reported as making up some 85 per cent of all mental retardation.

Though there are differences between these medical-style definitions and an educational definition, such as the recent DFES (2003a) version, there are some similarities that have implications for this option of retaining a MLD category. Despite the educational definition of MLD not referring to cognitive abilities, it is interesting that many LEAs continue to use some cognitive ability cut-off to define MLD (see Chapter 7). Though the DfES definition is mainly in curriculum attainment terms, it does also make reference to 'much greater difficulty than peers . . . in understanding concepts'. One of the differences between a medical and an educational definition is that the medical one is in more general terms and relates to different areas of social functioning. This is evident in the medical reference to areas of adaptive functioning, one of which is schooling. An educational definition has more specificity and this distances the relevance of medical definitions for school contexts and use.

As mentioned in Chapter 2, the DfES acknowledged that MLD was the most difficult of the SEN areas to define. It was the category which in consultation elicited the most critical comment: unclear, inaccurate and too broad. In this option, which considers MLD more like a disability than a variation of educational learning and attainments, MLD will be seen as a milder version of more severe intellectual impairment. This gives a central place to intellectual or cognitive functioning in the definition, like the DSM and AAMR definitions. The equivalent of the adaptive functioning criteria in an educational definition is the school-level attainments. This implies that the definition would include intellectual and educational attainment level criteria. From this perspective, it is clear that the recent DfES definition of MLD does not go far enough in giving equal significance to these criteria, nor does it set out how operational cut-offs will be used. This lack of specificity applies to both the educational attainment and to the cognitive ability criteria. Problems of validity about using test score cut-offs apply as much to educational attainment as to cognitive ability levels. Some of these issues were discussed in Chapter 2, and it is clear from the LEA survey (Chapter 7) that the unease about the MLD category is associated partly with the lack of specificity in national identification guidelines.

In this option, it would be conceded that there would be some error in the practical identification of children in terms of a set of criteria, however specific their formulation. The error can be reduced to a minimum in various ways. One would be to set out specifications for the quality of assessment procedures and test use. Part of this strategy would be to take account of the known error in test measurement (as in the DSM definition). Tests would have to be designed to represent and be relevant to all sections of the child population (taking account of ethnicity, class, gender and disability). Another aspect of strategy might be to require the use of qualitative and more interactive and dynamic forms of assessing cognitive abilities than the simple use of IQ test cut-offs. Another approach would be that MLD identification required evidence of additional educational provision having been tried without success (as in the DfES 2003a definition). However, to make this approach meaningful it would be necessary to specify what kinds of additional provision would be relevant. The question of specificity is relevant both to child and environment assessment criteria. Reducing error in these ways would require a considerable investment in research and development work, much more than in the past. In this option, some assessment error would be acceptable as MLD identification gives access to additional educational resources. These resources could be allocated to mainstream schools and applied in as inclusive a way as possible: more differentiated teaching programmes, smaller class sizes, etc. Individual identification does not necessarily imply a predominant focus on individual teaching. The individual educational needs can be met through a range of approaches, school-wide, class and group level as well as individualised. The purpose of individual identification is to give added and protected attention relevant to individual needs.

2 Abandon MLD as a SEN category: provide in terms of a social inclusion framework

This option represents a rejection of even the sophisticated version of the first option, outlined above. In approaching the identification dilemma it gives greater weight to avoiding the negative aspects of differentiated provision – the reduced opportunities and stigmatised teaching programmes, whether in special schools, special units/classes or significant withdrawal from mainstream classes. In this option MLD is considered to be less like a disability or impairment and more like a variation of 'normal' learning and attainment. This option picks up the traditional association between MLD and its various terminological equivalents and disadvantaged family and social backgrounds (Clarke and Clarke, 1974). The case for this interpretation is based on the relatively late identification of children, mostly until they have started at school, and the strong overlap in the social and personal characteristics of children with MLD and those with low attainments not identified as having SEN. Johnson (1998), in a North American context, has argued along these lines that it is difficult to distinguish between students with mild mental retardation (MLD), learning disabilities (SpLD) and behaviour disorders using current US definitions. She therefore uses the more generic term 'mild educational disabilities' to refer to these areas of difficulties in learning. Her position is that the issue is one of 'dysfunction versus disadvantage'; a choice which has practice implications.

However, this dichotomy can be taken to pose an overly simple individual deficit model versus a simple social/environment model. This could be seen as the distinction between the first two options, which are being examined in this final chapter. The individual deficit model does not necessarily ignore the significant environmental causation of learning difficulties, nor does it necessarily assume that appropriate interventions are 'treatments' aimed at remediation. However, it often does limit the focus of interventions to schools as this is the main focus of the SEN system of identification and provision. The case for the disadvantage position is rather that it merges the MLD (and other mild educational disabilities) with the wider group of children and young people who are *at risk of educational failure*. In the North American context, this broader group is referred to as 'at risk students' (Johnson, 1998), while in this country it is referred to within the social inclusion framework as those 'at risk of social exclusion' (DfEE, 1999). Johnson's model of risk factors and risk outcomes is causally interactive. Risk factors are characteristics of the students and their circumstances that 'predispose students to experiencing negative outcomes' (Johnson, 1998, page 224), with negative risk outcomes covering academic, social and personal failure. Her case for merging the mild educational disabilities group, and therefore the US MMR group or the UK-based MLD group into the wider at risk group is that the student-based risk factors are very similar to cognitive and behavioural characteristics of these disability-based groups. The benefit of the merger is that because the at risk framework also includes a range of environmental at risk factors (class, school, local neighbourhood, family, societal, etc.), the intervention focus is less limited and joins up with interventions outside schools.

In this option interventions for those currently identified as having MLD would become part of a framework conceptualised in terms of being at risk of educational failure or educational underachievement. Intervention in schools would be linked to preventive efforts that are interdisciplinary and more comprehensive. In the UK Dyson (2002), arguing along similar lines, has focused his criticism of the SEN concept and system for the disadvantaged group – not the 'disabled' group – in terms of its highly individual focus, which he contends deflects schools from addressing whole school issues. Dyson's position rests on a broadly based three-way distinction between disabled, disadvantaged and contended disabled groups within the SEN system, which resembles the OECD (2000) three-way distinction, discussed in Chapter 2.

Within the UK social policy context, Dyson argues that recent social inclusion policies (for example SureStart, Additional Literacy Strategy, vocational strand in Key Stage 4 curriculum, etc.), despite some of their weaknesses, have some promising features. First, they are pre-designed and focused on groups, while enabling some individualisation within their delivery. Second, they have a focus beyond the individual child and address 'whole school, inter-school or family and community issues' (Dyson, 2002, page 14). The similarities of this position with the North American model discussed above are evident. However, Dyson's criticism of the individualisation of the SEN system is over-done in seeming to over-dichotomise the difference between school-based interventions within the SEN system compared to interventions within a social inclusion framework. The SEN system is primarily an individualised and protected identification, planning and review system. In practice the provision decisions fit children into pre-existing programmes, with some adaptations, whether in special or mainstream schools. The individualisation is not mainly about 'inventing responses to children's difficulties on a case-by-case basis', as Dyson suggests (page 14). The individualisation, which is a process, does mark out the identified children from other children who might also be seen as at risk. However, those at risk who are not identified as having SEN or disability, for example those for whom English is an additional language (EAL) or those who receive the additional literacy strategy, also need to be identified in some way. There cannot be additional provision, whether in the SEN framework or a social inclusion one, without some individual identification system. There is a difference between schemes which identify individuals and either allocate additional provision to those individuals or to the system serving these individuals. As Table 8.1 shows, these can be found within the SEN and non-SEN additional provision frameworks.

As these examples show, it is not possible to represent the SEN framework as individualising provision and the social inclusion additional provision framework as targeted at groups or systems. One of the key differences is

Table 8.1 Allocations to individuals and systems within SEN and non-SEN additional provision frameworks: some examples

	SEN framework	*Non-SEN additional provision framework*
Allocate to individuals	Statutory assessment of individuals to decide about issuing Statements of SEN for additional resource allocation	Identify children to receive Additional Literacy Strategy provision
Allocate to systems	Formula funding of schools based on free school meal or attainment test cut-offs for School Action/School Action Plus provision	Excellence in Cities programme; Educational Action Zones programme

that individual allocation within the SEN framework (Statements) is more protracted, complex and visible, which arises from the legally backed 'contract' basis of provision to meet significant SENs. It is notable that the national move towards reducing the number of Statements (Audit Commission, 2002a) involves providing additional provision at School Action and School Action Plus stages, with individualisation being through individual educational plans and not Statements. So, there has been a move away from individual allocations even within the SEN framework.

This brings us back to the point that what characterises the SEN framework is not the systems of identification and allocation of additional provision, but what counts as a special educational need. Is SEN about additional provision that goes beyond disability to include those who are at risk, as in the OECD position (OECD, 2000), or is it about disability and impairment, as implied but not clearly stated, in the UK educational legislation and framework? If SEN is about disability in education (cf. the new SEN classification, EAL excluded as a SEN, etc.), then it is critical that the boundaries of SEN along the continuum of pupil achievements and learning difficulties are clearly defined. As Dyson (2002) argues, all those children whose difficulties can be addressed by a less cumbersome system should be removed from the SEN framework. Only those with significant disabilities, a much smaller percentage than the 3 per cent with Statements, should come within the SEN framework. In relation to the second option for the future of MLD, this means that MLD would cease to be a SEN category and not count as an educational disability. The arguments for this (arbitrary and uncertain cut-off, delayed school-based identification, overlap with other difficulties, similarities to those at risk not identified as MLD) imply that the boundaries of SEN will need to be more clearly defined. This would require more specific criteria for the two allied areas of learning difficulties – severe learning difficulties and specific learning difficulties – from which MLD has been differentiated.

Abandoning the MLD category and delineating the area of SEN as educational disability would imply a clearer demarcation between provision for disability and for disadvantage. However, that is not to dichotomise disability and disadvantage; a child can have a disability and experience disadvantage. The demarcation would enable an enhanced relationship between additional provision within the SEN framework and the social inclusion one. This might be achieved by continuing the process of reducing the number of levels of identification in the SEN Code of Practice from 4 (1, 2, 3 and 5 in first Code) to 3 (School Action, School Action plus and Statement in current Code) to 2 (School Action Plus and Statement). The reduction in levels from 4 to 3 has resulted in a step size reduction in the percentage of identified SEN children. This reduction could be continued in a further reduction from 3 to 2 levels.

Croll and Moses (2003), in comparing two national surveys of how teachers identify children as having SEN in primary schools, have found a notable increase in the percentage of identification: from 18.8 per cent in 1981 to 26.1 per cent in 1998. They found that learning difficulties (including general and specific versions) was by far the largest sub-group, with obvious overlaps with other areas of need, such as those related to emotional and behaviour difficulties. The learning difficulties group was also the one which showed the largest increase over this period. Head teachers attributed these increases to changes in pupil characteristics, associated with social changes in the neighbourhoods, and to changed procedures for identification. At least some of the increased identification could be attributed on this basis to the introduction of the Code of Practice system of identifying those with SEN without Statements. This would provide some justification for moving children from the SEN School Action level to additional provision not designated as involving SEN, that is educational disability (see Figure 8.1). This would require a tighter and more restrictive set of definitions of when schools were to identify children as having SEN at School Action Plus level. However, MLD would not be one of the areas of SEN in this option. In terms of the recent DfES SEN classification, which applies to pupils with Statements and School Action Plus only, there would be no MLD area.

One of the arguments against this option is that to abandon MLD as a SEN area would be to give up the legal protections afforded by the SEN framework (the question of the future of the system of additional provision through Statements, important as it it is, will not be discussed in this book). This has been argued in terms of the move away from Statements to additional provision at School Action levels in the current Code (Marsh, 2003). It applies as well to additional provision under a social inclusion framework. This is partly a question of the intensive assessment and identification

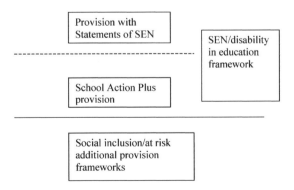

Figure 8.1 Delineation of SEN and social inclusion frameworks for additional provision

procedures within the SEN framework and partly about the additional provision that is person-led. There are several ways in which the school system can be enhanced to satisfy these conditions. One would be a commitment, with procedures at every level in the system (including legislation), to a more individualised or person-led system of needs identification and planning for all, not just those with SEN and those at risk of social exclusion. The other would be a greater commitment and investment in developing and reviewing differentiated and flexible teaching and learning programmes that were geared to individual need or diversity, including SEN and at risk pupils. There is a gap in current policy and practice about what counts as the flexibilities of 'normal differentiation' in relation to additional provision within the social inclusion and the SEN frameworks. Another argument against abandoning MLD in its entirety is that the MLD group is a very diverse one in terms of levels of low academic attainments/intellectual functioning and associated difficulties (cf. Crowther *et al.*, 1998 system of defining MLD discussed in Chapter 2). This leads on to third option for the future of MLD.

3 Abandon MLD for the majority, redefine a new, tighter category of mild mixed difficulties for the minority

This option adopts elements of the two above options. For pupils designated as having MLD with higher attainments/cognitive functioning and fewer associated difficulties, most of whom are currently in mainstream schools (see Table 2.2, page 14), they would cease to be identified as having SEN, as in option 2 above. For those designated as MLD with lower attainments/ cognitive functioning and more associated difficulties, many of whom are currently in special schools, they would be identified in terms of a specifically defined SEN area which could be called 'mild mixed difficulties' or its equivalent. Cognitive/intellectual functioning would not be a defining criterion of this new area, the defining characteristics would be low curriculum attainments associated with several other difficulties, such as sensory/ perceptual, motor, language/communication, behavioural and including cognitive/intellectual difficulties. This area would be distinct from severe learning difficulties in terms of the level of attainment and cognitive functioning. If this new SEN area is a viable educational disability category, it would be because of the impact of the non-cognitive areas of difficulties, such as the sensory/perceptual, motor and behavioural ones in interaction. This possible area of SEN might, for example, also include some children whose difficulties cannot be identified within one of the specific learning difficulties (such as dyslexia, dyspraxia) because of other associated difficulties (for example, attentional, behavioural, communication difficulties).

The viability of this option would depend on research-based evidence about the co-occurrence of difficulties in children currently identified as having MLD and children participating in social inclusion programmes. Data from epidemiological studies of whole child populations exists which can be used to undertake these cluster analyses of child level attainment, cognitive, sensory, motor, language, communication and behavioural characteristics. This type of research could also indicate how many co-occurring difficulties would define the area. Further research and development would be needed to inform decision not only about this third option but about the other two options too.

Concluding comments

Though the focus of this book has been the area of MLD, it is clear that it is not possible to deal with MLD, despite it being the largest area of SEN, without grappling with wider and more basic issues in the field of educating children and young people with disabilities and difficulties. The pervasive theme in the position taken in this book has been the presence of dilemmas of difference. This has linked the analyses across the range of issues and questions addressed in this book. It has also focused the discussion in this final chapter onto the question of identification. Real as opposed to false dilemmas call for resolutions, not definitive solutions; they require balancing tensions, accepting less than ideal ways forward and working positively with uncertainties and complexities. One of the aims of this book has been to illustrate how these general ideas apply in the particular circumstances of an important and much neglected area of SEN, that of moderate learning difficulties. We have discussed how far inclusion has gone in the MLD area, how schools and LEAs have proceeded and what their general plans are. But we have not examined how far inclusion will go for this group, partly because this involves wider policy questions about schooling and partly because we have ended with an analysis and set of options for the future of this group. Some of these wider policy issues have been discussed in Norwich (2002b).

We have picked up historical critiques of the MLD field and category and carried them forward into the current changing policy circumstances. Though the question of whether there is a future for MLD has not been answered definitively, it is clear that something has to change at a basic level. The Audit Commission (2002b), as an agency independent of the Government Department for Education and Skills, has called for a basic review of the SEN system. What change might look like for this contentious area of SEN has been sketched out in this final chapter. It is hoped that this book highlights many of the issues in this area of education, makes a contribution to wider debate about policy and practice in the SEN field and helps to define its relationships with wider issues about additional provision for those at risk of social exclusion within and outside the school system.

References

Ainscow, M. (1997) Towards inclusive schooling. *British Journal of Special Education*, 24 (1), 3–6.

Ainscow, M. (1999) *Understanding the development of inclusive schools*. London: Falmer Press.

Ainscow, M. and Tweddle, D. (1978) *Preventing classroom failure: an objectives approach.* Chichester: Wiley.

Ainscow, M., Howes, A., Farrell, P. and Frankham, J. (2003) Making sense of the development of inclusive practices. *European Journal of Special Needs Education*, 18 (2), 227–242.

Allan, J. (1999) *Segregation and educational reform*. Unpublished paper.

AAMR (American Association for Mental Retardation) (2002) Definition of mental retardation. AAMR website: *www.aamr.org*

APA (American Psychological Association) (2000) *Diagnostic and statistical manual* (4th ed.) Text review. Washington: American Psychiatric Association.

Armstrong, D., Galloway, D. and Tomlinson, S. (1993) Assessing special educational needs: the child's contribution. *British Educational Research Journal*, 19 (2), 121–131.

Audit Commission/HMI (1992) *Getting in on the Act: provision for children with special needs – the national picture*. London: HMSO.

Audit Commission (2002a) *Statutory assessment and statements of SEN: in need of review?* London: Audit Commission.

Audit Commission (2002b) *Special educational needs: a mainstream issue*. London: Audit Commission.

Avramidis, E. and Norwich, B. (2002) Teachers' attitudes towards integration/inclusion: a review of the literature. *European Journal of Special Needs Education*, 17 (2), 129–147.

Bailey, J. (1998) Australia: inclusion through categorisation, in T. Booth and M. Ainscow (eds) *From them to us: an international study of inclusion in education*. London: Routledge.

Balshaw, M. (1999) *Help in the classroom*. (2nd ed.) London: David Fulton.

Barton, L. and Tomlinson, S. (1984) *Special education and social interests*. London: Croom Helm.

Bear, G.G., Clever, A. and Proctor, W.A. (1991) Self-perceptions of non-handicapped children and children with learning disabilities in integrated classes. *Journal of Special Education*, 23 (4), 409–426.

Bear, G.G., Minke, K.M. and Manning, M.A. (2002) Self-concept of students with learning disabilities: a meta-analysis. *School Psychology Review*, 31 (3), 405–427.

Begley, A. (2000) The educational self-perceptions of children with Down Syndrome, in A. Lewis and G. Lindsay (eds) (2000) *Researching children's perspectives*. Buckingham: Open University Press.

Berlin, I. (1990) *The crooked timber of humanity*. London: Fontana Press.

Best, R. (2002) *Pastoral care and personal and social education: a review undertaken for the BERA*. Southwell: BERA.

Billig, M., Conder, S., Edwards, D., Gane, M., Middleton, D. and Radley, A. (1988) *Ideological dilemmas: a social psychology of everyday thinking*. London: Sage.

Blumer, H. (1969) *Symbolic interactionism: perspective and method*. Englewood Cliffs: Prentice-Hall.

Booth, T. (1996a) A perspective on inclusion from England. *Cambridge Journal of Education*, 26 (1), 87–99.

Booth, T. (1996b) Changing views about research on integration: the inclusion of students with special needs or participation for all ? in A. Stigson, P. Curran, A. Labran and S. Wolfendale (eds) *Psychology in practice with young people, families and schools*. London: David Fulton Publishers.

Booth, T., Ainscow, M., Black-Hawkins, K., Vaughn, M. and Shaw, L. (2000) *Index for inclusion: developing learning and participation in schools*. Bristol: CSIE.

Brennan, W.K. (1979) *Curricular needs for slow learners*. London: Methuen Educational.

Brennan, W.K. (1985) *Curriculum for special needs*. Milton Keynes: Open University Press.

Bryan, T. (1974) Peer popularity of learning disabled children. *Journal of Learning Disabilities*, 19, 577–640.

BPS (British Psychological Society) (1999) *Dyslexia, literacy and psychological assessment*. Leicester: BPS.

Buckley, S. (2000) *The education of individuals with Down syndrome: a review of educational provision and outcomes in the UK*. London: The Down Syndrome Educational Trust.

Burt, C. (1921) *Mental and scholastic tests*. London: B. King and Son.

Butler, R. and Marinov-Glassman, D. (1995) The effects of educational placement and grade level on the self-perceptions of low achievers and students with learning disabilities. *Journal of Learning Disabilities*, 27 (5), 325–334.

Caffyn, R. and Millet, D. (1992) From special to mainstream: perspectives of physically disabled children, in P.R. Jones and T. Crowley-Bainton, *Directory of Education and Child Psychology*, 9 (1), 64–71.

Camabra, C. and Silvestre, N. (2003) Students with SEN in the inclusive classroom: social integration and self-concept. *European Journal of Special Needs Education*, 18 (2), 197–208.

Carlberg, C. and Kavale, K. (1980) The efficacy of special versus regular class placement for exceptional children: a meta-analysis. *Journal of Special Education* 14 (3), 295–309.

CDC (Council for Disabled Children) (1995) *The pupil's view*. School SEN Pack. London: NCB.

Chapman, J.W. (1988) Learning disabled children's self concepts. *Review of Educational Research*, 58 (1), 347–371.

Cheston , R. (1994) The accounts of special education leavers. *Disability and Society*, 9 (1), 59–69.

Christensen, P. and James, A. (eds) (2000) *Research with children: perspectives and practices*. London: Falmer Press.

Clark, M., Dyson, A., Millward, A. and Skidmore, D. (1995) *Innovatory practice in mainstream schools for special educational needs*. London: HMSO.

Clarke, A.M. and Clarke, A.D.B. (1974) *Mental deficiency: the changing outlook*. London: Methuen.

Cleugh, M.F. (1957) *The slow learner*. London: Methuen.

Coard, B. (1971) *How the West Indian child is made educationally sub-normal in the British school system*. London: Beacon Books.

Cole, T. (1990) *Apart or a part: integration and the growth of special education*. Milton Keynes: Open University Press.

Coleman, J.M. (1985) Achievement level, social class and self concepts of mildly handicapped children. *Journal of Learning Disabilities*, 18 (1), 6–19.

Cooper, P. (1993) Learning from pupils' perspectives. *British Journal of Special Education*, 20, (4), 129–133.

Cooper, P. (1996) Giving it a name: the value of descriptive categories in educational approaches to emotional and behaviour difficulties. *Support for Learning*, 11 (4), 146–150.

Copeland, I. (1993) Is there a sociology of special education and integration? *European Journal of Special Needs Education*, 8 (1), 1–13.

Copeland, I. (2002) *The backward pupil over a cycle of a century*. Leicestershire: Upfront Publishing.

Corbett, J. (1996) *Bad mouthing: The language of special needs*. London: Falmer Press.

Cosden, M., Elliott, K., Noble, S. and Kelemen, E. (1999) Self-understanding and self-esteem in children with learning disabilities. *Learning Disability Quarterly*, 22 (4), 279–289.

Costley, D. (1996) Making pupils fit the framework: research into the implementation of the National Curriculum in schools for pupils with moderate learning difficulties, focusing on key stage 4. *School Organisation*, 16 (3), 341–354.

Crabtree, J.W. (2002) *Educational inclusion: the self concept of students with moderate learning difficulties*. Ph.D. thesis. Buckinghamshire Chilterns University College, Brunel University.

Crabtree, J. and Rutland, A. (2001) Self evaluation and social comparison amongst adolescents with learning difficulties. *Journal of Community and Applied Social Psychology*, 11, 347–359.

Crocker, J. and Major, B. (1989) Social sigma and self-esteem: the self-protective properties of stigma. *Psychological Review*, 96 (4), 608–630.

Croll, P. and Moses, D. (1998) Pragmatism: ideology and educational change: the case of special educational needs. *British Journal of Educational Studies*, 46 (1), 11–25.

Croll, P. and Moses, D. (2000) Ideologies and utopias: education professionals' views on inclusion. *European Journal of Special Needs Education*, 15 (10), 1–12.

Croll, P. and Moses, D. (2003) Special educational needs across two decades: survey evidence from English primary schools. *British Education Research Journal*, 29 (5), 730–747.

Crowther, D., Dyson, A. and Millward, A. (1998) *Costs and outcomes for pupils with moderate learning difficulties in special and mainstream schools*. Research Report RR89. London: DfEE.

Crozier, W.R. and Dimock, P.S. (1999) Name calling and nick names in a sample of primary school children. *British Journal of Educational Psychology*, 69, 505–516.

Crozier, W.R. and Sklipidou, E. (2002) Adult recollections of name calling. *Educational Psychology*, 22 (1), 113–124.

Cuckle, P. and Wilson, J. (2002) Social relationships and friendships among young people with Down Syndrome in secondary schools. *British Journal of Special Education*, 29 (2), 66–71.

Daniels, D. and Jenkins, P. (2000) *Therapy with children: children's rights, confidentiality and the law*. London: Sage Publications.

Davie, R., Upton, G. and Varma, V. (eds) (1996) *The voice of the child: a handbook for professionals*. London: Falmer Press.

Davis, J., Watson, N. and Cunningham-Burley, S. (2000) Learning the lives of disabled children: developing a reflexive approach, in P. Christensen and A. James (eds) *Research with children: perspectives and practices*. London and New York: Falmer Press.

Dee, L. (2001) *Whose decision? Influences on the decision-making process during the transition from school of twelve young people with special educational needs*. Ph.D. thesis. University of London.

DES (Department of Education and Science) (1978) *Warnock Committee Report*. London: HMSO.

DfE (Department for Education) (1994) *Code of practice on the identification and assessment of special educational needs*. London: DfE.

DfEE (Department for Education and Employment) (1997) *Excellence for all children: meeting special educational needs*. London: HMSO.

DfEE (Department for Education and Employment) (1998) *Meeting special educational needs: a programme of action*. London: DfEE.

DfEE (Department for Education and Employment) (1999) *Circular 10/99. Social inclusion: pupil support. The Secretary of State's guidance on pupil attendance, behaviour exclusion and re-integration*. London: DfEE.

DfES (Department for Education and Skills) (2001) *SEN Code of practice*. London: DfES.

DfES (Department for Education and Skills) (2002) *Consultation – classification of special educational needs*. London: DfES.

DfES (Department for Education and Skills) (2003a) *Data collection by type of special educational needs*. London: DfES.

DfES (Department for Education and Skills) (2003b) *Report of special schools working group*. London: DfES.

Detheridge, T. and Detheridge, M. (1997) *Literacy through symbols*. London: David Fulton.

Dyson, A. (1990) Special educational needs and the concept of change. *Oxford Review of Education*, 16 (1), 55–66.

Dyson, A. (ed.) (2002) Special needs, disability and social inclusion – the end of a beautiful relationship? in SEN Policy Options Steering Group. *Disability, disadvantage, inclusion and social inclusion*. Tamworth: NASEN.

Dyson, A. and Millward, A. (2000) *Schools and special needs: issues of innovation and inclusion*. London: Paul Chapman.

Dyson, A., Howes, A. and Roberts, B. (2002) *A systematic review of the effectiveness of school-level actions for promoting participation by all students*. London: *EPPI Centre Review*. EPPI-centre, Social Scence Research Unit, Institute of Education.

Edgerton, R.B. (1967) *The cloak of competence*. Berkley: University of California Press.

Education Pamphlet (1964) *Slow learners at school*. No. 46. London: HMSO.

Engel, G. (1977) The need for a new medical model: a challenge for bio-medicine. *Science*, 196 (4286), 129–236.

Epps, S. and Tindal, G. (1987) The effectiveness of differential programming in serving children with mild handicaps: placement options and instructional programming, in M. Wang, M. Reynolds and H. Walberg (eds) *Handbook of special education*. (vol. 1) Oxford: Pergamon Press.

Evans, J. and Lunt, I. (2002) Inclusive education: are there limits? *European Journal of Special Education*, 17 (1), 1–14.

Evans, P., Ireson, J. and Redmond, P. (1987) *Curriculum research for pupils with moderate learning difficulties*. DES Project report No. MLD (87)2. London: DES.

Farmer, T.W. and Farmer, E.M.Z. (1996) Social relationships of students with exceptionalities in mainstream classrooms: social networks and homophily. *Exceptional Children*, 62 (5), 431–450.

Farrell, A.M. (1997) *Accessing mainstream curricula in a special school: an illuminative case study*. M.Sc. thesis. City of Dublin University.

Felce, D. (2002) *Gaining views from people with learning disabilities: authenticity, validity and reliability*. Paper at ESRC Seminar on Interviewing Children and Young People with Learning Difficulties. Birmingham.

Festinger, L. (1954) A theory of social comparison processes. *Human Relations*, 7, 117–140.

Feuerstein, R. (1979) *The dynamic assessment of retarded performers: the learning potential assessment device, theory, instruments and techniques*. Philadelphia: University Park Press.

Finlay, W.M.L. and Lyons, E. (2001) Methodological issues in interviewing and using self-report questionnaires with people with mental retardation. *Psychological Assessment*, 1393, 319–335.

Fletcher-Campbell, F. (2004) Pupils with moderate learning difficulties, in A. Lewis and B. Norwich (eds) *Special teaching for special children?* Maidenhead: Open University Press.

Fogelman, K. (1983) *Growing up in Britain: papers from the NDCS*. London: Macmillan.

Fox, P. and Norwich, B. (1992) Assessing the self-perceptions of young adults with severe learning difficulties. *European Journal of Special Needs Education*, 7 (3), 193–203.

Freshwater, K. and Leyden, G. (1989) Limited options: where are leavers now? *British Journal of Special Education*, 16 (1), 19–22.

Fuchs, D. and Fuchs, L. (1995) What is special about special education? *Phi delta Kappa*. March 522–530.

Galloway, D. (1985) *Schools, pupils and special educational needs*. Beckenham: Croom Helm.

Gardner, H. (1993) *The unschooled mind: how children think and how schools should learn*. London: Harper Collins.

Gergen, K.J. (1977) The social construction of self-knowledge, in T. Mischel (ed.) *Self: Psychological and philosophical issues*. Oxford: Blackwell.

Gersch, I.S., Holgate, A. and Stigson, A. (1993) Valuing the child's perspective: a revised student report and other practical initiatives. *Educational Psychology in Practice*, 9 (1), 36–45.

Gipps, C., Goldstein, H. and Gross, H. (1985) Twenty percent with special need: another legacy from Cyril Burt? *Remedial Education*, 20 (2),73–75.

Glover, D., Gough, D., Johnson, M. and Cartwright, N. (2000) Bullying in 25 schools: incidence, impact and intervention. *Educational Research*, 42, 141–156.

Graue, M.E. and Walsh, D.J. (eds) (1998) *Studying children in context: theories, methods and ethics*. London: Sage.

Gray, P. (2003) Categories revisited: the emergence of a new epidemiology of SEN, in SEN Policy Options Steering Group (ed.) *Examining key issues underlying the Audit Commission Reports on SEN*. Tamworth: NASEN.

Grove, N., Bunning, K., Porter, J. and Morgan, M. (2000) *Guidelines to aid understanding of communication by people with severe and profound intellectual* . . . Kidderminster: British Institute of Learning Disability.

Guildford, J.P. (1967) *The nature of human intelligence*. New York: McGraw Hill.

Halpin, D. and Lewis, A. (1996) The impact of the National Curriculum on 12 special schools in England. *European Journal of Special Needs Education*, 2, 95–105.

Harter, S. (1983) The development of the self and the self-system, in M. Hetherington (ed.) *Handbook of child psychology*. (4th ed.) vol. 4, 285–385, London: Wiley.

Hastings, R. and Remington, B. (1993) Connotations of labels for mental handicap and challenging behaviour: a review and research evaluation, *Mental Handicap Research*, 6 (3), 237–249.

Hayden, C. (2000) Exclusions from schools in England: the generation and maintenance of social exclusion, in G. Walraven, C. Parsons, D. Van Veen and C. Day (eds) *Combating social exclusions through education*. Leuven: Garant.

Haynes, J.M. (1971) *Educational assessment of immigrant pupils*. Slough: NFER.

Heath, N.L. and Ross, S. (2000) Prevalence and expression of depressive symptoms in students with and without learning disabilities. *Learning Disability Quarterly*, 23, 24–36.

Hegarty, S. (1993) *Meeting special needs in the ordinary school*. London: Cassell.

Heiman, T. and Margalit, M. (1998) Loneliness, depression and social skills among students with mild mental retardation in different educational settings. *Journal of Special Education*, 32 (3), 154–168.

Hornby, G and Kidd, R. (2001) Transfer from special to mainstream – ten years later. *British Journal of Special Education*, 28 (1), 10–17.

Hugh-Jones, S. and Smith, P.K. (1999) Self reports of short- and long-term effects of bullying on children who stammer. *British Journal of Educational Psychology*, 69 (2), 141–158.

ILEA (Inner London Education Authority) (1986) *Special education – pupils' views*, Research and Statistics RS 1099/86. London: ILEA.

Jahoda, K., Markova, I. and Cattermole, M. (1988) Stigma and self concept of people with a mild mental handicap. *Journal of Mental Deficiency Research*, 32 (1), 103–115.

Jelly, M., Fuller, A. and Byers, R. (2000) *Involving pupils in practice: promoting partnerships with pupils with special educational needs*. London: David Fulton.

Jenkins, J.R., Jewell, M., Leicester, N., O'Connor, R.E., Jenkins, L.M. and Troutner, N.M. (1994) Accommodation for individual differences without classroom ability grouping: an experiment in school restructuring. *Exceptional Children*, 60, 344–358.

Johnson, G.M. (1998) Students at risk: toward a new paradigm of mild educational disabilities. *School Psychology International*, 19 (3), 221–237.

Jones-Davies, C. (1975) *The slow learner in the secondary school: principles and practices for organisation*. London: Ward Lock.

Juvoven, J. and Bear, G. (1992) Social adjustment of children with or without learning disabilities in integrated classrooms. *Journal of Educational Psychology*, 84, 322–330.

Kelly, G. (1955) *The psychology of personal constructs*. New York: Norton.

Kelly, N. and Norwich, B. (in press) Pupils' perceptions of self and of labels: moderate learning difficulties in mainstream and special schools. *British Journal of Educational Psychology*.

Kennedy, I. (1980) Unmasking medicine. *Listener* (6 November).

Kidd, R. and Hornby, G. (1993) Transfer from special to mainstream. *British Journal of Special Education*, 20 (1), 17–19.

Kiesler, D.J. (2000) *Beyond the disease model of mental disorders*. Westpoint, Conn.: Praeger Publishers.

Kirkbride, L. (1999) *I'll go first: the planning and review toolkit for use with children with disabilities*. London: The Children's Society.

Kloomak, S. and Cosden, M. (1994) Self concept in children with learning disabilities: the relationship between global self concept, academic 'discounting', non-academic self concept and perceived social support. *Learning Disabilities Quarterly*, 17 (2), 140–153.

Lewis, A. (1995) *Children's understanding of disability*, London: Routledge.

Lewis, A. and Lindsay, G. (2000) *Researching children's perspectives*. Buckingham: Open University Press.

Lewis, A. and Norwich, B. (2000) *Mapping a pedagogy for special educational needs*. Exeter: University of Exeter.

Lewis, A. and Norwich, B. (eds) (2004) *How specialised is teaching children with disabilities and difficulties?* Buckingham: Open University Press.

Lindsay, G. (2003) Inclusive education: a critical perspective. *British Journal of Special Education*, 30 (1), 3–12.

Lines, D. (2001) Secondary pupils' experiences of name calling behaviour. *Pastoral Care in Education*, 17 (1), 23–31.

Lipsky, D.K. and Gardner, A. (1998) Factors for successful inclusion: learning from the past, looking forward to the future, in S.V. Vitello and D.E. Mithaug (eds) *Inclusive schooling: national and international perspectives*. Mahurah, NJ: Lawrence Erlbaum.

Low, C. (1996) Sense and nonsense relocated, in SEN Policy Options Steering Group (ed.) *Provision for special educational needs from the perspectives of service users*. Tamworth: NASEN.

Lunt, I. and Norwich, B. (2000) *Can effective schools be inclusive schools?* London: Institute of Education, Bedford Way Series.

Lynas, W. (1986) Pupil attitudes to integration, *British Journal of Special Education*, 13 (1), 31–33.

Ma, X. (2002) Bullying in middle school: individual and school characteristics of victims and offenders. *School Effectiveness and School Improvement*, 13 (1), 63–80.

Male, D. (1996) Who goes to MLD schools? *British Journal of Special Education*, 23 (1), 35–41.

Madden, N.A. and Slavin, R.E. (1983) Mainstreaming students with mild handicaps: academic and social outcomes. *Review of Educational Research*, 53 (4), 519–569.

Maieano, C., Ninot, G., Bruant, G. and Benattar, B. (2003) Effects of placing adolescents in special classes: feelings of competence in cases of school failure. *Canadian Psychology*, 22 (2), 139–151.

Manset, G. and Semmel, M.I. (1997) Are inclusive programs for students with mild disabilities effective? A comparative review of model programs. *Journal of Special Education*, 31 (2), 155–180.

Marquand, D. (1992) *The progressive dilemma*. London: Heinemann.

Marsh, A.J. (2003) *Funding inclusive education: the economic realities*. Aldershot: Ashgate.

Marsh, H. and Shavelson, R. (1985) Self-concept: its hierarchical structure. *Educational Psychology*, 20, 107–125.

Marston, D. (1996) A comparison of inclusion only, pull-out only and combined services models for students with mild disabilities. *Journal of Special Education*, 30 (2), 121–132.

Martlew, M. and Hodson, J. (1991) Children with mild learning difficulties in a special school: comparisons of behaviour, teasing and teachers' attitudes. *British Journal of Educational Psychology*, 61, 355–372.

Mastopieri, M.A., Scruggs, T.T. and Butcher, K. (1997) How effective is inquiry learning for students with mild disabilities? *Journal of Special Education*, 31 (2), 199–211.

May, D. and Hughes, D. (1985) The prospects on leaving school for the mildly mentally handicapped. *British Journal of Special Education*, 12 (4), 151–158.

Meyer, L.H. (2001) The impact of inclusion on children's lives: multiple outcomes and friendships in particular. *International Journal of Disability, Development and Education*, 48 (1), 2009–2031.

Ministry of Education (1945) *Handicapped pupils and medical services regulations, circular 41*. London: HMSO.

Mortimore, P., Sammons, P. and Stoll, L. (1988) *School matters the junior years*. Wells: Open Books.

Nabuzoka, D. and Smith, P.K. (1993) Sociometric status and social behaviour of children with and without learning difficulties. *Journal of Child Psychology and Psychiatry*, 34 (8), 1435–1448.

Norwich, B. (1990) *Reappraising special needs education*. London: Cassell.

Norwich, B. (1993) Ideological dilemmas in special needs education: practitioners' views. *Oxford Review of Education*, 19 (4), 527–546.

Norwich, B. (1996) *Special needs education: inclusive education or just education for all?* Inaugural Lecture. Institute of Education, London University.

Norwich, B. (1997) Exploring the perspectives of adolescents with moderate learning difficulties on their special schooling and themselves: stigma and self-perceptions. *European Journal of Special Needs Education*, 12 (1), 38–53.

Norwich, B. (1999) The connotation of special education labels for professionals in the field. *British Journal of Special Education*, 26 (4), 179–183.

Norwich, B. (2002a) *Special school placement and Statements for English LEAs 1997–2001*. Report for CSIE, University of Exeter.

Norwich, B. (2002b) Education, inclusion and individual differences: recognising and resolving dilemmas. *British Journal of Educational Studies*, 50 (4), 482–502.

Norwich, B. and Kelly, N. (2004) Pupils' views on inclusion: moderate learning difficulties and bullying in mainstream and special schools. *British Education Research Journal*, 30 (1), 43–65.

Ochoa, S.H. and Olvarez, A. (1995) Meta-analysis of peer rating sociometric studies of pupils with LD. *Journal of Special Education*, 29 (1), 1–19.

OECD (Organization for Economic Cooperation and Development) (2000) *Special needs education: statistics and indicators*. Paris: OECD.

Oliver, C. (1986) Self-concept assessment: a case study, *Mental Handicap*, 14, 24–25.

Olweus, D. (1993) *Bullying at school*. Cambridge: Blackwell.

O'Moore, A.M. and Hilary, B. (1989) Bullying in Dublin schools. *Irish Journal of Psychology*, 10, 426–441.

Padeliadu, S. and Zigmond, N. (1996) Perspectives of students with learning disabilities about special education placement, *Learning Disabilities Research and Practice*, 11 (1), 15–23.

Pavri, S. and Luftig, R. (2000) The social face of inclusive education: are students with LD really included in the classroom? *Preventing School Failure*, 45 (1), 8–14.

Pavri, S. and Monda-Amaya, L. (2001) Social support in inclusive schools: students' and teachers' perspectives *Exceptional Child*, 67 (3), 391–411.

Polat, F., Kalambouka, A., Boyle, W.F. and Nelson, N. (2001) *Post-16 transition of pupils with special educational needs*. Research Brief no. 315. London: DfES.

Pritchard, D.G. (1963) *Education and the handicapped, 1760–1960*. London: Routledge, Kegan and Paul.

QCA (Qualification and Corriculum Agency) (2001) *Planning, teaching and assessing the curriculum for pupils with learning difficulties*. London: QCA/DfES.

Redmond, P., Evans, P., Ireson, J. and Wedell, K. (1992) Comparing the curriculum development process in special (MLD) schools: a systematic qualitative approach *European Journal of Special Needs Education*, 3 (3), 147–160.

Reid, G (2004) Dyslexia, in A. Lewis and B. Norwich B (eds) *Special teaching for special children?* Maidenhead: Open University Press.

Renick, M. J. and Harter, S. (1989) Impact of social comparisons on developing self perceptions of leaning disabled students. *Journal of Educational Psychology*, 81, 631–635.

Richardson, S.A. and Koller, H. (1992) Vulnerability and resilience of adults who were classified as mildly mentally handicapped in childhood, in B. Tizard and V. Varma (eds) *Vulnerability and resilience in human development*. London: Jessica Kingsley.

Roland, E. (2002) Bulling, depressive symptoms and suicidal thoughts. *Education Research*, 44 (1), 55–67.

Rutter, M., Tizard, J. and Whitmore, K. (1970) *Education, health and behaviour*. London: Longman.

Rutter, M., Maughn, B., Mortimore, P. and Ouston, J. (1979) *Fifteen thousand hours: secondary schools and their effects on children*. London: Open Books.

Ryan, J. (1972) IQ – the illusion of objectivity, in K. Richardson and D. Spears (eds) *Race, culture and intelligence*. Harmondsworth: Penguin Books.

Schulte, A.C., Osborne, S.S. and McKinney, J.D. (1990) Academic outcomes for students with learning disabilities in consultation and resource programs. *Exceptional Children*, 57, 162–172.

SCPR (Social and Community Planning Research) (1996) *Student voices: the views of further education students with learning difficulties and disabilities*. London: SCPR.

Scott, J. (2000) Children as respondents: the challenge of quantitative methods, in P. Christensen and A. James (eds) *Research with children: perspectives and practices*. London: Falmer Press.

Searle, J.R. (1995) *The construction of social reality*. Harmondsworth: Penguin.

Sheldon, D. (1991) How was it for you? Pupils', parents' and teachers' perspectives on integration. *British Journal of Special Education*, 18 (3), 107–110.

Siperstein, G.N., Leffert, J.S. and Wenz-Gross, M. (1997) The quality of friendships between children with and without learning problems. *American Journal of Mental Retardation*, 102 (2), 111–125.

Skrtic, T. (ed.) (1995) *Disability and democracy: reconstructing special education for postmodernity*. New York: Teachers College Press.

Smith, P.K. and Sharp, S. (1994) *School bullying: insights and perspectives*. London: Routledge.

Soder, M. (1989) Disability as a social construct: the labelling approach revisited. *European Journal of Special Needs Education*, 4 (2), 117–129.

Solity, J. (1991) Special needs: a discriminatory concept. *Educational Psychology in Practice*, 7 (1), 12–19.

Solity, J. and Bull, S. (1987) *Bridging the curriculum gap*. Milton Keynes: Open University Press.

Stalker, K. (1998) Some ethical and methodological issues in research with people with learning difficulties. *Disability and Society*, 13 (1), 5–19.

Stoll, L. and Mortimore, P. (1995) *School effectiveness and school improvement*. London: Institute of Education, London University.

Sutherland, G. (1984) *Ability, merit and measurement: mental testing and English Education, 1988–1940*. Oxford: Clarendon Press.

Tansley, A.E. and Gulliford, R. (1960) *The education of slow learning children*. London: Routledge and Kegan Paul.

Thomas, G. (1997) Inclusive schools for an inclusive society. *British Journal of Special Education*, 24 (3), 103–107.

Thomas, G. and Feiler, A. (1988) *Planning for special needs: a whole school approach*. Oxford: Blackwell.

Tomlinson, S. (1982) *A sociology of special education*. London: Routledge, Kegan and Paul.

Tomlinson, S. (1985) The expansion of special education. *Oxford Review of Education*, 11 (2), 157–165.

Tur-Kaspa, H., Margalit, M. and Most, T. (1999) Reciprocal friendship, reciprocal rejection and socio-emotional adjustment: the social experiences of children with learning disorders over a one-year period. *European Journal of Special Needs Education* 14 (1), 17–48.

UNESCO (United Nations Educational, Scientific, and Cultural Organization) (1994) *The Salamanca statement and framework for action on special needs education.* Paris: UNESCO.

Vaughn, S., Elbaum, B.E. and Schumm, J.S. (1996) The effects of inclusion on the social functioning of students with learning disabilities. *Journal of Learning Disabilities*, 29 (6), 598–608.

Vygotsky, L.S. (1978) *Mind in society: the development of higher psychological processes.* Cambridge: MIT Press.

Wade, B. and Moore, M. (1993) *Experiencing special education.* Buckingham: Open University Press.

Walker, A. (1982) *Unqualified and underemployed: handicapped young people and the labour market.* London: Macmillan.

Wang, M.C. and Birch, J.W. (1984) Comparison of full-time mainstreaming and a resource room approach. *Exceptional Children*, 5, 33–40.

Ward, K., Thomson, G.O.B. and Riddell, S. (1994) Transition, adulthood and special education: an unresolved paradox. *European Journal of Special Needs Education*, 9 (2), 125–144.

Warin, J. (2001) *Putting self esteem in its proper place.* Paper at seminar on dispositions in education, London: Institute of Education.

Warren, S. (2000) Let's do it properly: inviting children to be researchers, in A. Lewis and G. Lindsay (eds) *Researching children's perspectives.* Buckingham: Open University Press.

Whitaker, P. (1994) Mainstream students talk about integration. *British Journal of Special Education*, 21 (1), 13–16.

Whitney, I., Smith, P.K. and Thompson, D. (1994) Bullying and children with special educational needs, in P.K. Smith and S. Sharp (eds) *School bullying: insights and perspectives.* London: Routledge.

Williams, A.A. (1970) *Basic subjects for slow learners.* London, Methuen.

Williams, P. (1966) Some characteristics of educationally subnormal children. *British Journal of Psychiatry*, 112, 79–90.

Williams, P. (1993) Integration of students with moderate learning difficulties. *European Journal of Special Needs Education*, 8 (3), 303–319.

Wishart, J.G. (1990) Learning to learn: the difficulties faced by children and young people with Down Syndrome, in W.I. Fraser (ed.) *Key issues in research in mental retardation.* London: Routledge.

Wishart, J.G. (1993) The development of learning difficulties in children with Down Syndrome. *Journal of Intellectual Disability Research*, 37, 389–403.

Wooldridge, A. (1994) *Measuring the mind: education and psychology in England, c. 1860 – 1990.* Cambridge: Cambridge University Press.

Index